Up Smith Creek

**White Lion
Press**

Other books by George Smith

Asking Properly: the art of creative fundraising

Tiny Essentials of Writing for Fundraising

Up
Smith
Creek

**White Lion
Press**

Published by
The White Lion Press Limited
567 Ben Jonson House
The Barbican
London
EC2Y 8NH

©2011 George Smith/The White Lion Press Limited

ISBN 13: 978-0-9553993-4-3

ISBN 10: 0-9553993-4-3

First printed 2011

British Library Cataloguing-in-Publication-Data. A catalogue record for this book is available from the British Library.

Design and print production by em associates

Printed and bound in the United Kingdom by Bell & Bain Limited, Glasgow

For my beloved Stella

Contents

Part 1

The art and craft of asking properly: the fundraising years, from *Professional Fundraising* magazine

Part 2

The customers always write: reflections on decades of direct marketing, from *Direct Response* magazine

Part 3

Such is life: observations in the corridors of the almost powerful, from various sources

Foreword

**by Tony Elischer, managing director, THINK
Consulting Solutions**

George Smith was already a legend in fundraising circles by
the time I first met him, more than twenty-five years ago. I
was a young aspiring fundraiser full of hope and optimism,
working at the leading UK charity Help the Aged. The
trustee responsible for fundraising on their board at that time
was Harold Sumption, founder of the then tiny and very new
International Fundraising Workshop. Harold felt that I would
benefit from exposure to a real guru, so he introduced me to
George. A long and rich friendship developed and for several
years George and I even worked together, in the latter part of
the 1990s, as directors of the Burnett Associates agency
group. Throughout these years my admiration and affection
for George both as an individual and as a professional has
grown and grown.

So when we at THINK heard that Ken and Marie Burnett
were looking for help to put together this special collection of
George's articles my colleagues and I quickly volunteered our
support.

Fine writing is always in short supply in fundraising,
particularly in these days of emails, Twitter and such like.
Fine writing combined with fine thinking and a puckish wit is
sufficiently rare and valuable that it should be preserved,
treasured and shared just as widely as can be with as many
people as possible.

These articles contain a lot that you'll find useful.

They're brilliantly written, of course. This collection adds up
to a series of fine lessons in the writer's art. They're full of
clever insights, sharp observations and useful takeaways.

Though some of these pieces were written thirty years ago or more, they're all as relevant now as they ever were.

They're at times challenging, irreverent, perceptive, sad, moving, laugh-out-loud funny and incredibly thought provoking – often all in the same article.

We at THINK felt immediately that this is one book that really should be published. Once you've sampled it, I'm sure you'll agree. THINK Consulting Solutions therefore is not just happy to bring you this collection of the best of George's articles from the past three decades, we're proud and grateful to have the opportunity to do so.

Enjoy!
Tony Elischer

Preface

'One a day, to be taken at bedtime.'

This is a book for people who appreciate good writing. So, it's
not a book for everyone. But it is for you, so you should feel
proud.

George Smith writes for people who appreciate words and
their meaning, and how they work well when assembled in a
certain way, together. So this collection of his writings over
thirty odd years (read that as you like) will be valued by readers
of discernment, people who understand that words have
precise meaning.

George chooses and uses his words elegantly, deploying pearls
such as scrupulosity, seeping, pooh pooh, blather, and a
hundred other terms to which you will be unused and by which
you will be amused. Such is his facility with words that he's
able to create a silly but disturbingly realistic parallel world and
populate it with ridiculous but thoroughly believable types of
the advertising, marketing, supplier and client varieties. He
then imbues the ramblings and actions of these sorts with pace,
power, pathos, beauty, insight, sharpness, wisdom and a range
of other emotions. So it's the best of this that we've lovingly
assembled for you, here.

It'll help as you read if you also like fundraising and/or direct
marketing, as mostly, that's the stuff he wrote about. Well, no
he didn't. He wrote about innovation and passion, about
inspiration and pomposity, real meaning and shallowness,
inflated egos, simple truths and fine motives, slick subterfuge,
shallow sentiments and deep meanings. And a lot more
besides. He then planted these observational gems in the fertile
soils that are fundraising and direct marketing.

I suggest you don't try to devour these morsels at a single

sitting, but that you savour them slowly, bit by bit, over time. One each night really is a good idea.

For a flavour of the man himself though, you might have to dig a bit deeper.

Here's what avid fan Charlotte Grimshaw says about George, in his profile in The Great and Good Showcase on SOFII, the Showcase of Fundraising Innovation and Inspiration (www.sofii.org).

> 'George's chosen persona is the Luddite curmudgeon, baffled by modernity and resisting it with all the wit and humour at his disposal. Clients of his agency, Smith Bundy, will recall the typewriter proudly displayed (and in use) on his desk, when the world was moving rapidly to the desktop PC. He would still like to have you believe he would never own a computer if he could help it and, if he really had to learn to drive, he'd like to go no further than his local shops in Kent, preferably in a 1950s Ford Anglia.
>
> Yet this man has been one of the prime movers in some of the most innovative, world-changing thinking, writing and campaigning in the UK in the last fifty years. A man much more moved and inspired by the issues he writes about than he chooses to reveal and quietly passionate about making a difference. Hard to believe now that George started his working life as a production assistant for the Amalgamated Dental Company...'

Amalgamated Dental's loss, evidently.

A propos that typewriter it's well to remember that Smith was writing these pieces before the invention of the Internet, i-technology, even before the advent of the fax machine. A mobile device back then was a briefcase, in which one kept one's sandwiches. Tipp-Ex had been invented though and the post-it note was the coming thing in offices up and down the land. We tell you this merely to set the coming tales in the context of their time.

Please, enjoy this quirky, affectionate, information-packed tome.

Ken and Marie, publishers,
The White Lion Press

Acknowledgements

With thanks to Stella Smith; Carol Trickey and Steve Tully, for the illustrations; Kate Mazur; Paul Rowney; all at THINK Consulting Solutions, particularly Tony Elischer and Fiona Duncan; Terry Hunt; Derek Holder; Jane Fricker and Ernest Muller of em associates; Alistair Hall, for the photograph of the Olivetti typewriter on the cover; and Wilf the cleaner.

About this book

George Smith enjoyed many years as a much loved and looked-forward-to columnist of several leading trade journals, particularly *Direct Response* and *Professional Fundraising* magazines and the cryptically named *Local Government News*. From time to time he'd also pen a piece for national organs so there's an article included here from *New Society* and another from the *Financial Times*, plus at least one that never saw its way into print but which we deem worthy of inclusion all the same.

George wrote monthly columns and occasional features and it is the best of these that we have assembled for you here. He rapidly gained a reputation for irreverence, perception, the deflation of pomposities and, above all, fine writing. Many of these pieces are as relevant, or irrelevant, as they were at the time of writing. Others have been included for sheer curiosity value, or just because we like them. We think there are some real gems here, but of course it is up to you to make of them what you will. George once said of these diatribes that he wrote them in haste and repented of them at leisure. You can absorb them quickly or slowly, it's up to you.

This book is mostly a journey backwards in time across three productive decades of working at the noble trade of communication. It presents aspects of a curious life as seen through the eyes of the singularly unusual Englishman who was living it. The short introductions from the publisher are intended purely to shed light on aspects of whatever George was writing about that many people might otherwise not understand. Other than these and a bit of tidying and some clarification we have not added to it nor have we taken anything away.

The art and craft of asking properly: The fundraising years, from *Professional Fundraising* magazine

Time for one representative trade body?

April 1992

Fundraisers need a consolidated effort when looking to deal with the powers in Westminster.

First, a Labour MP worries at the prawns we have set before him at home and displays unexpected new attitudes to the issues of animal rights. Having assured him that all the prawns in question committed mass suicide after a long and fruitful crustacean life, we discover that our man is a born again animal rights lobbyist. He is spending lots of time with some of the major charities concerned and is about to go high profile on the subject. He is a politician whose new zeal for his fellow creatures will surprise many.

Second, I am accompanying a senior fundraiser to the mother of parliaments to discuss the, then, charities bill with a Government bigwig. Amidst two delightful hours that would have made an episode in *Yes Minister*, I hear the bigwig ringing the Home Office and demanding to know who drafted this infernal piece of half-baked legislation (this is a précis of his words but a fair one). And when the strutting civil servant tries to defend the mess my bigwig bellows, 'Did you actually talk to anyone before you drafted this?'

Third, I reflect on John Major's speech to the CAF conference at the end of last year. The Prime Minister told us all how important we are and how much his Government rated our work. On the spot, everyone fawned and clapped. Over lunch, however, it got a bit waspish. By the time the next issue of this magazine came out, its editor was prepared to be downright vindictive about Mr Major's lack of content as opposed to his charm and general niceness – though his expectations of conference speeches by PMs struck me as a trifle elevated.

The thesis? Broadly this: that charities are now well fused into the political process but still lack the overall influence and conference that should come from a sector that represents four per cent of GNP.

My Labour MP – a terrifying leftie in the public mind – is now prepared to see a voluntary

So, how will we be represented – as a collection of individual causes or as one integrated lobby?

organisation as a proper vehicle for effecting political change. He would have sneered at the thought a few short years ago. The stuttering civil servant thought that someone had talked to NCVO in the matter of the Charities Bill. And Mr Major was thanked for his vacuities. We are all political now, but not exactly central to any political process.

Individual charities know how to use the political process and then some. The current and brilliant campaign by the International Fund for Animal Welfare, launched after the fox-hunting bill, is an utterly worldly piece of politics. They have squeezed it on to the billboards before the election is called at which point it would presumably be illegal. A hundred or so Tory MPs are going to feel mightily victimised, and IFAW are to be congratulated on going for the political jugular with such panache and zeal.

The body politic is not going to take to this new style of ours. Charities are supposed to be nice, pottering after the political process and not interfering in the process itself. We may expect a few more bromides from the Commissioners on the difference between the two. And we may even have a great debate in the next parliament on the issue, for it is simmering in many an MP's postbag.

So, how will we be represented – as a collection of individual causes or as one integrated lobby? ICFM has done grand work on the new charities bill and the stately galleons of CAF and NCVO continue to sail through the corridors of power. But all these organisations have an individual remit – and politicians like nothing better than to divide and rule.

The case for an authoritative lobby for the voluntary sector – one strident voice and not a genial conversation. Years of zealous lobbying have failed to give us success on matters like VAT. We appear to have shed our political virginity in fundraising. Now, surely, is the time to be represented as the popular and important force that we are.

We do not have to look too far for models. British agriculture represents itself pretty full-bloodedly. And I understand that it is a smaller business than ours.

The importance of not being earnest

June 1992

The collecting tin could be as a red rag to the restless charitable masses.

Keith Waterhouse is a writer for whom I have a lot of time. He's happy to be a hack, producing tabloid newspaper columns, plays, novels and the occasional much-needed manual on how to write decent English. He is a denizen of that Soho watering hole where men and women of letters gather and growl at each other. I've seen him there, hirsute and shabby, he does a good growl.

He is of an age where growling is to be expected. Reasonable growling, I ought to add – not the insufferable snarl of an Amis nor the endless sneer of an Osborne. Waterhouse always comes across as a man of the people. He has always been very good at picking up emerging national norms and caricaturing them – look up *Billy Liar* or *Office Life* to see how skilfully he reflects silly old England in all its daftness.

I'm telling you all this because his most recent novel is all about us. *Unsweet Charity* was barely reviewed because its author is barely fashionable. And, where it was reviewed, it was reviewed badly. You will find it in hardback at the moment and the affordable paperback cannot be far behind.

I can't argue with the literary verdict. In all honesty, this is not my man on top form – perhaps he was too busy counting his winnings from the Jeffrey Bernard play. But it's worth the attention of any fundraiser who wants a glimpse of how we all look to the great world outside. The glimpse is less than flattering. We ought to be interested.

The book is a romp through Tom Sharpe land: lots of

boozing, sex, class strife, skulduggery and farcical plotting. You may not burst your sides but you may giggle just occasionally. It's a short book and it knows its own limits.

> Apart from that, we have been treated as a religion.

The basic joke is simply that a whole swathe of English culture has now been turned over to fundraising. The Home Counties town in which it is set is knee deep in charitable activity. Its pavements are forever occupied by costumed collectors and tin rattlers, its every activity is fuelled by good causes, its every committee is now dominated by the need to raise funds for something, be the cause increasingly esoteric. It is this manic cult that gives the book its predictable spin. Committee members vie with each other for power and rival causes vie with each other for the action, all of which is reasonably accurate. But the novel's considerable sexual activity is also fuelled in the fundraising hothouse. And that clearly is a scandalous canard.

No, it's not really a very good book.

As satire, it's too crude to make it. As farce, it's just a bit clumping. But we have to be interested that Waterhouse as social commentator has picked on us. It says that we are important enough to be deflated. This makes an interesting moment.

Think about it. We have always been above criticism. The very monument of a good cause has been sufficient for most people to shuffle their feet, metaphorically speaking, and adopt a serious expression – a little like the reaction evoked by the Royal Family.

Apart from the odd scandal and nine-day tabloid wonders we sometimes generate, nobody has ever had a bad word to say about the wondrous world of fundraising. Dickens had a little fun with our predecessors and I remember a brilliant send-up by Eleanor Bron at an early Amnesty concert. Apart from that, we have been treated as a religion.

And now here's old Waterhouse growling at what he sees as fashionable follies. This is a man irritated beyond measure at never being able to escape the clutches of the parade of good causes and permitting himself a wry observation that maybe all this do-gooding is just a knee-jerk reaction of a society that has forgotten how to fulfil itself politically and which has turned a waning sense of social responsibility into a social festival. Why else should we need to save whales by dressing up as those delightful mammals and walking the streets thus garbed?

That last bit is me getting overwrought and de-constructing Waterhouse beyond his means. But the irritation factor seethes through the book and we all know that irritation lurks just beneath the ground that we plough so thoroughly. At my commuter station each night I am greeted by the jangling tins of young medical students dressed as surgeons collecting for their local hospital. And every night I hear the tins jangle and I watch that irritation factor grow over people's faces. Another captive audience is getting restless!

There's no answer to the irritation factor but it's good to know that a good novelist has trained his gaze on us and felt able to put us down.

Read this book anyway. And give yourself a proper sense of distance.

Doing good with Dundee cakes

August 1992

If fundraising was left to village fetes, the voluntary sector would be a nicer, if poorer, place.

No sooner had I come back from doing my duty at the village school's summer fete when the bell rang. It was the good Doctor Wood, a neighbour, collecting for the lifeboats. Another couple of pounds changed hands, bringing the afternoon's philanthropy to nearly a tenner. I had acquired a tin of pink salmon in the tombola, a Dundee cake, half a yard of bedding plants and three RNLI stickers from Doctor Wood. This must have been about par for the flashier donors around here.

Say there's a hundred such plutocrats in the village and reckon that there must have been several hundred more contributing at a lower level. That's a couple of thousand pounds raised one Saturday afternoon in a small Kentish village. Repeat it several times a year (and we do) and the statistics begin to get awesome. Doctor Wood will be back in a week or two for Help the Aged and the church flower festival is next weekend. I forgot to mention that the Saturday morning shopping trip in our local market town featured a trad jazz band outside Boots and the young mums collecting for the local playgroup. Add another couple of quid.

Not that we remain unmoved between house-to-house collections and special events (did I mention that the Fun Run was last weekend?) judging by the car stickers around here, WWF has a fifty-per-cent penetration of all households and Christian Aid something similar from May through to

September. Our admirable Women's Institute is forever passing radical resolutions and ending the weekly session with a collection for something or other. Let it not be said that our wealth is other than modestly recycled by the week.

Of course, it is painless. It takes a misanthrope to avoid the jollity at the school fete and the chance to gossip with neighbours. Or to emerge without a Dundee cake and bedding plants. It takes a surly temperament to walk eyes down past the playgroup mums. And saying no to Doctor Wood would risk moral obloquy on a scale that would cause a frisson every time you walked into the village shop.

> Yet, I yearn for our beleaguered village school to ask those of us who can afford it to give lots more.

We all know each other, you see. That was Wendy behind the cake stall at the fete. The bedding plants are donated by Mrs Price. Doctor Wood marks the footpaths for us. I am known to be bohemian because of the Greenpeace sticker in the back of the Fiat and as the sole reader of *The Guardian* in the village.

This is idyllic fundraising for it must extract something like ten thousand pounds annually from a village of seven hundred souls by way of collective effort. Add in the private and discreet giving, and you can fairly double or treble that sum. Call it twenty-five thousand pounds a year from those seven hundred people; thirty-five pounds a head.

It is a sum that leaves us ahead of the latest CAF statistics for charity giving. If it were touted as an index of village philanthropy, we would be lauded in the local press as a citadel of decency and niceness. We are nothing of the sort, of course; we are merely buying Wendy's Dundee cakes and passing the time of day with Doctor Wood. Our giving forms a sort of licence to live here. In any sense of social responsibility, thirty-five pounds a head is not good enough.

But how do you make the difference? Doctor Wood is never going to demand a fiver for his RNLI stickers and there is a common understanding that a Dundee cake has its rightful price. Yet, I yearn for our beleaguered village school to ask those of us who can afford it to give lots more. But to provoke them to do so would be seen as a breach of local taste. I have actually offered my services in this mode. I was told that it would upset people. I know what they mean, for the intervention of full-blooded fundraising into a community so genuinely decent and altruistic would be alien and aberrant.

So, we shall remain under-achievers, giving less than we could because the manner of our giving is so pleasant. Stitch the geographic coordinates and you get the scale of the problem. In the South London streets that I left to move here, there would be no Doctor Wood to collect and not many doors that would open if he did. There are few Fun Runs around Brixton and trade in bedding plants is scant. The indices of wealth are probably similar but even our cost apparatus of giving is largely absent. Is the citizenry of yuppified Inner London good for thirty-five pounds a year?

Our giving, like so much else in this country, is imprisoned by our social structures, our national suspicion of change and virility, our acquiescence in the minimal gesture. It will take a bold charity to challenge these things. And I am far from convinced that such boldness would be fruitful. As my local head teacher said, we don't want to upset people.

Carpe diem – please!

September 1992

Fundraisers could be missing out on a multitude of atrocities.

A wavering monthly deadline imprisons a piece like this. For I write long before you get to read. And I write on the spur of a passionate moment, the cusp of a mood of outrage. In the morning I shall be pleased with myself that I can still have these feelings; for the moment the old Adam has come back with familiar vengeance.

I just saw the Serbian mortars exploding in that Bosnian graveyard. I saw children cowering behind gravestones who only wanted to put flowers on the coffins of their little murdered friends. I saw the old lady carried off, the mayhem, the panic, the terror, the tears. And I cannot forget that there are men in those hills, Western men (Christian men?) who look through binoculars, peer through gun sights and press buttons. Do they laugh? Are they pleased with themselves?

And last week I saw a television programme which told of the Turkish massacre of the Armenians in 1915, the century's first holocaust. I learned of the evacuations of a minority population and heard the survivors tell of the cholera, the dying, the massacres, the burning, the unbelievable callousness. I learned that seventy years of Turkish diplomacy and American stewardship of Middle East politics had denied me the knowledge of these atrocities. I learned that Adolf Hitler had said 'Who remembers the Armenians?' before starting his own holocaust.

So, I fast-forward my head to August 1992 when another vicious buffoon is talking of 'ethnic cleansing'. And I hear of new concentration camps and I see the same bewildered and fearful children and I see the mortar bursts in the graveyard.

And I hear that my country cannot accept refugees and that we must not take sides. And the next shot in my head is Somalia, the one after that Mozambique, the one after that an unnamed South African township. My head may be on fast forward but the film seems to be on rewind – this world of ours is running backwards into an old, dark terror. I wasn't around in the 1930s but it must have been a bit like this. There are ten million people like me this morning. They're outraged, they are moved, they are frustrated. When it was Franco bombing Guernica you had something to fall back on, a series of political demands to assuage the heartache. Arms for Spain! When it was Sharpeville the issue was ready-made. Anti apartheid! When it was Biafra the Oxfam ads were in the paper every day. Feed a child!

> But where are the charities? Or have I missed them?

I now expect nothing of politicians. Our disgusting pusillanimousness is par for the Foreign Office course And I can only suppose that the double-breasted opposition spokespersons are carefully considering their position in Tuscany. No vision, please, we're British.

But where are the charities? Or have I missed them? On the subject of our shameful refugee policy, I have seen only predictable letters in predictable papers by predictable people. But where are the ads, the mailings, the posters, the shouting? Where are the outlets for my outrage? Or, if you prefer, who will take this hundred quid I will freely offer up this morning to do something in the Balkans? It has all gone quiet. Freeze frame this moment, this morning of 5th August, accept that there are millions like me with consciences alerted and with hands inching toward chequebooks. Only no one is asking.

Perhaps charities have been advised by advertising agencies that August is a low-readership month? Perhaps someone is saying that it's too close to the ITV Telethon? Perhaps there

is a feeling that we must not rock the Foreign Office boat.
Perhaps (heaven forfend) all the fundraisers are in Tuscany?
Whatever the reasons for the silence, I sense the dead hand of
dutiful professionalism squashing the fine old instinct of
passion. However wrong or misguided I might be in that
judgment, I must be right in reporting the emptiness of a
morning when there was so much philanthropy about and no
one to wish it on. Like all good things, that mood will pass. If
Akabussi makes gold, Bosnia drifts down the page. If a
minister commits adultery, forget world hunger for a week. If
Jerry gets back with Mick, stop worrying about the
greenhouse effect.

This is the world we live in and always will. It is a world
where fundraisers need to make their own luck and force
their own issues on a public sated with junk news.
Sometimes, as now, the luck is made for them. In which case
there should be that wonderful surge of spontaneous decency
on which the British can still pride themselves. But, today, all
is quiet.

I did a four-minute rant in Birmingham on the need for
passion. This is a fifty-minute written rant on the same
subject. Both rants are based on my fear that we are
becoming technicians and not advocates, that we are
measuring opportunities and not creating them, that we are
beginning to settle for being suits and dresses ambling around
conference halls.

Carpe diem means seize the day. We just missed one and we
need all the seizable days we can get. The image of the
mortared Bosnian graveyard was just collected into our folk
memory and put alongside the Ethiopian tribesmen, the
Somalian children and the swollen bodies after a Bangladeshi
cyclone. Yet no one told us what to do about it.

As I say, this piece is written on the 5th August. I pray that it
will look silly, premature and wide-eyed by the time you get
to read it. Truly I do.

I know they do a good job, but...

October 1992

The days of a royal name on the letterhead of every charity may be numbered.

Let's be bloody tactless this month. Let's talk about the House of Windsor.

Strangely, I have always been fairly relaxed about the monarchy. My old mum was a stalwart supporter and what was good for my old mum was always good enough for me. There always seemed to me better things to worry about and on the few occasions when professional duties had me in a line shaking a royal hand, I had to confess to a certain *je ne sais quoi* and a desire to keep the photographs.

So these are not the observations of a rabid republican. I tend to turn into one late at night when we're on the umpteenth bottle and when talk turns to the British class structure, which I still take to be the source of most of our social ills. My regime would be Cromwellian and would therefore dispense of the monarchical apex to our society, but I have no desire to dispose of the current incumbents by way of lampposts or scaffolds.

But there is a symbiotic relationship between the royal family and British fundraisers and there always has been. There is a lot of cheap fun to be had in reporting the antics of charity managers and trustees who have fawned and grimaced and swooned in the presence of a royal personage. I have witnessed occasions when voluntary organisations have spent more time in planning the triennial forty-five minute visit of the royal patron than they have in organising their entire year's publicity programme. I have seen grown men become apoplectic when the desks in the accounts department were seen as less than shipshape before the princess passed through on her beaming way.

It is all slightly silly, but I know that the same applies when the visit is by the Lord Lieutenant's viceroy or the Under-Secretary for Important Things or when a third-rate television personality has accepted an invitation to attend a reception. We are a deferential lot and we like our little ceremonies. It looks good in the newsletter.

Only a naive or a nasty commentator would pretend otherwise.

The securing of royal support and patronage has always been seen as a priority for British charities and the press has recently been doing its homework and counting the myriad organisations with a royal on the letterhead. There can be no doubt that such patronage has been of value in fundraising, none whatsoever. The attachment of a royal has always conferred status and the presence of a royal has always extracted cheques from the audience. Only a naive or a nasty commentator would pretend otherwise.

But now? In my judgement, the recent travails of the royal family are going to mean a total reassessment of their social worth. A monarchy needs mystique to thrive and 1992 has seen a total shattering of that mystique. It is now known that they behave precisely as their subjects behave. No one who reads history should exactly be astonished by this revelation, but those appalling little creeps who sit in trees with telephoto lenses and who tap into telephone calls will have proved to be social engineers way beyond their grubby remits.

Exit mystique then. Exit personal dignity and deference and admiration. It may all be grossly unfair and vulgar but it is happening. And it must force charities, at least the worldly ones, to reappraise their royal relationships. Speaking with numbing crudity, I suggest that royals will have less fundraising value in future. I think it already true that certain members of that besieged extended family have zilch value as fundraising totems. I expect to hear of the odd social event that is cancelled because the royal drawing power is not what it was.

There is also a political dimension to this. I think that the government is going to have to make the odd constitutional rearrangement. The civil list may be curbed, the Queen's tax immunity adjusted, the whole monarchical act called into question. Mr Major is unlikely to be a Marat but he is shrewd enough to be a Talleyrand. He may have no choice, for a country having such a bad time of it may well begin to include some parts of the royal family in its list of scapegoats. In other words, the way in which we pay for our monarchy may become a hot political potato for the first time in a hundred and fifty years.

Fundraisers should pause in their traditional acts of obeisance. The institution is not going to be abolished but it is going through a profound sea change, it is no longer going to be a passport to social approval and visibility. Yet I have this uneasy feeling that charities will try and cling to the apparent status quo way beyond its sell-by date. I fancy that the last wide-eyed courtiers will be fundraisers, beguiling themselves that things are as they were. If they do, they will not feature in revolutionary tumbrils, they will simply be more and more ignored by the public at large. It will be a quiet and passive British tragedy. For charities will be marginalised.

I freely expect a postbag telling me that I am a cad. It is not inconceivable that I shall be challenged to a duel. In which case I nominate the darts board at Noordwijkerhout as my ground and the congres centrum's darts as my weapons. Double for start?

Nobody knows anything

November 1992

Now that the collapse of socialism has been followed so quickly by the collapse of capitalism, it is about time we hounded the experts from the room.

By experts I currently mean every politician, economic forecaster, Treasury bod, model builder, pundit, shaman, water diviner and young man in red braces allowed to opine from a bank department full of terminals, telephones and national flags. What has been revealed is what we have always suspected: that no one knows what the hell they're talking about. Expertise, be it Keynesian, monetarist, post-monetarist, interventionist, or outright totalitarian, is blow. If the pound is in free fall, then so is every wally who ever appeared on television to give us his views.

I hope we gnarled sceptics are allowed a wry smile. It's bad enough to hear about the new world role of the Finnish mark and the Swedish interest rates at five hundred per cent. It's bewildering to spend two weeks being told that the fate of the pound depended on a French referendum. It's sheer comic opera watching British interest rates changing with each edition of the *Evening Standard*.

It is finally comforting to learn that it's somehow all the fault of the Germans. When our trains cease to run, we discover it's the wrong kind of snow. When we get thrashed at cricket, Johnny Foreigner has been tampering with the ball. When the economy collapses we release our traditional demon from the pantomime trap door, beware the Bosch – Nicholas Ridley told us so.

It is experts who feed us this garbage.

On any honest appraisal, we should give more credence to taxi drivers, saloon bar bores, David Icke, or the Book of Revelations. Do you realise that the only man in British public life who has made a halfway-accurate economic forecast in recent years has been Arthur Scargill? A chilling thought.

> You can vote for an economic policy but you'll get out voted by five hundred currency dealers with red braces and little flags on their terminals.

So, let's stop deferring to conventional wisdom. It's rotting our brains and corrupting our politics. This New World Order of ours is revealed as a parlour game in which all the participants are blindfolded, stumbling around the room saying silly things to each other. Currencies don't matter any more, confidence in currencies does. You can vote for an economic policy but you'll get out voted by five hundred currency dealers with red braces and little flags on their terminals. They may even want to marry your daughters.

Say pshaw to them all. Examine your own worldly perception, your own uneducated common sense. You have nothing to lose but your sense of deference.

This recession, for example: it's not cyclical any more, is it? It's terminal. We are not buying things any more and only partly because we haven't got the money. We are buying less because there is less that we want to buy. The old aspirational hooks that made us big consumers are rusting. Our hi-fi systems are as good as our ears can cope with; our automatic cameras take perfect pictures; our dishwashers last for decades; we have even discovered that cars can last for more than two years; our children clothe themselves in Oxfam shops and Camden Market. The fax machines, the personal computers, the mobile telephones, the camcorders and the dimmer switches are mostly in place now. And mostly under used.

This is deathly news to retailers, large corporations, fashion houses and car manufacturers. It is already a headstone on the freshly dug graves of multinational computer companies. But it could be paradoxically good news for fundraisers.

Think about it. There's still an awful lot of money around, increasingly held by older people and increasingly being shoved into savings where it confers no benefit on society other than making the oldsters feel a little more comfortable. Some of this wealth may be occasionally unlocked to pay for a Saga Holidays' wingding or a new fruit cage, but Mr and Mrs Middle England are never now going to spark off a new consumer revival. Their annual five thousand miles of motoring can safely be conducted in their F registration model, their Max Bygraves records keep them immune from boxed sets of Madonna, their sensible tweeds make them unlikely to he found beating down the doors at Versace or even Austin Reed. Of all the people who've got enough, these people have an excess of enough.

In summary, then. We've got a newly impoverished society, we've got a younger generation who are going to have to build their lives via totally new economic mores, we've got an apparently endless recession and we can begin to talk about the end of growth through consumer spending. And, in the middle of this apparently apocalyptic state of affairs, we have millions of rich people getting richer. Many of them married our mother, or fathers.

Is this a case for specifically targeted fundraising, or isn't it? Hit the pause button and think. These observations are guaranteed LSE, Cambridge University, Bank of England and think tank free. I'm no expert.

The meejah fights back

December 1992/January 1993

If fundraisers fail to control the media, they can only blame themselves for the consequences.

Delegates to the twelfth IFRW who peeped outside the door at Thursday lunchtime would have been tickled pink by the sight of this writer looking dishevelled and jaded and being interviewed by a television team.

They were from Belgium and had come hotfoot from Charleroi to capture the world's greatest fundraising conference in all its frenzied glory. Our brief conversation was in a mixture of broken English (mine) and a gesticulatory form of Walloon (mostly theirs). But, even across the linguistic barriers, the first question was pre-ordained.

'Tell me, now that charities are big business, dee dah dee dah.' I can't honestly remember the rest of the question. It was the intro that thudded into my head with all the familiar force of a loyal oath. Why do journalists of any stripe have to precede any story about fundraising with that great dumb cliché about the fact that we are now big business? It sets us up as sinister. It is a short step to suggesting that we are devious and manipulative. Look, the media man is suggesting, look at all these fundraisers! They are drinking coffee together, they are having conversations in low, muttered tones! Many of them are wearing suits!

A couple of weeks later I was with the London branch of the ICFM offering an impromptu rant about the media. We could only be grateful that the media were not there, for the room boasted chandeliers, red wine, a man in a monocle, John Gray's latest tie and Rich Fox working the room like only Rich Fox can work a room. If we looked sinister in

Holland, we must have looked positively cabalistic in Belgravia. Thank heaven Jeremy Paxman was having his ego MOT'd that night!

The latest shock horror television programme on charity fundraising had appeared on Channel Four a few weeks before and indeed boasted a mini-Paxman whose eyes narrowed convincingly as he dug the dirt. The ritual incantation was made ... 'Now that charities are big business' and we were off, through a jolly Smee and Ford seminar, via a shot of Margaret

> It is the Eternally Pejorative School of Journalism: it could sniff around heaven itself and find sneering fault with the angels.

Bennett carrying an evil-looking computer tape somewhere near Godalming, ending up with a close up of Colleagues' [not a typo, Colleagues was an agency at that time: Ed] name plate in deeply-suggestive brass. Fundraisers sat around in small rooms intoning mantras about database segmentation. To the untutored eye, it must have been clear that do-goodery had fallen into the hands of a rather terrifying freemasonry of knavish exploiters.

The boy Paxman moved up gears in the second half. Using some fourth-form arithmetic to make the point that charities shouldn't have financial reserves, he presented a whizzy league table telling us that the top twenty charities had oodles of money, sufficient in some cases to pay their staff well into 1993. The poor old Guide Dogs for the Blind emerged as chief miscreants in the feckless stashing-it-away stakes: the inevitable Guide Dog-basher was found to amplify the point that charities had no business being businesslike. And so, the boy Paxman narrowed his eyes one last time. Next week, a searing exposé on how arc welding suppliers are failing the nation.

Actually we deserve this crap, or some of it. I gather that

some of the slagged-off charities tried to get together for a riposte after this disgracefully superficial programme. And I gather that the consensus was to keep the heads down, not to rock the boat, to let the dust blow away. Maybe such pusillanimity was correct, but it is an echo of the process of subjecting oneself to media scrutiny in the first place. Why bother when you know that the information you supply is going to be twisted to fulfil the stupid demands of formulaic journalism?

That formula is simply stated. At the level I am discussing, it says that any story should be adversarial and should contain the whiff of scandal or, at least, bad practice. It should offer a few heroes as set pieces but should concentrate on the villains. If they lack the proper villainy, suggest that they are smug buffoons. It is the Eternally Pejorative School of Journalism: it could sniff around heaven itself and find sneering fault with the angels.

Shrewd media operators know that you need to take the initiative. You need to overwhelm the nascent negatives with your own exciting positives. You need to create your own agenda and comment on that and not the media's predictable half-truths. Think what President-elect Clinton achieved this year. Remember what Gavin Grant achieved with the RSPCA. Use the media – otherwise the media will use you.

I'm just grateful that the Walloons stayed outside the door. If they'd come back later that night, they'd have copped some great footage. John Gray was doing a sort of tango, Tony Elischer was doing excerpts from *Grease* and Rich Fox was working yet another room. Sheer bacchanalia! Now that we're big business, we can really hold our drink. Bernard Ross, alternative as ever, remains a shining exception.

Good: the case for a re-launch

February 1993

The charity backlash of the me-generation is about to begin unless the giving public can awaken to their social responsibilities.

I don't mind you knowing that just before Christmas I was sitting in the Grill Room of the Savoy with a couple of very liberal captains of industry. I mean this: both captains were of distinctly liberal persuasion, responsible both for giving away large amounts of money and for convening other people to give away even larger sums of money. They were – and are – knee deep in good causes. The caviar was being spooned around, but don't see them as ogres – this is Big Gift country I'm reporting.

With thrilling lack of taste in the circumstances, talk turned to the Third World and a recent report that one of the captains had picked up suggesting that a generation of development aid to poor countries had been worse than a waste and had actually amounted to a block on the development of those countries. Somehow we moved on to London's homeless who must have been depicting a vivid need a hundred yards away from our burgundy. And then we got into social work generally and how it was a pity that all social workers lived in Islington, had never done a day's decent work in their lives and spent all their time training each other in the black arts of interference. Time did not allow, thank heaven, for a reactionary discourse on animal rights fanatics, sexual minorities and other tribes beyond the pale.

It was the taxi-driver school of social analysis and I bring you this reportage from the Great and Occasionally Good because it embellishes my belief that the Devil is beginning to get too many of the good tunes. We live in a jaded society, increasingly suspicious of the value of good, increasingly resentful that there are no apparent simple solutions to any evil. Apathy is beginning to seep through all of us, apathy born of scepticism.

Charities had better start taking this seriously for they have enjoyed a generation who were prepared to believe not just in altruism, but also in the achievement of altruism. If that generation now becomes tainted with disbelief and if they are succeeded by a generation with its heads stuck into Nintendo games, then we're all in for a troubling time. Philanthropy could quite easily become the pastime of the elderly, comfortable middle class – which it was until around 1960.

> Yet I hear no one prepared to admit that the conventional wisdom of twenty years ago was ever misplaced.

My fear is that many organisations are now so locked into their own tribal passions, cultures and vocabularies that the real hinterland of public communication is sliding past them as they leave the port where once they were anchored. I do not have to be reactionary to be bored and desensitised by those many organisations on my radio every morning baying for 'more resources' as the answer to any social ill. Don't they know that the country recently voted emphatically not to pay more in taxes?

We have fallen into the habit of simply putting a price tag on every social need. In recent weeks, I have heard school bullying attributed to boring playgrounds. I have heard the famine in Somalia attributed to debt charges. I have heard the Shetlands tanker disaster blamed on the government (and I do wish that opposition spokesmen would cease this habit of the predictable sound bite).

But the listening natives are getting restless. They read that there are now as many AIDS workers as victims, they read of social workers behaving like the Spanish Inquisition, they read about maniacal warlords in Bosnia and Somalia. And they increasingly cannot make the connection between the obvious evil and the promised good.

In the seventies I ran a campaign for mental health organisations that preached against institutional care and made the case for community care – a battle that we won. But, when I look around the streets of London, I cannot be proud of that victory. Yet I hear no one prepared to admit that the conventional wisdom of twenty years ago was ever misplaced.

Similarly, with the Shetlands tanker disaster: I have heard the blame fall on the tanker owners, the government and the Poles and Greeks who made up the crew. Only once have I heard anyone (and it must have been Greenpeace) say that such disasters will always happen if we allow oil to be transported across the world at the current rate of nautical knots. In other words – and let's say it loud – it is our fault for worshipping the internal combustion engine. The link between the dying cormorant and that lump of metal in the garage is a direct one.

We need more candour, a greater indication that we can still think imaginatively and liberation from our predictable vocabularies. For Good is currently in trouble as a concept.

A strange, old-fashioned, plea for respect

March 1993

The posturing of charities and agencies should cease if the two parties are to talk to each other.

It is a truth, universally acknowledged, that a charity in possession of a few bob must be in want of a consultant, agency, water diviner, shaman, guru, or some such external source of wisdom and fee.

It is a strange relationship that is sometimes created by this convention. Part deferential, part hesitant and suspicious, part hapless – the average charity regards its average supplier with a rich mixture of attitudes. It vests enormous aspirations in these relationships, works hard at selecting the right partners, then gets a little unruly when a few wheels come off.

I'd better declare an interest. I run an advertising agency, a rather nice and jolly one as a matter of fact and one with a few fundraising motifs on its escutcheon. But I am reporting from a wider world than the one viewed from downtown Kennington. For my IFRW hat seems to confer a somewhat above-it-all dignity in such matters. Clients and suppliers alike confide in me. They give me straighter gossip than I deserve. And I'm a bit restless about some of the venomous banter I hear. It smacks of the advertising jungle; and it is well worth avoiding if you have any feeling for what a charity, as opposed to a machine tools manufacturer, should be doing.

Venomous banter? Yes, really. I don't like hearing that Old Thingy up at the Greater London Fund for the Stoned is a time-wasting old git who's never at his fax after four in the afternoon. Or that Acme Direct are an over-priced bunch of

wallies where you get a new account man every time the
moon waxes. Even making allowances for the need to score
points, we should be able to do better than this.

In the immortal words of Bernard Ross, I'm arguing for a
little more respect around here. As a man of the world, I
don't expect perpetual
relationships between the
suppliers and the supplied.
Falling out of love is known to
be as commonplace as its
antecedent and none of us stay
moony forever. Even so...

> Too many good
> people waste time
> arguing about the
> wrong things.

It all starts with imprecision.
Imprecision of motive, imprecision of language, imprecision
of need. That's the client's fault and it's a fault often
compounded by the suppliers posturing beyond their rightful
means. It is a recipe for grief.

I lean to the humblest view of the supply side. I cannot speak
for the consultants, though I have increasing difficulty in
explaining to people that I am not one. But I can tell you
what an advertising agency does. It produces creative work
and ideas better than the charity can and quicker. It buys
media space and mailing lists more surely than the charity
can. Sometimes it can buy print cheaper or offer database
consultancy, but we are already wandering off the
mainstream agenda. In other words, an agency is a simple
thing. It does things that the charity cannot do quite as well.
Over and out.

About ten years ago the client class decided that it needed
something a little more elevated than such tradecraft. It
needed (dread phrase!) 'input'. This imprecise expression
conferred something mystical on the relationship, a belief that
you were buying not just the tradecraft but also a whole scad
of received wisdom. And a generation of received wisdom
was invented overnight – demand and supply, I guess.

The trouble with received wisdom is that it blots out original thought. And the trouble with over-deference to other people's received wisdom is that you tend to cop out of your own duty to be wise. This is why too many good people waste time arguing about the wrong things – I care less about the statistical propriety of the cell tests, more about whether the bloody mailing gets out next week. But such brawness of motive is maybe old-fashioned; it is barely input.

But then I am a simple soul I want people to argue more – about words and pictures and timings and ideas and invoices. I want them to wind each other up, to question the long words, to understand precisely what they are buying and selling, to congratulate each other, to share the occasional nemesis as well as the even more occasional hubris. I hate the idea that people are sullenly sitting through presentation-room rituals, passive and unquestioning, ready to backbite just as soon as the ritual is over.

The mores of advertising were bound to invade the culture of fundraising. But there are signs that the host culture is being swamped. By which I do not mean that fundraising is all nice and advertising is all nasty. What I do mean is that most advertising is pretty silly and that all fundraising is pretty damned important. We would do well to dwell on the difference.

Slow marching through Georgia

April 1993

American fundraisers seemingly know nothing, but it's hard to tell them so to their faces because of their joyful enthusiasm and appreciation.

The NSFRE conference in Atlanta was mind numbing. Two thousand delegates for a start, lurching around in downtown hotels that looked like sets for *Star Trek*, with lifts encrusted with fairy lights zooming noiselessly from the ponds on the ground floor to the hidden heights forty-five floors away. Hundred-foot silken banners fluttering in the atrium and tinkled Gershwin accompanying every meal and drink.

And if the environmental values verge on the oppressive, then the *bonhomie* or *bonfemmie* of American fundraisers compounds the very real feeling that you are part of something. This is no place for a typical Brit to go skulking around on the margins. Your badge will be espied in the lift, your accent will be overheard, your message box on the room telephone will be used – all in the interests of card-swapping and a five-minute conversation that the American party will always find useful, fascinating and somehow revelatory. Old-world business courtesy lives and thrives in the States; in Georgia it is probably enhanced by a certain antebellum style – it is a long time since a lady took my arm to go into dinner!

But, what are you part of? It is an event that feeds on itself. Simple things and banal observations are amplified by surrounding hype. The opening plenary comprised six speakers passing the verbal baton in a self-congratulatory relay race. Three rather humdrum copywriters in a session I attended were described as creative wizards. Any speaker is preceded by three minutes of educational history. 'It's wonderful to be here', said many a speaker.

Being here is wonderful: it could be the conference slogan.

It gives genuine satisfaction, make no mistake. Reserve your scepticism for European conferences. The American delegate is wide-eyed with enthusiasm, full chested with confidence, as respectful of the profession of fundraising as he is of the flag itself. Only in Australia have I met this combination of respect and enthusiasm. I envy it.

Great minds had obviously thought alike.

It does of course make the American fundraiser deferential. The creative wizards to whom I referred earlier would have been savaged in Birmingham or Noordwijkerhout. In Atlanta, they were honoured and thanked, sincerely thanked. Two hundred people left the room chattering about the banalities they had just heard.

It depends where you start, of course. The average European conference delegate comes from a larger organisation, better practised in the fundraising arts. The average American delegate is from a local charity, eager to get to first base. Time and again I heard direct mail speakers asked if there should be a message on the envelope, or whether a personality should sign the appeal, or whether it was worthwhile to personalise the salutation. We in the UK still ask these questions of each other but we have begun to suspect that the answers are marginal to the thrust of raising money on scale.

There was a delightful demonstration of the price to be paid for slavish deference to orthodoxy. Two teams of creative wizards were given a couple of days to come back to the direct response track with proposals for a mailing campaign on behalf of the Atlanta Symphony Orchestra. On the last day they each returned with a campaign that was practically identical. The envelope was the same size and colour, the one-page letter said the same things in the same order, the reply element was a lookalike. Great minds had obviously thought alike.

That, at least, was the verdict offered by the convenor. He – and they – felt that the orthodoxies had been proved and sound practice validated yet again just because half a dozen hacks had walked round the creative treadmill one more time.

No one seemed to grasp the opposite thesis: that these deeply boring and slender variants on a jaded theme were enervating the donor into total docility. We heard a lot about donor fatigue, excessive appeals through the post and the rising cost of donor acquisition. No connection was made between these factors and the lack of creativity with which we were confronted. And doubtless the guy from the New Mexico Boys Band of Albuquerque went right home to reproduce it all.

Sometimes in America you want to scream. I didn't of course. It would have been a mite discourteous, a bit like farting in church. Thus conscience doth make cowards of us all.

I actually wandered into someone else's convention while I was there. This was the Institute of Shopping Center Management who run to a newsletter called *Shopping Centers Today*, a university course or two and a whole publications programme on how to get the most from your mall. I just hope that the mall-owners weren't being told always to put the restrooms on the first floor, always to site the Body Shop nor' nor' east of the fountain, always to discount pizza prices on Thursday.

I bet they were though.

Diary of George Smith, aged fifty-two and a quarter

May 1993

Call the aged what you will, they'll still defend their unique culture to the bitter end.

The longer I live, the more the brain cells wane. This is a scientific truth, daily evidenced by an increasingly haphazard working style and a rapidly waning dress sense. Proved too by an ever more eccentric selection of anxieties. I used to worry a lot about things like workers' control of industry, the powers given to the European Commission and Third World debt. I now find myself worrying about why people wear baseball caps the wrong way round, why modern shoelaces won't stay tied, why I can't find a cassette of R Dean Taylor in my local Woolworth's. I have no more resolved these dilemmas than I have the first lot, but it interests me that this new self-given agenda is the classic mark of the curmudgeon.

I just looked that word up to find a far harsher definition than I suspected. I thought curmudgeons were simply miserable old farts. They turn out to be gloomy, bad-tempered men, misers or, heaven forfend, churls. I don't accept too many of these words. The old curmudgeon I want to be is certainly impatient, definitely waspish and dismissive. But finally a sentimentalist who proceeds from the absurd position that everything used to be better than it is now My curmudgeons are so touchingly daft that they deserve pots of affection if not respect. *One Foot in the Grave* is testament to the theory; Alf Garnett was an earlier one. We curmudgeons want to be loved a little.

All this maundering is brought on by the news that this is the European Year of Older People and Solidarity Between Generations. And that Help the Aged has solemnly posed the question as to what older people really want to be called. And that Age Concern has mounted a poster campaign bidding us to fight ageism by dwelling on the awful expressions used to describe persons of advanced years.

I wish to protest. Nobody told me that a year had been dedicated to my age group and that makes it a deeply undemocratic designation. And I'm by no means sure about this solidarity between generations that has gone similarly undiscussed. If you're asking me to beam fondly on Nintendo games, blokes with earrings, drum machines, yoof programmes on telly, the current English cricket team, or other demonstrations of societal decay, then I say pall and pshaw, and I bang my Zimmer frame down as I say it.

> I have to squirt these words out of a word processor when I yearn for the simplicities of carbon paper.

I'm allowed after all. I'm subject to ageism every day of my life. I have to deal with people who've never heard of R Dean Taylor. I have to squirt these words out of a word processor when I yearn for the simplicities of carbon paper. I have to argue with people who challenge my deeply reasoned view that Andrew Lloyd Webber should be hanged. The young people in my house behave disgracefully, playing loud music, drinking my booze, failing to wipe their feet, feeding the cats at the wrong intervals, using hair gel, disagreeing with me all the time. And they know about all these things I don't – things like computers and cars and chaos theory and identification of objectives. Solidarity with this lot? I'd sooner rejoin *Socialist Worker*; Paul Foot was always sound on hair gel.

So I have to argue the inevitability of gradualness on our

friends from the aged business. I'll buy the ageism bit with all the zeal of someone who's always wanted to be fashionably oppressed by something other than dandruff. But I jib at this inter-generational solidarity angle. I don't think we're ready for it. Let's kick it around in a decade's time. Statistically there'll be more of us anyway, and English cricket might have improved. Put a ring round 2003 and let's discuss.

Which only leaves us with the vexed question of what we should be called. Richard Ingrams seems happy with oldies and a lot of people make free with wrinklies. I note from the States that senior citizens have become truncated to seniors, a fact that I actually noted from a poster advertising a Grateful Dead concert. I imagine that pensioners is now lacking in political correctness, suggesting as it does a certain dependence on what used to be called the welfare state.

Oh, let's just call us curmudgeons. Now that we know that we're formally oppressed, we can start to behave badly. Don't forget we have years of practice, so the earring generation can start trembling in their shell suits. I expect massive subvention from Her Majesty's Government on the basis that the re-creation of the nineteenth century is an implicit part of their manifesto. Expect the first demo any day now. We'll wreck a few computer shops, march on Lloyd Webber's place and intersperse the harangues with good old R Dean Taylor. Best of all, we'll bore you to tears. Don't say you weren't warned.

Pick your own aphorism

June 1993

The next time you make an unreasonable request, you could be laying a path to the future.

I always used to use a Shavian aphorism in big speeches. I used it for so many years that I began to worry that my oft-repeated attribution to George Bernard Shaw might be something of which I've convinced myself – these things easily happen if you get used to the sound of your own voice.

It said this: 'That the reasonable man accepts the world for what it is. The unreasonable man does not. Therefore all progress is in the hands of unreasonable men.'

Neat, huh? And it certainly sits in harmony with my basic view that all things are impossible until you make them possible. Which sounds like so much hot air until you start to deck round the homily with a few real life examples. British fundraising is actually full of them and, if Saint Geldof is the patron saint of the doers tribe, then there are lots of less flamboyant examples knocking around.

Rich Fox is one. He arrived on our shores a few short years ago and banged on about the joys of telephone fundraising. He walked straight into the brick wall of British conservatism, suffered the delights of attenuated British decision making and listened patiently to the catch phrase of a nation, 'It will never work here'.

I sometimes think that that phrase should be etched into the national coat of arms, right below the lion and the unicorn. Translate it into Latin and it's a whole more pertinent than '*Honi soit qui mal y pense*' or '*Ich Dien*' or all those other tags that are good only for quiz questions these days. It's a reaction I've now heard attached to ideas like capital fundraising campaigns, direct mail appeals, research, company sponsorships and the professionalisation of charity shop staff. None of these things could work here; they all did.

The thought that the United Kingdom has a sort of cultural immune system that vaccinates it against outside ideas is merely daft and easily disproved. But we add to it a less worthy and altogether less endearing subtext which I also offer up for Latin translation and addition to the national escutcheon. It says 'It's all right for them.'

> When you played 'Simon says' as a kid at least you had to keep your wits about you.

By which we averagely mean that the other organisation is always better endowed, more popular, better managed, has a higher profile and is altogether luckier. Repeat the mantra often enough and you have the perfect mindset for doing bugger all over a period of years. I have heard medical charities whinge that fundraising is impossible at a time of high awareness on Third World issues, I have heard Third World charities whinge about the public's prioritisation of domestic issues. I have heard small environmental organisations complain about the large ones. I have heard head office complain about the regional organisers. I have heard regional organisers complain about head office. When all else fails, lay it on the trustees – it's always all right for them!

This is a dingy British echo of what the Australians call the 'tall poppy' syndrome, the habit of chopping successes down to size if they make you feel uncomfortable. The Red Cross may or may not have made fifty million quid for the Kurds but we enjoy the animus more than the achievement. It was all right for Whitlam and Gray – all they had to do was bell Jeffrey Archer and Harvey Goldsmith and the money flowed in. Nothing succeeds like excess!

Put together our national conservatism with our unworthy

habit of envy and you get an oddly paradoxical brew. For what we have too much of is deference, the belief that fundraising is about the simple repetition of previous practice, the sidelong glance at someone else's programme and its thoughtless replication, the unquestioning note-taking and thought-free debriefing. Mullin/Sumption/Strickland-Eales/Smith/Burnett say do this, and a hundred organisations do. When you played 'Simon says' as a kid at least you had to keep your wits about you.

If gurus were right all the time, they would be a damn sight richer than they are. All any of them can try to do is persuade people to think for themselves for they cannot in honesty report regular risk-free success or proven each-time-out method. And as an occasional strolling player on such stages, I have to tell you that the average audience wants the smack of authority more than the nuances of experience. It can be very frustrating.

The only aphorism that actually keeps me going is one I forged myself a few years ago. It says, 'You don't get what you don't ask for.' People like Geldof and Fox and Gray have proved it. So have a thousand others whose names we have forgotten and who are probably driving mini cabs in Stoke Newington. Fundraising is a risk business and never let anyone tell you otherwise. If you want to stay immune from ideas, or if you wish to wallow in the uselessness of envy, or if you get your rocks off by wringing your hands, then Lamont's green shoots give you an exit door to a new profession. Chartered accountancy beckons.

Never sneer at an Oscar

July 1993

Nothing succeeds like success, and nothing makes the cheeks glow more.

I've always taken a typically profound view about awards competitions: they are deeply meretricious, utterly meaningless, trivialising and altogether foolish. And I enjoy them like mad. Put it another way, they are incredibly daft and they make people happy. In an uncertain world, they are therefore a Good Thing.

I gather from the *Professional Fundraising* magazine awards in early June that such an annual event has been previously discussed in high places and dismissed on the basis that it would somehow give offence. By which I presume that the ICFM has looked at the idea and found it wanting. I find this rather depressing. A fast-developing profession should have the maturity to accept the predictable bad-mouthing and backbiting that come with awards in exchange for the exhilaration and pride that it offers the winners; and the general sense of aspiration that it offers everyone else.

Cerebrally it's daft. A handful of our peers shuffle into a room, pore over an unrepresentative entry of work, declare some awards, refuse to declare others and pieces of paper are given out to the lucky winners a month later amid handshakes, photographs and modest razzmatazz. Godlike omniscience is therefore granted to the judges. How on earth can you possibly know which is the best campaign in the arts or educational field? How can you really distinguish between senior practitioners in declaring a fundraiser of the year? What about the campaign that is difficult to precis and that offers too few of the glitzy graphic virtues that often catch the judges' eyes?

All this is fair comment, but total allegiance to it becomes uselessly puritanical, as dismal as the spectacle of those schools that eschew competitive sport because slobby kids can't play games and might need slob counselling for the rest of their natural. I think slobby kids can play games. I think everyone can win awards. Further, I think slobby kids should play games. And that everyone should win awards – eventually.

Having run an advertising agency for twenty years, I can testify to the value of professional awards. Inevitably, we have a wall-full of certificates and a mantelpiece-full of artefacts, though the louche days when they were used as doorstops is long over (the times are more serious and the risks of proprietorial eccentricity more pronounced). So I can vouch for the fact that they make people happy, that they add a little excitement to our dull lives and that they boost an organisation's morale. A trinity of excellent values.

> I think everyone should win awards – eventually.

And, without seeming patronising, I must report their particular value to young professionals. We gnarled old hands may be forgiven our sense of distance from such party games but watch a table of youngsters whoop and hug each other when they make the biggie. Only misanthropes would sneer at such displays of pride. The rest of us are allowed only a fond, knowing smile.

Having said that, George Medley's pretty acceptance speech on being made fundraiser of the year seemed genuine enough. And I can remember getting the gold award at the BDMA a few years ago for a Greenpeace campaign. Old know-it-all bounded to the stage and was sufficiently dislodged to give a clenched fist salute to the throng. If I hadn't been physically removed, I'd probably have burst into tears, thanked the printers and art-workers who made it all possible and made a speech announcing that I wanted to travel the world and work with children.

So, let this be an annual fixture. And let there be more entries and more categories. But, let there be just the one, authoritative competition, even if it takes some hard-bitten diplomacy between the Institute and *Professional Fundraising* to arrange it. The worst thing that can happen is for the apparent success of this first awards competition to spawn imitators. I have watched this happen in direct marketing where there now seems to be one a month. The currency gets devalued; the cynicism reappears.

And, while it may surprise my old adversary Paul Rowney to see this in print, I think we all owe him some sort of vote of thanks for getting that PFR show up and running so successfully at the Horticultural Hall. There was a bustle around, a sense that this was an event that for once coincided audience demand with value for money. Again, I hope it becomes an annual fixture and Paul can wallow in such warmth in the knowledge that I am unlikely to be so benign to him for a decade or so.

The fundraising caravanserai now moves on to Birmingham at the end of June and to IFRW in October. I submit that all these three events are relevant to British fundraisers and that all begin to have a definitive niche. When the ICFM launched the Birmingham convention, some people expected it to bring IFRW to its knees. What has happened has been instructive. Slightly fewer Brits now make their way to Holland and form a lesser fraction of a larger whole. The event has got larger and altogether more international; it has also got better, freed of its reliance on the British market. A healthy development. And better value for the Brits who do come.

Birmingham will also mature in different ways. As will the new Rowney event. I can't argue for a hundred flowers to bloom when it comes to fundraising conferences. But we seem to have three hardy annuals. Let's keep them well watered.

Seriously, let's be silly

August 1993

Shocking swimming pools is one thing, but shocking the world depends on a different set of vocal skills.

I have a friend who recently invested in a swimming pool. He is not a man who is at one with the mechanical world and he nodded politely through the two-hour briefing to which he was subjected by the bloke who came to tell him about pool maintenance. But he was delighted with the news that he had to 'shock' the pool every two weeks, the verb being one of the few words he had understood.

So, the two of us spent a silly afternoon jumping out from behind hedges and shouting 'waaagh' at 14,000 gallons of passive water. Then we leaned nearer and shouted, 'Come on out, mustard algae, the game's up'.

The news that 'shocking the pool' is a matter of chlorine concentrate and not of verbal abuse will be old hat to all you pool owners, but we enjoyed the difference. Being silly in a serious world gets ever more difficult. You have to leap at every opportunity.

All this came to mind when a genial cove with a beard approached me in Birmingham to say how much he enjoyed these feuilletons of mine and how he looked forward to a predictive monthly chortle via this free parade through my subconscious. I stuttered my thanks and tried to make the point that I thought I was being serious every month. He went away with tears in his eyes, giggling still at this further display of wit. You can't win.

Then again, there was the incident a couple of months ago when I mentioned the immortal name of R Dean Taylor in these pages. I received a fax from a very senior fundraising person whose normal reach on matters cultural is positively intimidating. She (oh heaven, what a giveaway) accused me of inventing R Dean Taylor and insisted that the name of the illustrious warbler must be a deeply meaningful anagram.

> So, that's one fundraiser who sees me as a Woody Allen and another who thinks I'm making like Jean-Paul Sartre.

So, that's one fundraiser who sees me as a Woody Allen and another who thinks I'm making like Jean-Paul Sartre. And, before we go any further, I'd like to point out that old Jean-Paul is a dead French thinker; he was neither an anagram nor did he play keyboards with Jethro Tull. Clear?

Actually, you know, making yourself clear is getting to be a muddied practice. The power of words, a subject about which I regularly opine, is vesting too much authority on that waning minority with the gift of the gab. We live in a curiously deferential society where articulacy is taken not as a means of transferring thought and opinion but as a positive and enhancing grace that confers immediate heavyweight status to the thought and opinion thus transferred. This is dangerous for both parties. Everyone occasionally talks crap; crap is not alchemised by superior presentational skills, meaningful pauses, or bursts of memorable rhetoric.

Hitler talked crap with terrifying power and with argument that seemed entirely rational to his audience. His spiritual heirs and assigns continue to do so in Bosnia. We yearn to relax into the comfortable simplicities of being told what to think, what's going on in the world, how everything is explicable if only you can accord blame and failure to forces beyond our control. Power ends with guns; it starts with words.

Is this a touch overwrought for a British fundraiser? I wonder. I watch Ian Paisley and I know that his verbal power has helped imprison the future of part of our country. I watch the pro-life and pro-abortion lobbies snarl at each other in the States and I know that we will suffer similar snarling here. I watch the politics of this country degraded by sound bites and trashy adversarial debates. All these examples are rooted in our increasing habit of using language as a ritual and not as a reasoned means of exchanging opinion.

Politically, we turn off. Professionally, we make notes. Such is our supine nature that we have come to regard any challenge to conventional wisdom as irreverent. And conventional wisdom is invented every single week. We run the risk of immersing ourselves in a cosy world where the responsibility for thinking can be shrugged off via some report writing here, a strategy document there, a new computer network somewhere else. At that point we live in a secondhand world. We have denied ourselves our greatest gift, that of original thought.

Any professional world finally divides into people who want to preserve things as they are and people who want to change things around for the hell of it. In reality you need both, but in fundraising you need a big, fat mischief-making faction for change at any time. We are far too important to get conservative. I still think we need to change the world, you see.

Irreverence is a proper thing. Heretics are usually innovative and always provocative. A sense of humour is finally a sense of proportion. That is why I reserve the right to be pompous in the morning and shout at swimming pools at weekends. I have long been accused of being a cynic; in reality I am a zealot with a bit of experience, a buffoon who remembers old songs.

But, with my luck, someone's going to write in and say that Jethro Tull was an agricultural inventor.

I know, I know.

A question of dignity

September 1993

If the needy and abused have the strength to stand up for their rights, the better off will feel more disposed to give.

There has been a great discussion recently in the liberal press about a dilemma which the chattering classes never thought to confront in their lifetimes. It is simply put: should you give money to the beggars you see on our city streets?

The very choice of words in that last paragraph implies an attitude. I said beggars. Substitute 'young homeless people' and the debate starts off on a different foot. The bleeding-heart tendency starts with a fifteen-point lead.

We are all confronted with this dilemma.

And our reactions to it are predictable, proper and wholly understandable. They also check out to a symmetrical extent with attitudes to fundraising generally.

Start with the Neanderthal attitude. You'd never give them money because they are a bloody nuisance, on drugs or booze, living off benefits and have never done a day's work in their life. Add phrases about breeding like rabbits and you have many people's attitudes to giving to Third World charities.

Continue with the thoughtfully negative attitude. You can't give them money because they are so many of them and you never know what good it does. Then again, they will probably spend it all on drugs and booze. And, besides, you don't like the way they all have dogs with them these days. At which point the thoughtfully negative attitude becomes an objectively Neanderthal attitude. Again, we have stumbled into an attitude to charity giving generally.

Then, you have the liberal cop-out attitude. You sometimes give them money but, really, the state should be doing something about it. Thatcher's Britain, more resources, blah blah blah. Ironically, this most progressive of attitudes is the least valid. Every time a journalist covers the story he finds out that any number of hostel beds were unoccupied that night. The uncomfortable truth for us leftists is that many young people in doorways have built a lifestyle around doorways. They'd quite like a council flat but they would probably miss their mates if they tottered off to that Salvation Army hostel.

There is no point in trying to be wise about such an issue without saying how you react to it yourself. So I'll come clean. I don't give money to these people because they frighten the life out of me. I can dip into any of the previous rationalisations to explain the fact that I regularly turn the other way (which is literally what I do most nights).

> There are plenty of unpopular causes around and few of them are cuddly.

But I don't bother. The fact is that they alarm me, these people. The younger ones remind me of what might have happened to my own children, the drunken ones disgust me as all drunks do, the aggressive ones make me aggressive in return. If this is need, I lack the grace to cope with it.

But this year – or was it last year? – someone did something to change these perceptions. The Blessed Anita Roddick funded something called the *Big Issue*, a very handsome street newspaper on and around the homelessness issue and which is sold by homeless people. Very good and professional it is too. So, you can give and rationalise your giving. You are buying something, a function somehow more wholesome than the scattering of coinage. I guess the average donation has shot up as well.

But the main visible effect is on the people selling. They now stand where they used to sit. They have developed a nice line in patter and they are sometimes very funny. Last year's mendicants have become this year's salespersons, if indeed they are the same people. Dignity and cheerfulness have entered the equation and I now find myself buying the *Big Issue* regularly. It may be a ritual salaam, but someone has found a means of parting me from a few pounds a month that was previously denied.

I shouldn't get overwrought about this.

The *Big Issue* has neither solved the problem nor dispersed the public hostility that I recorded earlier. Many of the mendicants are still terrifyingly battle-scarred from life's wars and it is still irritating to be accosted thirteen times in a ten-minute walk.

But, if this new venture has sapped some of the total despair from the issue, it will have done much. We want to believe in these bright-eyed young people and their jokey banter. We can cope better with this image; we are not forced to disdain them because we fear them. They are suddenly like us, only poorer. And, so we begin to understand better. And to give.

I think of a lot of causes when I think of this. I think of the AIDS charities and the barrier they face in trying to convince a surly community that wants to believe that the cause is a tribal and alien one. I think of those charities working with the diseases of the elderly. I think of those heroic organisations currently trying to restore our historic national decency on the question of refugees.

There are plenty of unpopular causes around and few of them are cuddly. All I can urge on their proprietors is a greater presentation of human dignity for I believe it to be a much under-employed idiom in fundraising. We are bewildered by this awful and complex world we see every night on television. Nothing works any more, nothing ever seems to get better. But bewilderment need not make us all reactionary. Give us the images of human dignity and we can still respond, I'm sure.

I need to see those kids standing up straight and laughing. I need to see AIDS victims as people like me. I need to see Alzheimer's victims as my own parents. I need to see those refugees as neighbours, not tearful dependants. I want to identify with human need. Don't we all?

There'll be a session devoted to the Third World aspect of this at IFRW this year and it will be fascinating to see how it plays. If you can't get to Holland, try and catch the excellent photo exhibition that the Terrence Higgins Trust are moving around the country. You may go in slightly homophobic and all that. You'll come out a better human being.

Let's hang on to what we've got

October 1993

Knowing when you've run out of steam is to be to your credit. Recalling Walker Brothers B sides is not.

I have a friend who can chant the names of the entire New Zealand cricket squad who toured our shores in 1957. Cricket buffs will know that this is the height of mental recall, the equivalent of remembering the Eurovision Song Contest in chronological order or the names of all Mrs Thatcher's education ministers. You have to be slightly barmy to store away such things.

And I have always been thus barmy. I am probably the only man in Kennington who can tell you the name of Harry Truman's vice president, give you the state capital of North Dakota, identify Norma Tanega's only hit and remember that Bristols were once cigarettes. Indeed I have occasionally incurred folding money by mastering such arcane material. There was the occasional pub quiz. There was the regular Trivial Pursuits trouncing of my children when I insisted that pocket money changed hands on the basis that it was positively character forming to get a grip on such marginalia.

And there was the crowning moment when I was asked to co-author the *St Michael's Book of Trivia,* a belated attempt by M&S to cash in one the pub quiz market. The book sold in dozens. I got my royalties in returned Y fronts.

Barmy, then. And insufferable, too. We all hate a know-all. And so we should, even if the knowingness covers nothing more profound than Millwall left backs and Walker Brothers B sides. A man's brain cells deserve better than to be assigned to the endless compilation of such stuff. Surely the prime purpose of the cerebellum is to learn and not to digest. There are only so many brain cells in there and they get to be a waning resource in middle years. I am positive that my failure to grasp the merest principle of quantum physics is rooted in an earlier decision to burden the little buggers with south London tram routes.

But, now that the said little buggers are signing off by the year, I begin to nag at the whole question of knowledge, experience and wisdom. For we tend to merge all these qualities for our greater comfort, and in doing so we miss the precise meaning of each word.

Experience is unchallengable and it is a chronological thing. If you have served a charity for thirty years, you sure know all about it. You can remember the last six directors, you can remember when the entire staff could meet in an Anderson shelter, you can remember when the old Duke of Gloucester told you to keep up the good work.

We may be paying too high a price for continuousness and longevity.

Knowledge does not always follow experience. Sepia-toned anecdotes do not make you the master of risk analysis or the nuances of the latest legislation. Indeed, it would be conventional if your longevity made you the enemy of such knowledge. Pshaw, you may cry, in my day we did without this computer stuff. A Remington typewriter, some sheets of carbon paper and a day's work for a day's pay. And we still had change for a packet of Spangles.

But wisdom – where does that come in? At what point do you acquire it? At what point, more importantly, is it attributed to you? Are you wise because you have done something, because you have spoken about it, because you have written about it? Or, because you are experienced or knowledgeable? Or old?

I'm in this vein because I have recently decided to stop doing some things that I have been doing for years. Professionally speaking, that is. I have decided to resist the vanity that comes with an assured position in life, to smile fondly and with total disbelief at the siren voices that tell me how much I will be missed, to wander out of a few tents and peer down a few new crevasses.

There is nothing either heroic or mystical about this. I have merely come to the view that I have exhausted whatever mental seams I have been mining in these several incarnations. I do not think myself wise, I do not consider myself particularly knowledgeable. And, while the experience is validated by everything from a birth certificate to liver spots, it doesn't impress me and I don't expect it to impress anyone else.

The fact is, that we all hang on too long in our conventional modes. There are plenty of reasons why professionals do, things likes mortgages, kids, pensions. But in the world of charities, we may be paying too high a price for continuousness and longevity. I think particularly for trustees and boards of directors and even those splendid volunteers who have been running the Tunbridge Wells group since 1961. We can respect their commitment, but can we truly respect their contribution?

Think of the House of Commons. Once elected, five-sixths of its members know that they have a job for life. They may start with zeal and panache but within two terms they are jaded functionaries, incapable of original thought, as grubby and conventional as Dickensian clerks. The place stinks of uselessness and we all pay the price.

Now, think of a House of Commons where no one was allowed to serve more than two terms, where it was agreed that you were there to innovate, to achieve, to move the furniture and then sod off. Oh boy, what a prospect that would be!

We all have our sell-by dates. We should acknowledge the fact with great candour. To do so is not to deploy the pejorative phrase 'being past it'. It just signifies that human beings are very good at one thing for a part of their lives but cannot be expected to be very good infinitely. Would caps not be thrown in the air if your trustees were appointed for a two-year, non-recurring period?

Try a trivia test on your seniors. If they can remember the Four Preps, send for a tumbril. If they have never heard of the Four Preps, they are distinctly unworldly and should never have been there in the first place. If *you* have never heard of the Four Preps, then I don't know what the world is coming to.

How green is your jargon?

November 1993

If jargon is the enemy of meaning it has no place in the mailing packs of professional fundraisers.

I just discovered a new word. I discover new words every day but most of them turn out to be unusable in common parlance. Ziggurat is a pretty good example. It is, of course, a pyramidal Sumerian temple with terraced stories. But you just don't need it very often. 'What a super ziggurat!' is a rare thing to say outside Sumeria; use it at home and you could be misconstrued.

But this new word defines an everyday function. You offer up your credit card or smart card to the retailer, right? He or she passes it through a machine, right? It validates your status as a cardholder and gives you permission to deepen your debt. So, what verb defines the passing of the card through the machine?

The word, I have to tell you, is 'swipe'. My British Airways handbook tells me so, as in 'you must ensure that you swipe your Executive Club membership card through the automatic card reader'. Not a lot of people know this.

A swipe in my dictionary is 'to hit violently with a swinging arm, or 'an inaccurately aimed blow'. 'Swipe me, guvnor' we used to say when we were lovable Cockneys all those years ago. And surely it was demotic for petty theft as in 'Sir, Grimshaw minor has swiped my protractor'.

So, how did it come to describe this most technical and advanced of electronic functions? Is it one of those dreadful acronyms like ROM and DOS? I think we should be told.

And another thing. Why does everyone now say 'there you

go' when they used to say 'here you are'? No wonder Johnny Foreigner gets confused at our verbal ways.

I speak as a man with all the moral authority of someone who has just written the dread words 'resource implications' into a report. What I meant was that we should discuss the money side. What I said was that we should discuss the resource implications.

Isn't it interesting that a statutory verb always attaches itself to this new gobbledegook? Resource implications are always being discussed, assessed or outlined. Issues are always being addressed. Information is always being sourced. Data is always being retrieved.

Because we are constantly addressing problems, we are never likely to solve them.

Here are some phrases I have plucked from an incoming report on my desk: 'consumer typology', 'cost transparency', 'validate the top-line analysis', 'team bonding', 'key windows'. I can wrestle with this terminology, I can decode it, but I am left with the distinct impression that, whatever this bloke is selling, it's going to be bloody expensive. Or dear, as we used to say. Or 'having significant financial impact' as he might say.

Let's be honest. We all select modish words to define ourselves and our professional value. A certain dignity attaches itself to the command of a knowing vocabulary. But we should pause before this automatic collation of jargon and begin to appreciate that the loose and unthinking deployment of fashionable gibberish is an enemy of concise meaning, a cop-out that restricts precise or original thought.

Issues are there to be resolved; problems are there to be solved. The new fashion for 'addressing' both these nouns carries with it a subtext for inadequacy – because we are constantly addressing problems, we are never likely to solve them. Every politician who gabbles on about the infrastructure is denying the electorate a better understood discussion about more prosaic things like trains, hospitals and roads.

Which, of course, is at least half the point of these arcane languages. They are deliberately used to confuse, to mislead, to sell. The legal profession is a good example of how you can get away with it for hundreds of years.

My point was made – and made better – fifty years ago by George Orwell. This is from *Politics and the English Language*:

> 'Modern writing at its worst does not consist of picking out words for the sake of their meaning and inventing images to make the meaning clearer. It consists of gumming together long strips of words which have already been set in order by someone else, and making the results presentable by sheer humbug.'

Amen to that! I use this column to make a familiar point because I see signs that fundraisers are disappearing into the abyss of verbal sloppiness and pompous doublespeak. I have already seen a mailing that asks for resources and not money. Saving the infrastructure cannot be far behind.

The best of our communication uses simple and vivid words and uses them with passion. Have you ever stopped to think of what a beautiful product name Greenpeace has? But we live in an age where someone is probably advising Feed the Children to rename themselves Nutritional Support for the Younger Person.

I joke, but only just. Actually the joke's on me. In the hour it's taken me to write this squib, I've learned that I'm the only person at Smith Bundy who didn't know about 'swipe'.

A tall fellow-director sneered at my ignorance. 'You've been too long removed from corporate bodies', he said. To which I can only reply that he's spent too much time hanging out with computer companies. Yah boo!

Goodbye to all this

December 1993

Admitting you got it wrong is often the only route to getting something right.

This is the last regular column I shall write for this journal. There is no great significance or weight to be attached to this minor event; I just get bored with the sound of my own voice and I have to believe that others share the boredom. Besides, I don't get paid for it.

Writing a free-ranging piece like this every month is a strange privilege. There is no brief and I have never seen it as an opportunity to sell my varied wares. Anecdotes from Smith Bundy or IFRW stray in from time to time but they have always been deployed to make a general and not a particular point. Or indeed, a joke. I remain keen on jokes.

But humour is a dangerous commodity. I have always argued that a sense of humour is merely a sense of proportion, but you would be amazed at how imperfect a perception that is. The offence that can be given by the slightest hint of levity is astounding. People ask me why I'm always taking the piss… I remember one piece in a direct marketing journal where I used the name of Buxtehude because he was the most obscure German composer I could think of. An indignant list broker wrote to me; he had been stationed in Buxtehude after the war. Why was I having a go at him?

But, then I suppose dropping names like Buxtehude is just a trifle poncy. Anyone reading such a piece can be forgiven for believing that the writer is trailing his cultural coat, airing his lordly views via crafty syntax and knowing analogies. You get to use poncy words, too. Some people enjoy that; others find it obscurantist. Another poncy word.

And views are difficult things to have. They get to be Views, which get to be Opinions, which get to be Professional Judgement. Repeat them strenuously and often enough and they get to be Minor Theology.

The point about having views is that they should be capable of total and regular revision. Is there anything more insufferable than someone who knows the absolute truth all the time? We pay a terrible price for dogmatism in politics and we should not wish to reproduce that useless banter in a profession like fundraising. I would predict a five-point opinion poll leap for John Major if he had the courage to say what he knows to be true about some of the policies he inherited.

The free thinker is forever branded as the heretic, the boat rocker, the piss taker.

Rail privatisation probably seemed a reasonable piece of Tory politics when it was encoded into their last manifesto. Eighteen months later it is clear that the idea is inoperable. No one wants it, the market is sceptical, the advice of the civil servants is implacably negative. And the bill will be presented to the next parliamentary session.

Far better that Major or MacGregor should stand up and say that they have changed their minds, that they have done a lot of work on the proposal and found it lacking. The country would salute such candour. And I should point out that this is no party political point I am making; the Labour Party has paid a terrible price for continuing to offer policies way beyond their sell-by date. Dogmatism drowns original thought. It is the historic enemy of honesty.

In fundraising, I find myself saying out loud that supporter recruitment via direct mail is no longer cost-effective, a braw view and a contrary one to the one I have peddled for a decade. I have reached it through observation of the market; the growing resistance of people to direct mail, the formulaic techniques we are all using, the weight of competition, the actual response figures that often sit on my desk.

But to say such a thing is to risk the wrath of every vested interest involved in the field, and they are many. The letter columns of the trade press will likely fill with stories of continuing success in direct mail recruitment. My own daily colleagues will accuse me of rocking the boat. List brokers will write me outraged letters and buttonhole me in watering holes.

These are small prices to be paid for saying what you think and I am much too old to be worried by such social obloquy. What worries me is the defensive posturing that so readily sets in in a world where everyone seems to be selling something to someone else. And what also worries me is that the free thinker is forever branded as the heretic, the boat rocker, the piss taker.

You see it in far more important areas than mine. The recent consultancy report on the future of voluntary organisations is a classic case. The entire voluntary sector descends on the proposals like lion on sheep. Lo, even the holy Charity Commission is offended and comes, teeth bared, fighting out of its cave. Someone actually asks if we are to overturn two hundred years of decently ordered practice in the matter of charity regulation.

Put it like that and I find myself in the unlikely position of supporting a Tory think tank. Anyone who imagines that the system we have is anything more than the Great British Fudge is deceiving themselves. The Charity Commission may be a fine and ethical thing but it has about as much connection with current charity practice as the MCC has with English cricket. I rest my case.

And has anybody actually read this report?

It turns out to be slightly dotty but full of interesting perceptions about charities seen from outside. It is actually a progressive piece of thinking that comes to no real conclusions because it is mindful of its very advisory status.

But it is provocative. It seeks to change things. It takes a radical look at what we do.

And so we rail at it, or seem to. I guess British charities were always finally conservative but I am troubled at the extent to which such conservatism is now embellished with all the trappings of a defensive lobbying group. I still believe that we are here to change the world, a task that sits ill with the defence of every known status quo.

Exit the heretic. Stage left.

Who's an oxymoron then?

February 1996

On his welcome return to the pages of *Professional Fundraising*, George ponders on the social risks run by fundraisers.

When I entered the advertising business on the reasonably shrewd basis that girls in advertising were prettier and more forthcoming than girls in banks and building societies, I soon learned to apologise for my calling at parties. If you moved in leftish circles, the fact that you were a humble production assistant did not insulate you from the scorn of chaps with convincing beards, badges and scarves. Working in an advertising agency? How could you? These Holy Joes and their doomish ladies were always doing integrity-packed things in libraries, schools and town halls; you were sorting out process engraving (ah, dear dead phrase!) for the Ford Motor Company. Moral obloquy was immediate and total.

It was worse with direct marketing. By now, it was probably a dinner party at which you had to stutter your chosen profession. 'So you're the bastard that sends me all that junk mail', said the man with avocado streaks in his greying beard. 'I don't know anyone who ever responds to that stuff.' You prepared your set routine about the Consumers Association, Book Club Associates and the fact that his wife was clad top to toe in mail-order Laura Ashley but to no avail. You remained a professional pariah.

I'm beginning to worry that fundraisers might be at equal risk. The British have long been characteristically two-faced about their charities. They celebrate them, indeed they support them with true and heart-warming generosity. But they positively hate the idea that anyone should be paid for eliciting that generosity. Fundraisers live in a moral no-mans land; they can be honoured for the end that they achieve, but trashed for the means by which they secure that end. Which is a bit like finding the Gulf War totally justified but rueing the bombs we dropped.

We can never win this eternal battle for esteem. Just as the public is willing to call for enhanced public services and reduced taxation with no apparent sense of irony, so it demands that a charity spends zilch on administration and is run forever by volunteer ladies opening envelopes in a back room donated by a noble benefactor. Professional fundraising is an offensive oxymoron for anyone who claims to recall a voluntary sector that was truly voluntary. Offer up some documented history of our field and it will be waved away as the special pleading of the smart-arsed apologist. Some people need to believe in the Royal Family, in Tony Blair and in the internet and some people need to believe that charities were once run by mild-mannered, eternally grateful nice people who did it all for love. Why confuse any of them with horrid facts?

> Offer up some documented history of our field and it will be waved away as the special pleading of the smart-arsed apologist.

And yet, and yet... I am concerned that we may be risking a true cleavage of understanding between us, the askers, and them, the asked. If an ordinary member of the public stumbles into the bacchanalia that is every fundraising conference's last night, they might be forgiven a slight frisson of distaste. Who's paying for all these drinks? Those suits, those dresses? The average soiree in our business looks and sounds identical to a convention of motor traders except that more women are involved. It is a long way from the Cause.

As a regular participant in such bacchanalia and the

occasional convenor of social excess, I am in no position to offer moral homilies. What are we supposed to do anyway? Sing hymns? Chant the ICFM code of practice? Most fundraisers are dutiful little souls. They deserve their occasional tipple and the sight of John Gray's waistcoat collection.

But can we do something about the mutual backslapping at these events? I played the Canadian convention a few weeks back and the annual dinner was an orgy of introductions from one worthy to another before the hired speaker stiffed the entire hall with a speech that was verbal Mogadon. British fundraisers, being an unruly lot, would never quite settle for this degree of starchy formality but there are signs that we may be heading in the same direction. Last year's awards ceremony at Birmingham certainly crossed a threshold of taste, presentation and self-satisfaction. And some delegates found it hard to take.

I don't mind fundraisers getting pissed. I do mind them getting too pleased with themselves. It is an entertaining fact that we produce only a small part of British charity income. It is an even more instructive fact that the vast majority of people raising funds are in fact volunteers. Too much preening on our part is bad for our souls

But I still don't quite know how to explain the fundraising function at parties. Mind you, all those lefty librarians seem to have retired on index-linked pensions, having voted Tory for donkeys years. The last time I mentioned Greenpeace to one of these veterans of the duffle coat, he practically spat at me as in days of yore. Greenpeace – how could you?

Seems like you can't win.

A voice from the regimental database

April 1996

This month's column sees George pulling rank with fellow donors.

I just received an appeal addressed to Major Donor. None of this clever personalisation, I'll have you know – no Dear Mr Smith. Just my rank, respectfully set above six hundred words of passionate pleading, Dear Major Donor.

I like this. I'm a man who narrowly escaped National Service and, therefore, failed to have a Good War. I even kept out of the Officers' Training Corps (OTC) at school and formed the Alternative OTC, a bunch of fellow-refuseniks who smoked behind the bicycle sheds while our contemporaries paraded in the playground, did aircraft recognition and became adjutants and corporals. When I realised that my early tendency to drop out was denying me this sort of status, I promptly made myself a wing commander of the Alternative OTC – Dennis Armstrong, I seem to remember, became a rear admiral.

So, the acquisition of military rank in middle years is an unexpected bonus, beside which honorary fellowship of the ICFM pales just a little. I like being Major Donor. I shall now buy a swagger stick and swagger with it. I shall grow a clipped moustache. I shall write to the *Daily Telegraph* quite a lot. It goes without saying that I am now wholly in favour of the re-introduction of National Service.

Only one thing worries me: we majors need a hierarchy of other ranks in which to thrive. I need a commanding officer, dammit, and I can't think that the charity concerned is writing to people who outrank me donation-wise and calling them General Donor. And what about the chaps in the ranks? I see them now, bulling their standing orders, saluting me as I pass at the annual general meeting, singing their cheery working-class ditties around the campfires. Are they addressed as Private Donor? I doubt it. I think they are addressed as Dear Friend – a typically slipshod form of salutation in today's fundraising army. It is no wonder standards are slipping

Perhaps we should look further afield to find an appropriate hierarchical vocabulary. I shall not idly sacrifice my new-found majorship but I am happy that

> All this sounds much more fun than that crummy old donor pyramid.

we should consider public school language. Thus I can become Donor Major on the basis that lesser oiks can be addressed as Donor Minor. A first donation qualifies you for New Boy status and bounders like me can bully them and get them to toast my crumpets. The Director of Fundraising (the Beak, of course) could appoint a Head Donor from the top percentile of the database each year and allow him to make the vote of thanks after Redmond Mullin addresses us at Founder's Day. I'd hope for a prefectship out of all this and you can certainly count me in for the annual dance with the girl donors over at Wilkinson's House at the National Trust.

All this sounds much more fun than that crummy old donor pyramid. I never liked being in that pyramid anyway. There were tens of thousands of you at the bottom as humble Enquirers. We lost a few when we became Responders and then even more when some of us turned into Donors. But we still had to hold the rest of them up! We were just like the lower ranks of those pyramids formed by noisy Germans at Costa Brava swimming pools, staggering and straining while others climbed on our backs.

And how insufferable some of them were! Those Committed Donors, for instance ... always giving themselves airs just because they could decode direct debit mandates. Worse were the Covenantors, lean-faced donors forever jabbering texts from John Knox. And with Big Gifts you really had to keep your temper. 'I started as an Enquirer myself before I became a Big Gift,' one of them told me, 'mind you, that's when an Enquirer really meant something.' Straightforward elitism, if you ask me.

We didn't mind Legacies being down at the bottom of the pyramid. They were the true aristocrats – good manners, fine breeding. And they were also totally dead.

No, we've come a long way in fundraising terminology. When a man such as myself, from humble origins and once a mere Donor, can rise without trace through the structure and acquire the rank of Major Donor for a reasonably modest outlay, then we truly live in a world of relationship fundraising.

My wife, the memsahib, has been instructed to iron my puttees. I am going to play with my soldiers in the war room, as the conservatory is now called. I met a Legacy Pledger the other day. Damn fine chap, salt of the earth and all that. Could be good for three stripes – if he learns which way to pass the port.

Lies, damn lies and charity statistics

December 1996

Administration costs are readily accepted by today's sophisticated donors. But should donors be given further financial information to enable them to make a more informed choice?

I do not know Paul Rees of Relate International who wrote so provocatively in last month's issue of *Professional Fundraising*, but it would be churlish to deny that he has a point.

The point, if you missed it, was that charities with apparently vast reserves should pause a little before unleashing major fundraising programmes. How can you need more money, he asks, if you have millions of pounds in the bank? And he makes a terrifying suggestion, 'To enable potential donors to make informed choices as to which charities to support, why not make it the norm for each charity to print its last year's income, expenditure and reserves on all its appeal literature, newsletters, forms and so on. Can anyone give me,' he says, 'a good reason why not?'

I will offer two reasons, though neither of them will give Mr Rees satisfaction. The first is that donors do not make informed choices – they make emotional choices. The myth of the financially literate donor poring over balance sheets to decide the best venue for his or her philanthropy is pleasing but daft. The fact that Guide Dogs for the Blind has £184 million in the bank will probably not deter one donor in a hundred from giving – they like Labradors, they want to help the blind and no amount of objective data about the financial comfort of the organisation or, indeed, the anxiety about the appropriateness of the product itself will stop the legacies coming in or the collecting tins jangling in the pubs. Both things have been well publicised in recent years. It has made little apparent difference to the organisation's income.

The chicanery was always bad and it's getting worse.

The second point is altogether more important. For even the keenest-eyed donor would be perplexed by the average charity's presentation of its finances and therefore of its current needs.

There is much chicanery afoot in the pie charts, the percentages and the statistics. The chicanery was always bad and it's getting worse. We run a grave social risk if we do not acknowledge the dishonesty and try to do something about it.

Lies, damn lies and statistics... the aphorism is an old one and we certainly live in a world where statistics are mangled daily to serve interest or rhetoric. Thus, we either have the fastest growing economy in Europe or we are somewhere between Albania and Papua New Guinea, according to political taste. We spend more money on health care every year and close hospitals regularly. The National Lottery reduces personal donations by six per cent and charity income mysteriously grows. You can pick and choose between these statements – they are doubtless underpinned by some statistical credence.

It is sad, though, that charities seem so happy to join the game. I am looking at a pie chart as I write. It offers slivers of expenditure called 'information costs', 'recruiting', 'direct expenses on subscriptions and donations', 'general marketing costs' and 'administration and central management expenses'. This could be a diligent attempt to itemise the organisation's running costs for the benefit of its supporters. Sadly, I think it is an attempt to mask the picture of an organisation whose expense ratio (to use the old-fashioned term) is around the 50 per cent mark. Neither that basic fact nor the means taken to conceal it are at all unusual in British charities.

Today's donor is reasonably sophisticated. He or she knows that it costs money to run a charity and that the cost of administration is a proper cost. But he or she would be alarmed by some of the percentages that now pertain. And he or she would likely be incensed by the verbal trickery regularly applied to denying them the knowledge. Too often we betray their trust and the betrayal is often childish. I went looking for the accounts of one charity earlier that year that stated in a mailing that it spent just 15 pence in the pound on administration. Only the most absurd figure juggling could justify the claim.

The answer can only be the standardisation of such financial reporting. It is an old demand and it would take an almighty effort to defend the integrity of such standardisation. But we are sitting on a time bomb here – the plurality and creativity currently applied to the process offers a rich field for any journalist who wants to put the boot in.

Transparency is a vogue word but charities, of all institutions, should apply it. We currently offer opacity as a substitute. It does not become us and it is dangerous. The asset value of a charity or the number of years' running costs it has stashed away is a matter of fine financial judgement that most donors will not seek to apply. But knowing how the charity spends my donation is a simple right, one that should not be demeaned by the organisation's fear of the truth being understood.

In search of baubles

February 1997

How many fundraisers are actually making the New Year's honours list and is it really for want of trying?

Now you know and I know that twice a year the honours lists are earnestly scanned by many in the voluntary sector just to check which of their colleagues or acquaintances have secured a gong.

They pretend otherwise, of course, but I have seen many a fundraiser in early January put on thick spectacles so as to scan the published lists from top to bottom. And I am quite willing to believe that newspaper readerships soar on the days in question, such is the interest among charity wallahs.

I love this annual ritual for it combines prurience and spite, two qualities that characterise a young and growing profession. There are those amongst us to whom three palace-awarded letters after their names confers lifelong serendipity. Indeed, there are some who begin to express growing impatience – out loud at that – at their continued absence from the rolls. Actually, an awards system that seems to prize a veteran volunteer above an upwardly mobile, well-connected professional strikes me as entirely proper. But I can still sense gritted teeth in some quarters when the good lad who chairs the Halesowen branch goes to the palace and the high-profile charity executive doesn't.

Two of my direct marketing mates turned up on the honours list this year. Not for services to junk mail, I hasten to point out, but for that most mysterious and delicately phrased of commendations – 'public and political service'. Far be it from me to record that at least one of them has single-handedly been keeping the Conservative Party going in Scotland these last troubling years. He is an all-round good egg who richly deserves (see how quickly the pusillanimous language sets in!) his new initials.

You'll probably remember that John Major tried to open up this process a few years back bidding all of us to write in with nominations, sort of an awards charter, probably. What you may not know is that he and I share a Brixton background and that, indeed, we coincided on Lambeth Borough Council – from slightly different political perspectives, you understand. And, if the other buggers can flaunt the old school tie, why shouldn't I? On the basis that 'you don't get what you don't ask for', I wrote up. And, at risk of breaking the thirty-year rule and probably incarceration, I want to share the correspondence with you.

> Dear John,
>
> Remember me? Other side of the council chamber, long hair, foul-mouthed. You were on housing, I was on libraries. Remember the bacon sandwiches?
>
> Anyway, John, I made my way in life. Went into advertising, wrote a lot, went into fundraising, became a columnist on Professional Fundraising. Which is why I'm dropping you this line.
>
> Any chance of an award this year? Anything will do. If there's the odd K knocking around, I wouldn't complain. But a nice little OBE would do. I'm not proud.
>
> Do let me know. If you want dozens of letters saying how much I deserve it, I can easily write them (it's what I do for a living) – Ken Livingstone will probably put in a word.
>
> Look forward to hearing. Love to Norma.
> George Smith
>
> PS I still think Chelsea are crap!

Imagine my dismay at the reply I received in response (below) to this well-crafted missive.

> Dear Mr Smith,
>
> The Prime Minister has received your letter of the 8th inst and begs me to inform you that he remembers you well.
>
> He also asks me to tell you to sod off. Further, he wishes to make clear that Chelsea under the aegis of Mr Ruud Gullit are magic and will wipe the floor with your bunch of tossers from White Hart Lane.
>
> Yours faithfully
> Malcolm Timeserver, Private Office

Okay John, if that's the way you want it!

Chances are, the follow-up will go to Prime Minister Blair in any case. I think I'll start networking New Labour – I know a man who once touched the hem of Blair's duffle coat. Then there's abroad with a glittering array of possibilities. I just heard that Charlotte Grimshaw has been offered the vacant throne of Albania. But it's probably only a rumour.

Job-speak – a user's guide

March 1997

When you're seeking a new job, it's not what you know it's how you explain this to potential employers.

If I had to earn a living writing this column then, presumably I would have to apply for the position of writing it. As it is, I can offer my monthly gibberish to an uncaring world without subjecting myself to the due processes of recruitment, assessment and interview. The status of the gentleman-amateur still has its virtues.

For it is clear that I would never survive these processes of personal selection. I have to waddle regularly through the thickets of recruitment advertising by charities; it keeps me up to speed with the state of the fundraising job market.

Everyone tells me how difficult it is to 'find the right people'. Dare I point out that this is partly because of the verbal infelicities that now attach to the process?

Charity ads have fallen into the hands of those human resources-wallahs. Within recent memory they were of course personnel officers, a grand enough title for most people but one clearly doomed by the fact that most of us understood what it meant. Power in today's world stems from incomprehension and titular aggrandisement. All visualisers are now art directors and I understand that there are people called resource development managers. I speak as someone who used to be a writer but should clearly be re-designated as written language executive.

One look through charity recruitment ads demonstrates not just the ceremonial style of the new bullshit but the verbal poverty that stems from it. There are certain words in the English language that now only occur in such ads.

'Commensurate' is one, as in 'your remuneration package will be commensurate with experience'. Which can only mean that they will pay you as little as they can get away with. There are a lot of little games played around this phenomenon – watch out for the 'competitive remuneration package'.

I also like what I must describe as the 'booming vocative', the use of a disembodied second person verb to state certain personal necessities.

I also like what I must describe as the 'booming vocative', the use of a disembodied second person verb to state certain personal necessities. Thus, 'You'll be highly motivated', or 'You will be a graduate'. This last one really gets up my nose, suggesting as it does that the privilege of poncing around a college for three years bestows a lifetime's dedicated brainpower and restless intellectual energy.

Then, there's the word 'possess', a comparatively new entrant in the field. It has usurped 'have' in job-speak and is usually gummed together with the booming vocative as in, 'You will possess good interpersonal and motivational skills', or 'You will possess proven team-leadership skills'.

I like all these new skills. 'Oral communication skills' are what we used to call talking and 'interpersonal skills' are presumably getting on with people and going to pubs with them. And I have just spotted 'the ability to handle multiple priorities', which is presumably what most of us do every time the phone rings when we're in the loo.

But, if there is one thing that marks out the successful applicant from the also-rans, it must be the word 'strategy'. Time and again a job ad will specify the need for a 'strategic thinker', or indeed demand, 'You will think strategically', or, at the top end of the market, 'You will possess proven strategic thinking skills'. Tactical thinkers can go take a jump. They probably didn't go to college anyway.

There is equal symmetry in the description of the workplaces that demand such strategy. They are always 'hard-working', the incumbents forever 'working under pressure', or in 'a pressured environment'. Which is why you have to be 'self-motivated', or 'highly focused', or – wait for it – 'personally receptive to the demands of a high pressure working environment'.

Do the conveyors of these ads pursue the same verbiage into the interview? Do they boom at the applicant and say, 'Do you possess sugar for your coffee?' or 'I note that your feet are commensurate with your legs'. Are you asked to demonstrate your oral skills by reading a leaflet out loud, or your strategic skills by twisting the knob on one of those new office coffee mugs? I do hope so.

Only once, and donkey's years ago, did I find myself in such a situation, sitting uncomfortably before a Knightsbridge management consultant in application of a very sexy job. 'Is there anything in particular you are afraid of?' said the bullshit pioneer. 'Yes,' I said gravely, 'falling over. I don't like falling over.' The man made a very large note on his pad and I got shortlisted.

The job was running Apple for the Beatles.

Sadly for western civilisation, Paul put his oar in and Allen Klein got the job. I've still got the rejection letter somewhere. I guess my interpersonal skills just weren't strategic enough.

Why shame the punters when you can threaten them?

April 1997

In this month's column, George tackles the 'aggressive' tactics used by direct marketers.

In today's paper the World Cancer Research Fund is being calumnified for those 'aggressive direct marketing tactics' that we all know and love. Apparently a recent pack goes through the motions of asking for volunteers on the way to the Big Ask. It embroiders the 'No' option on the reply form with this form of words, 'I am sorry I will not be able to help as a volunteer. But I wanted to let you know now so you will have time to replace me in my neighbourhood. I enclose my contribution of £10, £15, £25, more...'

This is certainly as crass and as ugly as fundraising can get. Or is it? I don't doubt that the constant tweaking of the minutia of the fundraising art produces dividends. Add a moral threat to the standard 'No' box and doubtless guilt seeps over the mailing list, propelling lots of nice old ladies on to the active donor file.

But why stop at low-level moral blackmail? Why not elevate the role of shame, fear, threat and aggression to the whole process? Most of the buggers don't respond anyway – what have we got to lose? Wording such as the above merely suggests guilt and social obloquy and even the suggestion is a sly one. We should up the ante, postal rates being what they are.

We are actually halfway there with those door-to-door survey packs that are going to be lining doormats this summer. They used to ask reasonably credible questions; they now say things like, 'Many murder victims die a horrible death – by strangulation, knifing, gunshot wounds, or battering. The murder often takes quite a long time and the victim sometimes ends up in a pool of blood. Do you think this is a good thing or a bad thing? I exaggerate, but only a bit.

> We should do more testing on that somewhat limp statement – it sounds a bit self-consciously revivalist to me.

We have, of course, invented so many clichés of communication that the only task we have left ourselves is the embroidery of those clichés. We allow our donors only to give to us via the declamatory YES, succeeded by the substantive statement, 'I want to help the aardvark lead a long and meaningful life'.

We should do more testing on that somewhat limp statement – it sounds a bit self-consciously revivalist to me. How about, 'YES, some of my best friends are aardvarks'; or 'YES, I am a fairly sad person and a serious legacy prospect'; or 'YES, I agree – an aardvark is not just for Christmas'. Let the donor speak, I say.

But the fun starts with a negative tick box.

The word NO can be followed by all manner of self-revealing statements. Do it often enough, compile the tested responses and you have a verbal database of quite enormous profundity. Fie on your focus groups when you can get the punters to say things like, 'NO, I am as poor as a church mouse'; or 'NO, I am the meanest bastard you ever wrote to'; or 'NO, I hate aardvarks and, come to that, all insectivorous quadrupeds'.

You could certainly develop the shame-making WCRF gambit even further. How about, 'NO, I'm much too smug and secure to worry about aardvarks. I wear colourful cardigans, admire Noel Edmonds, drive a Range Rover and am almost unbelievably unpleasant.' For it could be argued that the average reply form is a very boring rectangle indeed, one that merely offers a verbal square dance to the reader – tick the tick box here, docey doh and honour your prompt boxes.

Why not admit that this space is a field of honour, no less, where fundraising battles are won and lost? Why not use it to say exactly what you want to communicate? I always wanted to start a lapsed re-activation letter with the words, 'Look, you bastard' in place of the traditional rueful personalisation. It's in the same spirit of straight talk that I offer the following suggestions for reply forms.

'If we don't do five-to-one on this appeal, I'm probably out of a job.'

Or, 'When are you going to get up off the pot? It cost a lot of money to recruit you and you've sent sod all to the last five appeals.'

Or, 'There's some very big geezers on our local committee in your area and they get really upset when people in your postcode don't respond. A big donation could spare you untold aggravation and perhaps save your kneecaps.'

The terrible thing is that messages like this would probably work. When you're as boring as we are most of the time, the merest sign of life is likely to be welcomed beyond its means.

Let the aged help

May 1997

It is a sad truth that an extraordinary opportunity is going begging because fundraisers have ignored the potential of the 'gilded generation'.

It looks like there are ten million old people in this country, ten million and rising. The percentage of the population now aged 60 or more is approaching twenty-one per cent and you'll have seen the projections for the growth of that percentage in the next century. One in four of the entire population will soon be old.

The extent to which this known phenomenon is ignored by fundraisers is fascinating. For it is not ignored by other marketers. The railway stations and airports are thronged by beaming, vigorous travellers who have been targeted by Saga. These same people are the big purchasers of TESSAs and other savings products as financial service companies know full well. These people spend millions weekly in garden centres and keep large chunks of the West End of London in lights.

For the central point about old people is that they are astonishingly rich. I have pointed out elsewhere that they are historically rich, the richest people who have ever lived. They are arguably the last generation to profit from a lifetime career, from secure pension provision and by startling fortune in the property market. You do not have to have done anything remarkable to have assembled a seven-figure asset by the time you stop working; six figures is utterly conventional. It is sadly unlikely that future generations will enjoy these components of wealth creations. For the current concentration of wealth in the upper age groups is a finite phenomenon, only very recently visible and likely to disappear below the horizon like the Hale Bopp comet.

We know all this. We have heard all about it at seminars, read about it in the press. If we have been exposed to Ms Judith Nichols, we will have learned the characteristics of this new fundraising market. They are active, these people. They are physically active, sexually active, socially active and culturally active. They are so active it's sodding unfair – here are all these rich people poncing around, doing what they want, never having to go to meetings, living on their savings, rarely touching their capital, lying in bed all morning and growing world-class Swiss chard. I stayed at a five-star hotel recently. The noisy splashing in the pool came not from the traditional Germans forming pyramids but from dozens of white-haired folk with figures like Brad Pitt. Well, the chaps anyway.

We should have the wit to develop products and messages unusually appropriate to it.

Let us be keen-eyed about this. A good proportion of one fifth of the population is loaded and leisured. It is financially secure and has quality time on its hands. It is having all the fun that the rest of us deserve. And what is the conventional depiction of this gilded generation by fundraisers? We think of them as legacy prospects. Oh, and as shop assistants if they are female. For the fundraising mindset is that old people are poor and frail, not to be disturbed by us lest they tumble from their Zimmer frames. If we categorised millions of young people or black people or female people with such blandness we would offend liberal opinion. But liberal opinion goes totally untroubled by the startling caricature that is Victor Meldrew. (Don't get me wrong – I think we should laugh at everything. But the basic joke in that show is about being old and therefore silly.)

So, in ignoring the potential of this market we are at once patronising and incompetent. We have all the science and the statistics with which to reach this market. We should have the wit to develop products and messages unusually appropriate to it. We should have the skills to overcome its known problems. For the problems exist all right – these people have probably never been charity donors on any scale; they think of a donation as something placed in a tin; they are likely to be politically reactionary. But they are real people. They grieve over suffering and love their grandchildren. They may even suffer the odd twinge of guilt as they see the interest on their deposit accounts making them richer every passing month. And they might be happy to be confronted with the opportunity to devote some of that marginal income to doing good.

It is a sad truth that this extraordinary opportunity is going begging because most fundraisers are young and see their natural audience as themselves. Thus, the continued quest to recruit 'young professionals' or (and I quote from a brief 'the critical 25-44 generation'). I tell you two things about this age group. First, it hasn't got as much money as its elders. Second, it will inexorably get older itself.

Sure, I'm an Old Fart myself. But just for the record, I'm not in the age group described above. Not for ... oooh ... months.

Do you seriously want to be famous?

June 97

Fundraisers mustn't think that they are going to get famous just by standing up and saying how urgent their causes are or how much they need money.

My wife was on the radio recently. Or wireless as we call it in the Weald. At least she says she was. She was interviewed by a girl reporter about the millennium thrash we're having in the village, and the resultant transmission apparently happened during a three-hour swathe of records and local banter. The lady from the post office said she thought she recognised the voice. So, that's the wife's fifteen minutes of fame.

My own last media exposure had me invited onto a telly programme where a panel of academics and human resource-wallahs were discussing stress or rather Stress. It was chaired by that American professor with a silly name who bobs up on all these things. I seem to recall that my contribution consisted of sulking bodily on camera, saying that stress was all a load of bollocks and trousering my cheque. I do try to elevate the intellectual level wherever I go.

Anyone can, of course, now play the media game. All those zillions of channels and stations need human fodder to sustain them and it is a rare fundraiser who will have missed the point, such is our celebration of the new god, Awareness. Pay your dues to Awareness and regular income shall be yours – reticence is the road to financial shortfalls. And charities must all go to the Fame School.

But they mustn't think that they are going to get famous just by standing up and saying how urgent their causes are or how much they need money. This is poor and fustian stuff: they need an Issue. And Issues must by Addressed, Urgently and as a Matter of Priority.

Take my friends down at Sinister Action, the pressure group set up to fight for justice for the left-handed community. They could just go on telly and rant about the lack of left-handed doors, the fact that all weather forecasters are right-handed and that Alan Mullally is in and out of the English cricket team. But, not wanting to appear to be mere ranters or craven mendicants, they have done that most media-savvy of things. They have Commissioned a Survey.

And what a mound of fascinating attitude they have uncovered! Apparently seventy-three per cent of us would be unhappy if our daughters were to marry a left-hander. Fewer than five per cent of us claim to have had a left-handed sexual partner in the last twenty-four hours, while a massive eighty-one per cent agree with the statement that left-handers have been unfairly stigmatised in the media. Phrases like 'left winger', the survey points out, are now widely used to convey a total lack of fashion sense and inability to serve in government.

> All those zillions of channels and stations need human fodder to sustain them.

With material like this under the belt, it was a short step to the *Today* programme on the morning of publication. Solemnly Humphrys intones the ritual words , 'A survey due to be published later today ... ' and we are off. There is the earnest young spokesperson from Sinister Action talking of the reality of the left-handed culture and how government should devote more Resources to the Issues that the Survey reveals and which must be Addressed. Urgently and as a Matter of Priority. There is the junior minister uttering sympathetic noises and Welcoming New Initiatives when Resources Allow.

There will of course be an awareness advertising campaign to capitalise on this communications coup. Well, there'll be a couple of whole pages anyway. The headlines will say things like 'Left-handers have rights too', or 'All we want is even-handedness' and the coupons will be natty little trapezoids, the size of your thumbnail. Later that afternoon there'll be a photo call to launch the poster campaign. Well, the poster anyway – there's only one and it's unveiled by one of the few soap stars to be openly left-handed. It features a torn picture of Allan Mullally and the headline 'Left out again' and it makes page seven of *Professional Fundraising*. It's only fair to report that all this creative work had been produced pro bono by a top-line advertising agency. Well, fairly bono anyway.

I managed to talk to Malcolm Gauche, director of communications at Sinister Action, later that evening when he'd finished his exhausting round of interviews and chat shows. 'Went the day well?' I asked. 'Magnificent,' he said, 'the left-handed Agenda has never been so High Profile. And this is just the beginning. For the National Left-Handed Awareness week in July, Anne Widdecombe has agreed to gig with the Spice Girls.'

'I didn't know she was left-handed,' I said. 'She isn't,' said Malcolm, 'but she needs the publicity.'

Let's be conventional

July 1997

Smith's first law of conference networking: you will never find the person you are looking for. But you will meet this other person every five minutes.

There used to be conferences. Now there are workshops, conventions and heaven help us – symposia. This week I actually did a symposium. Long words were acquired that will be deployed with great gravitas this next twelve months. You want to know what 'disintermediation' is, or who the 'category killers' are? It'll cost you – I charge significant coinage for consulting in such language.

But all such gatherings enjoy a certain symmetry, however they are titled or whatever the price tag. And you need modest familiarity with special verbal and physical body languages to cope.

There is the 'conference down glance' for a start. This enables you to demonstrate proper courtesy to the unknown person who just greeted you with unnerving intimacy (a particular problem for middle-aged men who've haunted the conference circuit for years). The conference down glance enables you to briefly clock the fellow delegate's name badge without being seen to do so, a gracious facial swoop that will have you responding in seconds 'Damien, by all that's wonderful! And how are things at Phallic Software?'

You need to practice this at home. The down glance needs to be the merest movement of shoulder and eye. I have seen flustered out-of-practice delegates resort to the old untied-shoelaces gambit and pretty pathetic they looked. Two words of advice though: if your enthusiastic greeter is female and you are male, do check that she is wearing a badge before applying the glance. If she is not, your zeal for etiquette could be misconstrued. And do look out for the later stages in any conference when delegates start to swap badges. Just apply common sense in this situation. Otherwise you will get a response like, 'Do I look like Damien from Phallic Software? Surely you remember me Gloria Mundi from the Bewildered Fund?'

Also invaluable is the 'beady-eyed room scan'. This is a great boon for those many occasions when you are merely hanging out at a conference. You are knackered, you half want to go back to your room but you want to stay a dutiful delegate. You stumble into a room, probably a bar, that looks full of people who want to sell you fleet insurance or personalised balloons. They half turn to you, sizing you up as an interesting person/reasonable prospect.

I met Damien from Phallic Software in a corridor.

A balloon man begins to make towards you ... it is time for the beady-eyed room scan. Just narrow the eyes and pretend to be looking for someone. Small up-and-down gestures of the head and a growing frown will help make the point that you are a person with a mission, not idly to be interrupted with talk of balloons or fleet insurance.

This is, of course, first cousin to the 'brisk clipboard walk'. Whichever conference you go to, you will spend most of your time walking down corridors. And corridors are dangerous places. Personalised balloon salesmen and fleet insurance wallahs live there, lurking behind columns, ready to entrap the unwary delegate. I met Damien from Phallic Software in a conference corridor.

You enhance your chances of corridor survival with the brisk clipboard walk. Stride, don't ramble, perhaps apply the beady-eyed scan (see above). Always affect a clipboard on the basis that it suggests not just power but local, vital and confidential power. Get it right and balloon man will stay lurking, in the belief that your purposeful walk suggests that you have just be warned by security that terrorists have seized the keynote speaker. And that you are looking for David Ford to help you start negotiations.

All of which brings us to Smith's first law of conference networking: you will never find the person you are looking for. But you will meet this other person every five minutes. Thus, the hot prospect, genuinely interesting speaker, or otherwise beautiful person will apparently be vaporised. But that scrofulous old git who always comes to this conference, who supports Manchester United, sings Carpenters' songs in the bar, shows you a photograph of himself with Noel Edmonds and probably sells personalised balloons ... you will meet him in every room at any hour of the day.

Which is why you have to fall back on 'conference banter', a sub-language that permits verbal courtesy while stopping short of meaning. 'How's business?'; or 'How's things?'; or 'Enjoying the conference?' are the classic openings of conference banter. Its characteristics are that you either cannot hear or cannot give a toss about what the other herbert is saying, but you can still manage the 'knowing nod' or the 'fawning smile', the facial accoutrements of conference banter.

Sometimes, in playful or surrealist mood, I punctuate the dutiful verbals with something like, 'Of course, you can never have too many coat hangers'; or, 'That girl's looking up my trousers.' I still get the knowing nod, the fawning smile, even on occasion something like, 'You're dead right there'.

That is why video conferencing is a dead duck already. It just doesn't offer the fun component of interface with fellow delegates. And you never get to meet personalised balloon salesmen.

Read any good t-shirts lately?

August 1997

Does wearing the t-shirt make you part of the gang?

Once upon a time I was wandering around a shantytown in Kenya and I came across a bloke whose engaging smile survived a total lack of teeth, who greeted me in gummy Swahili and who was sporting a familiar t-shirt. Mysteriously my new Kenyan friend was wearing the colours and logo of the British Lung Foundation.

So how did this item of garb find its way to Nairobi? Had it been given away by the British Council, recycled by Oxfam, parachuted in for some local emergency? My mate didn't know and I can't believe that this estimable charity had started a local chapter. The fact is, that t-shirts have become a strange new currency, sullenly finding their way around the world, bearing ill-understood legends and incomprehensible names.

Stick around long enough in fundraising and you're going to amass a whole collection. My own wardrobe boasts specimens from Target Direct, Smee and Ford, the International Fundraising Workshop, the Management Centre, Greenpeace and a host of other causes and events. They should nudge the memory but somehow they don't. Did I really participate in the Great Walk to Brighton or someone's 1982 mail order day? And what is the provenance of that rather upmarket number which has the Royal Mail thanking me for being there? Where was I, for heaven's sake?

And no one ever remarks on them. In a world where the t-shirt is ubiquitous and where the display material on them can range from American universities to pop groups, from restaurants to newly launched software, readership is minimal. Sad though it is, I have to record that no one – but no one – has ever stopped me in the street to express amazement that I know Smee and Ford, the legacy people. No one has ever slapped me on the back to say that they too were on the Great Walk to Brighton. No one has ever crossed a room to compare notes on Target Direct.

There is one current exception. A couple of weeks ago my daughter returned from Glastonbury, naturally with the festival t-shirt. For a modest consideration she lets me wear it and it has proved seriously eyebrow-raising among one's peer group. This is a recent conversation recorded verbatim.

Peer group member: You didn't go, did you? All that mud!

Self: Of course, I was there. The band always play Glastonbury.

PGM (incredulously): I never knew you were in a band.

...and greeted my explanation with a rueful, 'Well, it takes all sorts.'

Self: We only play the big festivals these days. Retro spots in the acoustic tent. Sort of early Tim Buckley and James Taylor. I play dobro. Twenty years ago Ken Livingstone used to sit in on keyboards.

PGM: What's the band called?

Self: Used to be Girls Wear Brassieres. Now we're just a quartet we go out as the Four Skins.

PGM (ruminatively): I had no idea...

T-shirts rarely spark off conversations of this quality though. And they rarely help you bond with other members of the human race. I was once sporting my Greenpeace solar energy job in Waitrose when I found myself at the checkout next to a bloke wearing an authentic Rainbow Warrior t-shirt. I mumbled something like, 'Good old Greenpeace, eh?' He looked at me scornfully and told me to piss off.

Actually perceived affiliation to Greenpeace is a weeny bit of a problem. The postman once commented on the amount of Greenpeace material being received at Smith Towers and greeted my explanation with a rueful, 'Well, it takes all sorts.' And my new Greenpeace Visa card is already causing scenes in restaurants, with waiters nervously edging me and my chosen bimbo off the premises with undue alacrity, doubtless fearing that we are about to change into wetsuits and abseil up the kitchen wall because they use fossil fuels on the seared tuna. The WWF Visa card, on the other hand, often leads to fond smiles and remarks as to how nice the tiger looks.

> The WWF Visa card, on the other hand, often leads to fond smiles and remarks as to how nice the tiger looks.

T-shirts will be worn in Birmingham, I'm sure. All I can ask delegates is that they make the effort to sustain the conversation that the apparel has started. If you see the Legacy People, pretend to have seen them in an episode of *Flash Gordon, Flash versus the Legacy People*. If you see Ken Burnett in his Scottish t-shirt, say that you had no idea he was Scottish. If you see the Target Direct t-shirt, ask in the kindliest way whether the rumours about Stephen Pidgeon are true.

Shan't be there myself, I'll be at home playing with my dobro.

Do you seriously want to be serious?

September 1997

A light-hearted look at the more 'serious' side of things.

In the early days of Smith Bundy I always wanted to have a checkout in reception. Clients would bring their copy, layouts and finished artwork (oh dear dead phrase) there in a basket or a trolley, a junior member of staff would rack up the cost of their purchases on a big till and the clients would pay on the spot. We would accept credit cards. I even invented some dialogue for said staff, 'A mailing, two revised adverts, three media schedules and a concept... Brenda, aren't we doing a special offer on concepts this month?'

I tried to share this and other fantasies with clients. They used to chuckle nervously, look for the exits and sometimes moved their business to other agencies where the proprietor could be guaranteed to be of sound mind. Mind you, eccentricity occasionally had its due reward – I once won a sizeable piece of mail order business when the client team from Manchester arrived early while I was washing my hair in the sink. 'Are you really George Smith?' asked the marketing director. 'I could be' I said. 'Would you mind passing that towel?' We worked with Marshall Ward for the next seven years on the implacably professional basis that we were more fun than the other herberts.

It wouldn't do these days. Agency pitches are solemn hard work, preceded by large briefing documents from the client and ending with spiral-bound submissions from the agency, the whole event choreographed to the minute.

There is much frowning and note taking. Regiments of

people are involved. Both sides regroup after the presentation to de-brief each other. Another meeting will always be arranged.

Similarly with the interviewing process. Apply for a job more senior than a car park attendant and you will be sent a small feuilleton of paper relevant to the post concerned. Get shortlisted and you will be subjected to a beady-eyed interview aimed at plumbing the heart of your soul. Get seriously shortlisted and you will suffer a barrage of tests and procedures to determine your intellect, your role-playing capacity, your ego, your id, your bonding skills and your command of Excel and water pistols. There's a forest around here that is regularly given over to recruitment weekends where earnest executives zap each other with blob guns, the game monitored by chaps in glasses with clipboards. They all want to be computer salesmen.

> The replacement of human conversation by earnest verbal ceremony can make for mediocre choice, whether of the individual or the company.

My hiring process was always a little more relaxed. I hired Terry Hunt because he read interesting books. I hired Chris Barraclough because he was good on old pop records. I hired Kate Mazur because she was a good bloke who could handle a cricket scorebook. Colleagues could always tell when an interview was going well – they heard the scotch being opened and conversation turning to the virtues of the Dead Kennedys, the superiority of Lorenz Hart over Cole Porter and why Andrew Lloyd Webber should be hanged just after Norman Tebbit. No one queried the relationship of such banter to the stern disciplines of direct marketing. Nor should they have, with salary levels quaking around the hundred-quid-a-week level. Plus luncheon vouchers I might add.

I am not impressed by the New Seriousness.

The replacement of human conversation by earnest verbal ceremony can make for mediocre choice, whether of the individual or the company. Tick boxes are ticked, points awarded, verdicts reached through an accumulation of collective judgements geared for propriety and not for flair. You hear the phase, 'He interviewed very well' and it usually means that the applicant has said the correct things with apparent conviction. The occasional applicant with attitude, the one who might want to challenge the brio – will be seen as a loose cannon – mad, bad and dangerous to know.

Which was, of course, the contemporary description of Lord Byron. Would he have got a job as a poet-in-residence? Would John Prescott have made it via role-playing tests? Blair probably would. Would Spielberg have passed an interview? Actually he dropped out of movie school and just parked his backside at Columbia Studios without asking; by the time the guvnors found out, he'd written the screenplay for *Duel*. Talent rarely emerges via the newly formal techniques of selection. You end up with Mike Atherton or Graham Taylor.

I think I'll pop down to our neighbourhood forest and behave badly. I'll dress up as a moose and confuse both job applicants and chaps with clipboards. They'll probably offer me a job after a psychometric test or two. If your software house turns up for a presentation with the OHPs being carried by a moose, know that we will have scored a small victory for the human race.

Infantile musings

October 1997

George mulls over the reasons why we might want to change the world – and make a donation in the process.

Great news from Smith Towers. Borrowing the first person announcement plural from Mrs T, I can announce that we are going to be a grandfather. The daughter married with such breathtaking expense on the lawn last year has gone for it, succumbed to my frequent readings about the horrors of childlessness from the public prints, witnessed my flamboyant knitting of mittens and collecting of soft cuddly toys, and has announced the arrival of a person and heir next spring.

And there is suddenly a spring in my step as well. We can change nappies again. We can dandle and make goo-goo noises. We can haunt the Early Learning Centre, study books of likely names (will Ringo and Ziggy again be considered by the memsahib?). We can plan trips to zoos after an earnest discussion about the political correctness of such excursions. We can turn the spare room into a nursery. I can have a Meccano set again.

I have already reported this programme to the happy young couple. With terse forbearance, they have made the pettifogging point that the child will be essentially theirs and that the role of grandparents is normally expected to be marginal and occasional. I am, in short, not to get too excited and silly about it.

What me? Middle age offers serenity and continuous if repetitive delights, but I have to tell you that true excitements get to be increasingly well spaced. The last time I was as excited as this was when Botham clobbered the Aussies and the time before then was the birth of my second daughter earlier the same year (I debriefed the Headingley score to her minute by minute as she slept soundly in her cot). General elections, Gulf Wars, World Cups, family weddings, Oasis albums, Spielberg movies – I have enjoyed them all. But nothing matches the anticipation of a new nipper, even one-stage removed. And perhaps especially when one-stage removed.

For the relationship between child and grandparent is famously the most easeful, natural and beautiful in the whole gallery of human relationships. The wrinklies can afford to be indulgent for they have mere walk-on parts in the process of rearing. They don't have to shout, scold or complain; they can simply beam and dandle at irregular intervals. No wonder children warm to these benevolent old things for they offer kindliness, support and fun with nary a nasty world. At least, that's what I hope for.

And as my heart soars, my wallet lightens. Being happy, I feel philanthropic and altruistic. This child will hopefully live through a good chunk of the next century and all my old 'change the world' rhetoric comes flooding back for now I have a discernible and personal interest in that world. For the moment I am a very warm donor.

Charities cannot easily be expected to identify these personal moments of serendipity among their supporters, but they might well consider how better they could service those moments. The only time that the key events in human life are listed as fundraising opportunities seems to be in a legacy leaflet where the personal stocktaking that follows a marriage, a birth, a house-move or a retirement is seen, quite properly, as a nudge to make a bequest. But why isn't a charity gift seen as a natural thing to make when something momentous happens? The greeting card business was the only retail sector to emerge unscathed from the recent recession. Think about it.

Celebration, private human celebration, is an undervalued

asset in fundraising. The death of Diana, Princess of Wales tells as much about ourselves. It teaches us that we are not totally cynical, that we are capable of unexpected emotion and respect. And it teaches us that many people's reflex reaction to an emotional event is a charity donation, a thank-offering. It would not be opportunistic to mark the lessons and offer the donor greater help at the happy times as well as the sad times.

Celebration, private human celebration, is an undervalued asset in fundraising.

I know of only one charity product on the market that matches my current state of mind. Greenpeace has an upcoming scheme for grandparents that targets old farts like me and tells me that the Greenpeace agenda is worth supporting for future generations. I never doubted that, but I guess that they will be writing to me about it soon (probably phoning after this piece is published). Believe me, they will get a result.

But forgive me if I have to dash. I'm going up to the loft to get out my Dinky toys and blow the dust off those old jelly moulds. So much to do – and only eight months to get ready!

Facts and factoids

November 1997

If something is published it must be true – or is it?

What everyone seems to have missed in the endless discussion about the Information Age, the Information Super Highway and the Information Revolution is that information (the demotion to lower case is quite deliberate) is often bunk. What we call information is often nothing more than opinion, hearsay, special pleading, or selling copy. It is rarely objective, seldom provable, and only constant repetition gives it credence. Say something with authority on radio or television, repeat it as often as invited, and somehow it will get to be fact, at least for the majority of people too indolent to quiz it. It is a strange new alchemy that turns the base metal of the press release into the gold of received wisdom. If something is published, it must be true.

History proves at every point what a lot of cobblers this is, how necessary it is to distinguish the actual fact from the printed factoid. If there had been books pre-Galileo they would have told you of a flat earth. Combustion was solemnly reported to be the property of an element called phlogiston. Alchemy was indeed a science, with many a university chair dedicated to its development. All a long time ago, I agree when communications were sparse, publication irregular and information slow to congeal.

Not now of course. I have a friend who last Thursday contributed some information to the Internet. A jazz buff, he had bumped into a site where the origins of the word 'jazz' were being discussed. It was the work of moments to invent some hilarious banter about itinerant Arab workers turning up in New Orleans at the end of the last century from the town of Hejaz and bringing their strange syncopated music with them. When asked what it was called, the uncomprehending Arabs could only say 'Hejaz'. The rest you know. This nonsense is now bouncing around in cyberspace, doubtless to be imbibed by many a saddo.

In other words, we know absolutely sod all about what has happened.

But fundraisers can surely discern fact from factoid? Think again. I am staring at a headline in a respectable newspaper that says, 'Charity income dives in the wake of Diana fund'. It is the latest derivation of a story that has been peddled regularly since 1 September and which has even turned up in the ICFM Bulletin – that the spontaneous public giving to the Diana, Princess of Wales Appeal Fund has knocked general charity income sideways. For all I know the story will be echoed in this very edition of *Professional Fundraising*.

A figure is always mentioned – the Diana appeal has raised £150 million. I first spotted this figure in *The Times* on the Thursday before her funeral and it seems to have been constant for the intervening six weeks. But it is always the text for charities supported by the Princess to express anxiety that donors may think them too well endowed to need more support. And for other charities to bewail the likely effect on their own income. A familiar figure from the sector is always wheeled out to amplify this fictional scenario and to suggest that Something Should be Done.

Thus does a combination of factoids become *fact*. The last version of the same story was that, again, the National Lottery was going to decimate voluntary income. It didn't, though lots of interested parties will go on pretending that it did and the media still find it a repeatable fact, 'Only three years after the National Lottery diverted massive income from British charities, the new Diana, Princess of Wales Appeal Fund threatens to hit struggling good causes yet again.'

Let's pause for a moment. These are the current facts of the matter at the time of my writing. First, no one knows the size of the Diana fund. Second, no one knows anything about the nature of its support – personal or corporate, widows' mites or large donations. Third, no one knows (and never will know) how much of this giving will prove to be spontaneous, specific and supplementary rather than replacement activity for other giving. Fourth, no organisations will yet have their own definitive income figures for the weeks in question.

In other words, we know absolutely sod-all about what has happened. There is a vacuum of fact and we have succeeded in invading that vacuum with guesswork, for the media – like nature itself – do indeed abhor a vacuum. Thus is Information invented.

There is a danger here that the voluntary sector could become the whingeing sector in the public mind. Whatever happens is a threat, a danger, a reason why Something Should be Done. At which point we resemble the British farming lobby, a group that perennially complains about wind, heat, cold, rain, drought, consumers, supermarkets and subsidies. Farmers were once admired. Now they are too often seen as bad guys, knocking down hedgerows, chemicalising our food, complaining about everyone and everything.

A fanciful analogy? I wonder.

Synecdoche, synecdoche... we all fall down

December 1997

Why do people use one word when ten will do?

I was at a meeting last week when an otherwise-intelligent bloke said that he needed to buy into a central management resource.

I'll run that phrase by you again in a minute or two, so don't worry. But let me report in the meantime that this was a divisional head who felt he was (I'm going to have to say it) under-resourced. In other words he had lots of work to do and didn't have enough staff. And so it was that he needed to buy into a central management resource.

Ever eager to acquire new variants on the English language, I pressed him further. What, in the name of arse, was he talking about? He gibbered things about data entry, significant overload and surplus resources in the marketing department. Only when I had him pinned to the floor with a Stanley knife at his jugular did he feel able to unburden himself with short words. It turns out that his Emma is overwhelmed while Tracey in marketing has visibly got nothing to do. Hence the gibberish. 'Could Tracey help out with some typing?' seems a reasonable translation.

It could have been worse. At least he didn't say 'paradigm' or 'synergy' or 'saliency', three words that crept into management language like thieves in the night somewhere around 1990. And he didn't meld the bullshit with one of today's no-brain clichés such as 'moving the goalposts' or 'at the end of the day'. He could have done with ease, 'At the end of the day, we can't move the goalposts – we'll just have to buy into a central management resource' loses nothing as a sentence, merely adding eleven meaningless words to the original ten.

The last paragraph contains one of the first bottlings of 1997 management- speak. I refer, of course, to the expression 'no-brain' – more often expressed as the noun 'no-brainer'. I first heard it in California (where else?) a couple of years back and it began to surface in British marketing circles about the turn of this last year. What I like about it is what I like about many examples of management-speak – it can be used for totally different meanings. Thus, a no-brainer is either a decision so obvious that it brooks no debate or something that is simply stupid. That last Spielberg movie was a no-brainer but so was the director's intention to have large dinosaurs in it. This won't do at all – language can only afford modest elasticity if it is to offer clarity. And even instant clichés deserve universal understanding. Pompous or what?

There I mischievously go again, though purely in the interest of demonstrating how very easy it is to gum words together and giving them the whiff of the zeitgeist. Which brings me back to my intelligent divisional head who wanted Tracey's help. If he had expressed himself in such demotic terms he would have seemed a whingeing office empire-builder. But as Bullshit Man he walks taller, swirling his daft vocabulary around like Darth Vader's cloak. We all quail when we hear such utterances and few of us would dare say, 'What exactly is a paradigm?' out loud.

As I've regularly pointed out over the years, the main purpose of management-speak is to sell familiar things for more money. This is how copywriting became a quaint old habit akin to blacksmithing. The client now wants 'creative input', a far more diffuse and expensive commodity. Anyone concerned with 'identifying and addressing issues' must be a superior life form to anyone actually doing things. And anyone who can skilfully attach the word 'strategic' to his humble function will be creaming it. If I were a carpenter, I wouldn't be buggering around with chisels. I'd be a strategic carpenter, willing to help you identify wood issues and addressing them as part of an over-all strategy for timbered infrastructure.

But as Bullshit Man he walks taller, swirling his daft vocabulary around like Darth Vader's cloak.

Fundraisers have latterly had to subscribe to this new language lest they be thought a primitive sub-species. Charities talk of 'brand ownership' and 'giving retentives' and being 'donor-focused', but these are all borrowed terms, derivative from mainstream marketing. We are now bounden to contribute our own dedicated vocabulary. Can I kick it off for the New Year with the word 'synecdoche'? It means, 'A figure by which a more comprehensive term is used for a less comprehensive or vice versa; as whole for part or part for whole.' Which is about as useless as a word can get.

Not that that should stop us. It has a ring to it. And it will take a brave fundraiser to blow the whistle on it. Make this the Year of the Synecdoche. You have nothing to lose but your brains. A real no-brainer, if ever there was.

Client: **Lemuel Sweat International**

Present: **Lemuel Sweat,** MD

Nigel Luncheon — Voucher, MBS, Ass Brand Mgr

William Blake, Copy Writer

FIRST DRAFT COPY:

woolly quadruped

'And did those feet in ancient time
Walk upon England's mountains green?
And was the (holy lamb) of God
On England's pleasant pastures seen?
And did the (Countenance Divine)
Shine forth upon our/clouded hills?
And was (Jerusalem) builded here
Among those dark satanic/mills?'

choose something Joe Public will understand

are we stuck with this?

REWRITE!

The customers always write: reflections on decades of direct marketing, from *Direct Response* magazine

Is this column legal, decent, honest and truthful?

January 1981

Legal, decent, honest and truthful was a mantra for all advertising at the time, and it's one worth revisiting. George though is always at his best when taking the mickey out of the system and here he has a chance to shine.

A lot of cynical people in this business, the sort of people who start magazines for example, expected me to get all waspish this month on the subject of the BDMA awards. You know the sort of thing: the iniquity of £30 tickets, the irrelevance of a Roy Castle cabaret, the irony of we stern-faced men of business slapping each others' backs and handing out baubles... writes itself, doesn't it? Well, someone else can do that piece. We won one, so there. And anyone daring to suggest that the BDMA awards were other than an event of dignity, grace, probity and infinitely wise judgment is obviously peddling sour grapes. Yah boo...

No, I've got better things to write about. The ASA Case Report No. 68, for one. Have you seen it? It's sternly embargoed until the 10th December on the apparent presumption that the reported malpractices of such enterprises as the Pro-Tek Construction Company and the Runnacleave Hotel are bound to inch Lady Diana Spencer off the front pages. Mind you, any headmaster's report that lumps together companies like the foregoing with the likes of Barclays Bank and Boots and offers even-handed wiggings to all of them is obviously in the finest traditions of British jurisprudence.

A word of explanation might be in order round about now. You won't need telling, or at least shouldn't need telling, that the ASA is the Advertising Standards Authority. It's the one that isn't the CAP or the EEC or the BDMA – it's the one with the tick mark and the bold claim that 'if an advertisement's wrong, we're here to put it right'. Which is a deft slogan of the first order, begging only questions like the definition of wrong and the logistics of putting it right. But, never mind, the ASA is quite certainly on the side of the angels when it comes to the ethics of advertising and to underline the point it boasts a Reverend Paul Flowers on its council.

Now, the ASA produces a case report every month that summarises a number of the key cases that have crossed its collective desk. As a guidebook both to the highways and the byways of British advertising and as a psychological snapshot of the state of mind of the Consumer with an upper case C, the ASA Case Report takes some whacking. I commend it wholeheartedly to all fellow lovers of the human pageant. It makes great bedtime reading.

Much of the warp and woof of it will be familiar to mail order operators. Seasoned old hands will snigger at the innocence of the party who tried to describe his mahogany-veneered tables as mahogany tables. Most people I know will be delighted to learn that it was a readers' offer from the *Observer* that has incurred wrath by getting the size of its duvets wrong. And anyone who ever worked on a travel account will be pleased to hear that the postbags are still full of complaints from people who've paced out the distance from the hotel to the beach and found the linear measurements contained in the original brochure a trifle on the optimistic side.

And the special lobbies are still at it. Someone in Abingdon has complained about JR's halo in the recent Heineken poster and a fellow zealot in Acton objects to the headline 'let us

Spray' on a re-spray ad. The women's movement surfaces regularly as well, though any advertiser crass enough to use a headline such as 'Like a bit of spare?' for a tyre service, or a nude lady in conjunction with the copy line 'Come and meet our friendly staff' deserves all they get. This latter by the way, was for the Surrey Glass and Door Company and the complaint was upheld. Quite right too.

As I say, much of this is predictable. But what gives me the biggest buzz is the glimpse you get of the really eccentric stuff that goes on, usually out in the sticks. Would you have believed, for example, that Alpine Sports could actually produce an ad with a headline as eclectic as 'Still crazy after all these sales?' and combine it with an illustration of an apparently insane man in a straight jacket? Or that Barratt Developments could wax lyrical about the town of Buxton in the Goyt Valley when it is in fact situated elsewhere? Or that someone could actually contrive the fraught claim 'Grow up to 100 lbs of potatoes from just 4 seeds'. All three got a wigging from the ASA, but all this is routine, fustian stuff compared with the misdemeanours of the Protector Lamp and Lighting Company of Eccles, Lancashire, who contrived to have a shot of the Duchess of Kent holding a mining lamp in one of their ads. Here the complainant was not 'disgusted' of Dewsbury or 'mother of four' of Windsor. It was in fact the Lord Chamberlain's Office, a situation that has evoked a full-blooded apology from the miscreants and a promise never to do it again. I should hope not.

One wonders what sort of a life they lead down at the ASA, what sort of conversation goes on during tea breaks. Anyone charged with the responsibility of holding the ring between the country's scoundrels, incompetents, chicanery artists, professional moaners and outright loonies deserves the grateful thanks of the nation. Take the issue of the Runnacleave Hotel, for instance. Being some three hundred yards from Ilfracombe beach, it saw fit to describe itself as a 'sea-front hotel'. Well, someone from Cambridge thought that was a bit strong and the ASA agreed. Acknowledging that the hotel 'was near the sea front', they point out that the hotel does *not* in fact face the sea, which presumably means that the back of the hotel *does* face the sea. Can you imagine the verbal gymnastics that must have gone on at Torrington Place before the verdict was handed down, the special pleading and advocacy on behalf of those several thousand sea-front hotels that would shortly find themselves other than sea-front hotels? The rhetoric must have been elevated, the nuances of the argument explored with verbal scalpels. But now we all know. Sea-front hotels face the sea and are usually located within three hundred yards of the sea. One waits with bated breath for the next test case concerning a sideways facing hotel two hundred yards from the sea. This one will run and run...

... it is nice to know that someone is trying to muster good deeds in a naughty world.

The language of the ASA's judgements is headmasterly throughout, only rarely giving you a glimpse of the irritation and frustration that must pervade the daily grind up there. I mean, it's one thing to be vested with the responsibility of defining legality, decency, truthfulness and all that high-flown stuff – it's quite another to be greeted with a letter signed by twelve citizens of Canterbury complaining about an ad for a new album by Sniff 'n' the Tears in the *New Musical Express*. Any normal reaction to an ad showing a partially clothed woman attempting to close the door against an intruder ought to start and end with a deeply felt yuk. But the ASA found themselves unable to uphold the complaint despite the fact that they found it 'worse than distasteful'. No, on balance, they regarded it 'as reflecting the pop music industry's prediliction for the startling and bizarre'. Which strikes me as a suitably sniffy form of words. I think I detect the hand of the Reverend Paul Flowers in that one.

I do not envy those who have to do this job. On balance, I am glad they do it, for it is nice to know that someone is trying to muster good deeds in a naughty world. But why is it that the bureaucracy which inevitably sets in as a result of well-meant, do-gooding legislation, statutory or voluntary, finds itself so soon and so often wallowing in trivia? Millions of advertising pounds are being spent this Christmas on persuading people to get drunk. We still sanction the complacent hypocrisy of permitting the promotion of cigarettes. The Companies Acts still allow villain after villain to abuse the status of the limited liability company to rip off customers, suppliers and employees. And all the ASA are allowed to do is to pronounce on the precise definition of a sea-front hotel. Frankly, I regard the spectacle of intelligent people being charged with exploring the rights and wrongs of incorrect duvet sizes and imprecise hotel locations as grotesque. It is a ritual salaam to the woozy idea of better business practice. We ought to be able to do better. But I bet we never do.

Sir, I'm worried. I think the computer is cracking up

March 1981

Laser personalisation, then a novelty prone to more cock-ups than conquests, was always going to be an easy mark for George. A lot of people still remember this piece with affection.

I want you to know straight away that I'm a man who eschews decorations, baubles, qualifications and other meritocratic gewgaws. Yes, I'm strictly a University of Life man, School of Hard Knocks and all that. Show me a client who talks of employing MBAs, and I'm reaching for a glossary. Confront me with a client who trails his university degree on his business card and I'm agog with indifference. Come at me with your wretched initials and be sure of a snarling response and the news that Ian Paisley got to be a reverend by sending off a subscription to some ersatz institution in Kentucky (true, you know). All in all, I'm a down-the-line give-me-your-Christian-name-and-surname-and-cut-the-crap-sort of operator.

Well, like all such quasi-moral postures, my own needs immediate qualification. I have to confess to having produced a business card once that boasted certain initials. It was the year in which I succumbed to the siren song of a British Institute of Management mailing that made it quite clear that British management would pass quickly into terminal decay unless I joined the said institution. For £12 a year I could ensure that my voice was heard at the commanding heights of the economy, could help thwart the socialist menace, could receive *Management Today* every month, could, in general, prance around the body politic as an acknowledged member of the management class. Indeed, I could, after certain bona fides had been checked, regale myself with the letters MBIM.

Well, reader, I was a slip of a lad at this stage and the opportunity to suffix my humblest of names with a few initials was too much to resist. Twelve hard-earned pounds found their way into the maw of the ruling class and I was an MBIM overnight. I demanded no great courtesies from my colleagues, allowed my wife to continue to use my Christian name, in short allowed this new mantle of perceived privilege to drape my shoulders with a certain becoming indifference. Some are born to it, others have it thrust on them, some send up their twelve quid… it was ever thus.

But, as I say, I did have a business card printed that boasted the said initials. And that business card found its way around. And that styling found its way on to a variety of mailing lists through whatever process of buying, selling, compilation and swapping one can only guess at. All I know is that a continuing amount of mailings that reach my desk boast this suddenly quaint appellation – George Smith, MBIM. And I have to confess that it gives me a little frisson of nostalgic something-or-other every time I see it.

Last month, I received such a mail shot. It came from a mailing house and it breathed the sort of whoopee creative approach that occurs to people in this business when they feel a real need to strike out and shake up an entire industry. It consisted of a blank piece of paper in the form of a letterhead. To which we were all obviously intended to reel back in a flux at the sheer audacity of it all. In fact, I suspect half the industry reeled back in indifference at the covert message that someone else had invented a whizzo means of letter enclosing. And the other half of the industry fell about laughing that a major mailing house had committed an enormous cock-up.

All was revealed a day or two later when the follow-up arrived.

It started with the unquestionable statement that, 'You may have been intrigued by the unusual message you received a few days ago', and went on to explain that 'the envelope and letter were made by a unique machine that adds a whole new dimension to personalised computer mailing for greater consumer response'.

A fine thing to want to communicate, you may say. If you've got it, flaunt it. If you've got a machine that 'cuts, trims, encloses up to four inserts, makes and seals the envelope', then cut loose, baby. And, if you reckon that an event of this import deserves communicating via such a brio-packed creative approach, all power to your corporate elbows, *mes braves*.

And the other half of the industry fell about laughing that a major mailing house had committed an enormous cock-up.

No, I'm all for the wonders of the new technology. I'm happy to believe that lasers can beam, ink can jet, cheshires can cheshire, and that we can all look forward to a brave new world where catalogues get bounced off satellites, where Viewdata will have us all riffling through our domestic data banks before deciding which pub to go to, where customers can access products in the comfort of their own homes with the ease that Scotty beams up Captain Kirk. I'm all for it, I tell you. The only corollary I've got to the process is to advise caution. For my Compumailer mailing fell from grace not through the hysterical aren't-we-wonderful brio of its creative approach, the validity of which is, after all, infinitely arguable. It reached major chortle status not by sending me a blank piece of paper, but by addressing me as Mr Mibm.

Yes, really. The computer programme which underpins this piece of technology has obvious difficulty in distinguishing a chap's surname from his qualification and there it is, as bold as brass: 'Dear Mr Mibm'.

And, if you find that pretty rib-tickling, stick around, because this is obviously one personalisation technique that eschews that old beginning of the line or para constraint and can whack your name right there in the middle of the mailing. Which, I'm sure, is bound to shovel up the response a treat when it gets the name right.

When it doesn't, it's a gas. This particular mailing boasts one of those short, penultimate paragraphs that render the whole message into an eyeball-to-eyeball number. And which offered to me the never-to-be-forgotten question, 'Still interested Mr Mibm?'

It was better than that, actually. Two days later, by virtue of that mastery of duplication technique that is the British mailing industry's hidden subsidy to the Royal Mail, I received another mailing shot along the same lines. This time, I had ceased to be Mr Mibm and had become his first cousin, a Mr Mibw. Dear Mr Mibw, it stated and it went on to confront me with that same deathless question, 'Still interested, Mr Mibw?'

If this is the 'whole new dimension to personalised computer mailings' count me out. Because, if I had been transformed into Messrs Mibm and Mibw, then I have to believe that fellow toilers in the business were finding themselves addressed as Mr Ma or Ms Msc Econs or even, just conceivably in a roughneck industry, Mr Obe. At least you can pronounce Obe – indeed it sounds like you ought to be prime minister of Nigeria, But Mibm? How the hell do you pronounce it for a start?

No, it's back to the drawing board, I fear, the Compumailer may slice up paper like Sunblest slice up bread but the end result looks just about as compulsive. Get my name wrong and you're attracting derision, not interest. Attract derision and you deserve all you get. I just talked it through with Mibm and he's of like mind. We're going to check it out with Mibw when he gets back from lunch,

In which we segment an entire industry in terms of highly spurious psychographics

April 1981

Another favourite and recurring theme for George is the tendency of others to elevate direct marketing from a simple means of shifting a product to an academic art or science. Someone mentioned in this article first time around apparently threatened George with solicitors, so we've renamed him here as 'Mr X'. Well, we're not *Private Eye*, you know.

'All this new technology is a crock of shit.' The comment came from a senior practitioner of the direct marketing art at the recent DMMA conference in Paris and it was the sort of heartfelt aside that comes from over-exposure to earphones, hotel coffee and earnest presentations about the current state of the Finnish book club market. Neither wild horses nor enormous retainers will drag the name of the guilty vulgarian from me, though I had better record right now that it was neither Mr Len Ford nor Mr X, two worthy gentlemen who can confidently be expected to eschew both the proposition and the crudity of expression contained therein.

But it *was* an existential moment, I tell you. My anonymous pundit was speaking from the heart and it reminded me, not for the first time, of what a funny lot we all are. Wide-eyed and guileless, we subject ourselves to a lot of banter about things like the new technology and the electronic cottage and de-massification, and then snarl into our fruit juice that the whole thing is a... well, let's just say a mess of pottage.

Not everyone, mind. There's always someone who emerges with a new glossary with which to dazzle his loved ones and clients in the months to come. In fact, we all do a bit of it. But what appeals to me is the total distinction between the Jack-the-Lad response to such weighty matters and what we might call the more professional response. There will be those who will have returned from Paris wheezing with merriment about how many Twiglets they put away at the Donnelley party and there will be those who are even now beginning sentences with,'Of course, Toffler put his finger on it in Paris'. In which case, they will be referring not to Alvin's penchant for crumbly canapés, but his inspirational view of all our futures.

The distinction goes beyond merely staying studiously serious most of the time or affecting cheerful irreverence – in fact, survival in direct marketing involves an interplay between the two. But there is a deeper difference that, for lack of a happier epithet, I'm going to have to call attitudinal. There are those among us who see direct marketing as a whole new art form or science. And there are those who are in it to shift products and make a few bob. Either side will claim allegiance to at least part of the other philosophy, but ultimately the instincts of the one are different from the instincts of the other.

It all reminds me of those childhood stories of public school or university life where the entire *dramatis personae* was more or less classifiable into 'aesthetes' or 'hearties'. Aesthetes, you may remember, were swottish characters who could conjugate verbs, decline Virgil and all that sort of thing. Typically, they wore glasses, were absolutely rotten at games, sneaked to the housemaster and blubbed when ragged. By the time they got to university they were into soppy poetry, velvet suits and cups of tea with tweedy dons.

Hearties on the other hand were all round good eggs and were certainly where our sympathies were meant to lie. They were always scoring crucial tries, getting into scrapes, smoking behind the pav, ragging swots and generally comporting themselves like direct marketing delegates.

Now, before the entire industry rises before my eyes and attempts to shuffle to the Harry Wharton side of the line, let me tell you that the view from Clapham is a little more congested than that. The hearties in this business are an endangered species, in danger of being nibbled out of hearth and home by the aesthetes. You've got to mean it to be my kind of hearty. It's no use affecting heartiness in the taproom and then perjuring yourself with distinctly swottish behaviour at the next important meeting, a charge to which most of us plead guilty, prattle though we might about extenuating circumstances.

My hearties are those wonderfully refreshing people who see a distinct affinity between direct marketing and street trading, who call products 'lines' and customers 'punters', who see a rate card as something to be trumped, who are happy to refer to an exquisitely-crafted timepiece as a 'Cartier knock-off,' whose reaction to the trading standards officer's visit is to buy him lunch, who probably think that the ASA is the outfit that sends moon probes out of Houston.

John Bloom was an archetypal hearty, a man who single handedly reinvented the washing machine market. Tony (whatever happened to...?) Alkin was another, and the mention of both names will send shivers down a lot of spines. But their successors still thankfully inhabit the undergrowth of British mail order. In a world of flow charts, segmentation analyses, seminars and workshops, we need their bravura, their feel for a bargain, their instinct for a selling message.

To an extraordinary extent, the enterprises which now dominate our business, whatever their current style or practice, started life as slightly irrational ideas, financed on a wing-and-a-prayer basis, but making it finally on the basis of proprietorial pride, individual judgement and sense of adventure.

> ## A hearty, for instance, asks for ideas; a swot talks of input.

I'm not going to attempt to do a Darwin on all this anthropological stuff – not for the money Rowney pays me, I'm not. But a few Attenborough-like hints about how to spot the respective species might be in order.

A hearty, for instance, asks for ideas; a swot talks of input. The one wants to run the offer that weekend, the other talks of testing it in the Orkneys' edition. Swots call meetings, hearties say it all on the telephone. The hearty insists that no one drinks port any more because the man at the off-licence told him so, the swot has five pages on the market penetration of fortified wines in 1977.

Me, I'm on both sides and so are you. But you can have a lot of fun dividing up all sorts of third parties into one camp or the other. And who knows where it might all end? We could even have two different conferences and use up those few remaining virgin dates on the calendar.

For just £1,400 you can talk to your clients on glossy paper... a never-to-be-repeated offer. Till this time next year.

May 1981

George enjoyed poking fun at the weekly trade mag of the advertising world, *Campaign*. Well, it did take itself rather seriously. And whenever it descended into the grubby world of direct marketing it quickly appeared to get its metaphorical knickers in a twist.

One of the great reasons not to have annual awards is the opportunity to deny trade magazines the easy financial pickings that come in such situations from a narcissistic industry that loves the idea of talking to itself at vast cost.

I refer of course to the house ads which follow in the train of such events like the last few floats in the Lord Mayor's show – a distinctly unseasonal observation brought on by having received two letters in this morning's post, each of which is grubbing for the same hard-earned readies with a distinctly similar proposition.

The first was from the very same magazine over which you are currently dozing. The message was simple and predictable: immediate fiscal doom awaited my company unless we bought an ad. That's an overwrought precis, obviously, but that was the gist of it. For the price of a two-week holiday in Sri Lanka I could communicate with the great and the good in our business via these illustrious pages. Fair enough, lads, fair enough – we'll sell a few layout pads and take a big, big classified – at least we know where we are with you.

The other missive was from your favourite parish magazine and mine: *Campaign*. And it should surprise no one to learn that *Campaign* is devoting a special edition to direct marketing next month, After all, nary a week goes by without *Campaign* devoting a special report to something, and the editorial probity which underpins such events is no more or less than the *Financial Times*' regular interest in Nigerian banking, new developments in arc welding, or wherever else soft advertising money is coming from that season.

What got me was the tone of the letter, written with ineffable precision to the wrong address. How's this for openers? 'Over the past year or so *Campaign* has been devoting more and more editorial space to the subject of Direct Marketing.' Let's pause there and express bewilderment – all I've seen in *Campaign* recently about our great business is a picture of Brian Halsey looking terse in his boardroom in illustration of some dumb story about an account he had some time ago, and a picture of John Watson looking even terser in the street with his new oppos.

But, to continue – 'On December 11 *Campaign* will be devoting a substantial number of its pages to informing its readers about changes and developments in Direct Marketing... This issue presents itself as a unique opportunity for you to promote your company to your clients in an editorial environment one hundred per cent relevant to your needs... Take advantage of this offer by calling me now.'

Pretty terse, huh? All I've got to do is ring this herbert now and arrange for him to deploy a four figure sum on my behalf so that I can promote my company to my clients, a process which normally goes on day in and day out via humble little telephone calls and earnest chat in darkened hostelries. And what on earth an editorial environment one hundred per cent relevant to my needs might be I can only ponder over.

It all makes me wonder, and not for the first time, how the likes of us look to the likes of them. We swim around in our little goldfish bowl and they swim around in theirs. Once a year they come among us in their god-sent mission to part us from our petty cash.

> And what on earth an editorial environment one hundred per cent relevant to my needs might be I can only ponder over.

Well it's Christmas and you have to fall back on the bromides about them only doing their job. So they are. Even if their board does seem to boast two Simons, even if they do make millions, even if Heseltine had something to do with it and even if everyone photographed in *Campaign* always looks so bloody miserable. Let's agree that they are nice chaps really and wonder how this 'Special Survey on Direct Marketing' actually came about...

Scene: Campaign's editorial office. Vivaldi is heard softly in the background interspersed with quiet rustling of banknotes being counted and the murmurs of space reps ringing their brokers.

Enter: an ink-stained hack in a state of excitement.

Inkstained hack: Hold the front page. I've just had a tinkle Jerome Fandor is leaving OTE for SM. Apparently his new appointment as Joint Deputy Creative Director on Tuesday hasn't worked out. He's already left, taking his rubber plant and half the business with him. I've got the new creative team at SM

	assembled on a traffic island in Portland Place and I'm just organising a snappy poo.
Editor:	Good work, Millington. (Tersely into intercom): Hello, production? Kill that front-page story on the Hand Shandy account moving to Castor and Pollux. We've got a biggie to replace it.
	(Swivels round in leather chair to address the space rep who has been quietly waiting for an audience.) So, you think we should do a Special Report on Direct Marketing, do you?'
Space rep:	Certainly I do sir. Direct marketing is going positively boffo right now. And they're having a big do at the Dorchester next month.
Editor:	The Dorchester, eh? I wouldn't have thought they'd let the scruffy blighters in...
Space rep:	Oh, it's all different now. They're one of the most important elements in advertising...well over £250 million is spent every year...
Editor:	(impatiently): Yes, yes, yes. I met one of them once. Awful little tick. Kept going on and on about results. Totted up the bill at Langan's on a calculator, as I remember. Grotesque!
Space rep:	Ah, but sir. They're *real* people – very unaffected – and they *do* take house ads. I've seen some of them. Not the same class as our television production companies, mark you, but they do try...
Editor:	Yes, I suppose so. I expect most of them are off the beaten track?

Space rep:	That *is* a prob, sir. There *are* some in WI, but most of them are fairly scattered. Places like Richmond, Kennington, Swindon (editor's face wrinkles in disgust). I believe they even have some in Shropshire!
Editor:	So we'll have to send them some literature. What do they call it?
Space rep:	A mailing shot, sir.
Editor:	That's it, a mailing shot. Can we organise one? Just wrap a few long words around the rate card. I understand they like long words.
Space rep:	Will do, sir. I'm sure it can be bigger than Point of Sale North of the Border if we really try.
Editor:	(tapping out cheroot on chukka boot): Let's hope so. Now please let me get on with it. Amanda seems to have made her annual boo-boo over my hotel reservation at Cannes...
	CURTAIN

I'm sure it wasn't like this really. But it ought to have been, I tell you.

Bad news, I'm afraid, Sir. We only made £216,000,000

October 1981

In this piece George calls a serving minister of the Crown daft and predicts with precision the subsequent explosive growth of household distribution. He makes some other points too.

In a business that prides itself (with some reason) on its occasional dementedness, it is good to have Sir Keith Joseph around as a fixed mark of higher lunacy. By which I am not deferring to the *Private Eye* line that our current Minister for Trade and Industry is an outright headcase who disappears to the funny farm on occasion. I am merely recording that he is the cabinet minister who seems to end up with all the lousy lines.

This untoward excursion into the thickets of political comment is brought on by the news of the Post Office's unsatisfactory profit performance over the year. At which stage, I am already using the *Daily Telegraph*'s language to tell the story. That profit figure, you may remember, was a crumby £216 million – a figure that is pshawed out of sight by the leader writer of the *Telegraph*. Only the Giro made its targets apparently. Telecommunications could not even rustle up 4.5 per cent on turnover and the mails, our own little sector of under-achievement, came up with what the *Telegraph* calls a derisory 1.1 per cent. Derisory indeed – I just hope Nigel Walmsley has the good grace to do the decent thing and fall on his envelope slitter. The idea that you can run a modestly competent public service and still only finish up with a bottom line of £216 million to give to BL is an obvious offence against reason.

That at least seems to be the reaction of Sir Keith's department, which is quoted as expressing 'concern' that financial targets had not been reached. For our mates at the Post Office it must be a bit like passing twelve O levels, flunking on dressmaking and reading the dread words 'can do better' on your end of term report.

> ...headmaster Joseph's rigorous judgements on how much money sections of society are to screw out of other sections.

I will not dwell on my own belief that the Post Office is pre-eminently a public service which has as much business turning in huge profits as the Fire Brigade would have in publishing a tariff for carrying people down long ladders. What troubles me is the predictable results which now stem from headmaster Joseph's rigorous judgements on how much money sections of society are to screw out of other sections. The Post Office is putting up its rates, which is as dumb and as indefensible as this traditional response of British commerce usually is.

I wish I could have a year off to study the effect that inevitable price rises have had on consumer demand over the last twenty years especially in the public or quasi-public sector. It is now well-attested that fare increases have a mathematically predictive effect on fares bought and people conveyed by public transport. It is obvious that newspaper circulations have slumped in the same inverse proportion to rising cover prices. I don't know – but I suspect – that fewer people send Christmas cards than did a few years ago, a reflection not of a mass seizing up of Yuletide goodwill, more of the cost of transmitting said goodwill to the nearest and dearest. In the more advanced sectors of the world like

Scandinavia and, more exotically, the Greater London Council, these revealed facts of public utility life are beginning to seep through into the body politic. Hoping that they might seep through to a cabinet boasting Sir Keith is obviously a bit like hoping that Norway will win the Eurovision Song Contest.

Which brings us to direct marketing which has currently, if rather belatedly, got the shakes. And while I do not pretend that the Post Office is there primarily to service the likes of you or me in our god sent mission to introduce the delights of yes/no stamps and free prize draws to the great British public, I still cling to the belief that a significant part of Post Office profitability in recent years has been due to the explosion of direct mail activity. And it has to be admitted that, whatever our individual or corporate frustrations with that organisation, it has mostly deserved the wave of new business which we have given it, for it has sold itself, developed its service, positioned itself at many a point as a true helpmate in the difficult business of earning an honest copper in an uncertain world. The Post Office today compared with the Post Office of a decade ago invokes comparisons of Tony Blackburn's BBC with Lord Reith's and, while I have distinctly mixed views about the latter, I have nothing but enthusiasm for the former.

> ... what more erudite scribes would probably call the interface between cause and effect.

I'll leave any clichés about killing the goose that lays the golden eggs to someone else. I will merely report what I know to be true: that direct marketing and mail order companies are currently facing some very delicate equations which lie at the heart of their business. Easy pickings are currently scarce, banker situations thin on the ground, the scale of risk is becoming intimidating. And here's the rub: postage charges are one way or another the biggest cost of any promotional package or venture. To increase them now is to divert many people's intentions away from enterprise and toward caution. People will experiment less, postpone some programmes and reduce others. In short, they are likely to do less mailing. I doubt that the Post Office will notice the difference immediately but they might well do with their bottom line two years hence. But, by then of course, Sir Keith may be out to grass and that nice William Rodgers may be making with the bromides.

I suspect that one or two businesses will cease to function over the next twelve months. I suspect that a lot of major companies now inching their way into direct mail will promptly inch their way out again. I suspect that we are all going to have another intelligent look (probably belatedly) at the potential of household distribution. Some of this would probably have happened if the Post Office had held their prices but more of it will happen when they raise them. It is less cause and effect than commercial psychology, what more erudite scribes would probably call the interface between caution and enterprise.

I tell you something. If Sir Keith Joseph comes to your door in three years time posturing as a consultant, give him a frosty look and a we'll-let-you-know. I'm not saying he will, I am saying he's daft enough.

Save the emu, to hell with the ostrich!

January 1982

George considered this piece an example of how to write an article when you've got nothing to say. Writing it convinced him that everything in direct marketing is funny, if you want it to be. Worth saying that, don't you think?

Someone out there knows something about ostrich feathers that I don't. And it's probably the same party that wrought havoc with the Japanese shaving brushes. And the macaroni and the pickles and the plastic flowers. Yes, there are more things in heaven and earth than are dreamed of in our philosophy, even if Walter Schmidt *is* running a symposium on it.

I'll tell you what I'm on about. It's the Post Office Guide, a volume to which I recently repaired in order to look up some fustian piece of information about what you can and cannot do with PO box numbers. Like all big books, it turns out to be a positive minefield of completely gaga facts and figures. Have you read it recently? You should, I tell you, for it could determine your whole business future, particularly those of you whose thoughts are beginning to turn to overseas expansion.

Did you know, for instance, that you couldn't send filth through the post? Well you can't, so there. It says as much on page 73 of our dog-eared copy of the Post Office Guide. In a long list of prohibited articles (inland post section), it says it as bold as brass: Filth. A one-word paragraph sitting smugly in a sea of leading.

And there's more where that came from. For the list of prohibitions goes on to describe lots of other products that you were about to launch in a crazed attempt at diversification. Most living creatures are right out for starters. But you'll be glad to hear of the exceptions: 'bees, leeches and silkworms', to name but a few. Then 'certain parasites and destroyers of noxious insects intended for the control of said insects'. Then again, you can mail 'certain other harmless creatures in packs approved by postal headquarters'. Anyone about to market tarantulas or gerbils in polylope bags would seem to scrape through.

But it's when you turn to the overseas section that your eyes begin to glaze over with the wonder of it all. What stories must dwell between the lines of those close-knit pages! What long-forgotten tragedies must underpin this extraordinary recital of dos and don'ts! What hidden diplomatic history must lie behind the beachcomber-like eccentricity recorded here!

> ...now that you know, don't blame me when the *Guardia Civil* puts its Iberian finger on your collar for running around Ibiza with a cribbage board.

Some things are more obvious than others. I didn't need telling, and neither will you, that contraceptives are a mite controversial in Catholic countries. And everyone's inhibitions about butane gas lighters, small arms, radioactive materials and viruses as the subject of mailing campaigns strike me as entirely reasonable. But can you figure why you can't send playing cards to the Balearic Islands? Neither can I, but now that you know, don't blame me when the *Guardia Civil* puts its Iberian finger on your collar for running around Ibiza with a cribbage board. And does anyone know about these ostrich feathers? You see, when it comes to exporting to the States (and you can forget gold bullion, potatoes and cotton seed oil in this direction), you come right up against the para which prohibits feathers and skins of wild birds except (and this is what I want to know about) ostrich feathers. Now, this is either some dapper piece of legislation on behalf of the bird protection lobby or someone in East Jesus, Nebraska, is planning to corner the market in Lily Langtry hats. I don't know which and I think we should be told

New countries can and should be forgiven the obvious whims and eccentricities of their postmaster generals on the basis that such gentlemen are likely to have to change their jobs quite rapidly every year or so. And I quite appreciate that many of these countries have fledgling industries to protect from the likes of us. So far so rational. But does anyone really know why Uganda should make a special prohibition of Japanese shaving brushes? You can lather away in Kampala with a brush from Taiwan, Korea or from Bridgnorth, but the Nipponese version is strictly frown material, postally speaking. All I can think of is that Milton Obote hates Japanese shaving brushes or that the wily Nips bought an entire year's coffee crop from Amin and paid him off with shaving brushes. There has to be some such explanation, I tell you.

As I say, it's a Third World country's right to defend its industries. But what do you reckon is going on in Sri Lanka, which is currently prohibiting more things than you ever dreamt of? When I tell you that the list runs from account books, albums, calendars, via exercise books, picnic baskets, the wonderfully ambiguous rubbers, sunglasses and waste paper, right through to wire clips, you'll begin to share my concern that Colombo is poised to make a great leap forward via world domination of the office stationery market. Again, you are warned.

And, if you still had hopes of coining it in Kabul, just forget it. Afghanistan gets very first prize for the most eccentric collection of prohibited articles anywhere the world. Nothing logical about this list, I can tell you, for those wily Pathans will have nothing to do with ashtrays, chewing gum, fancy postcards, handbags, macaroni, plywood, pickles and plastic flowers. What I like is the precision on the postcards. When was the last time you heard a postcard described as fancy? Do they mean dirty or just ornate? Come to think of it, why pick on macaroni as an offending pasta? Anomaly freaks can obviously have a whale of a time inundating Kandahar with Charles and Di postcards and tagliatelli.

Finland is nordically rational compared with all this. I nearly said sober until I remembered that they have quite an alcoholic problem up there. (I know of one mail order cosmetics company whose beer shampoo reached brand leader status because Lapp lushes chose to treat the follicles from the inside.) And here again the Post Office Guide punctuates human experience for us, telling us in black and white that samples of alcoholic beverages are prohibited unless addressed – and I haven't made this up – to Alkoholiluki OY. And oy to you too, my Finnish friends – I'll be routing my alcoholic samples in quite a different direction. The same goes for my ostrich feathers and pickles and clips. Now that I know where I can't send them, it could be the start of a whole new business. And if you hear anything on the Japanese shaving brushes, just let me know.

Say, yes, you bums. Otherwise Sherwood Forest will have to be used for the follow-up

March 1982

George sticks his neck out and gets it chopped off. He of all people should have known that if a pack keeps appearing, chances are that it works.

When I was a slip of a lad, much given to long words and literary conceits (*plus ça change*, did I hear you say?), I had an English master who used to boom at me from a great height with a phrase that still echoes down the years. 'Incandescent, Smith?' he would boom, settling on my proudly-touted epithet of the week, doubtless culled from the bit in *Reader's Digest* which offered to increase my word power. 'Incandescent? We don't need words like that in a second form composition. Have you swallowed the dictionary?'

Interestingly, I next heard this phrase from the lips of a Kaleidoscope executive who scratched out the name Buxtehude from some deft wordplay I'd written on behalf of a posh radio, to replace it with a jokey little reference to Tony Blackburn. Again, my protests on behalf of a little culture in all things were swept away with the accusation that I had swallowed the dictionary. Fair comment you will probably say – the pretensions of the literati should be quashed wherever they surface.

Well, I'm going to get my own back here and now. For, while there are few signs around that direct marketing operators have swallowed anything more verbally demanding than Harold Robbins, there are signs aplenty that too many people have swallowed the textbook.

For someone has now produced the ultimate mailing shot. It's the *Gone With The Wind* of mailings, pulling together every hint you ever picked up, every case history you ever noted down, every technique that you always meant to test. It's a direct mail tribute to a flagging papermaking industry and it's spread all over my desk right now. And I want you to know that I'm a man with a big desk.

If you haven't received it yet (and I didn't exactly ask for it), the package is selling a three-months' trial subscription to *Which?* magazine, a promotional device which its proprietors have been peddling successfully for as long as most of us can remember. I don't know whether the off-the-page ads are foundering, or whether those canny loose insets are falling on deaf ears as well as on the floor at W H Smith's, but something has obviously happened to have tempted the Consumers' Association into the ethically-iffy area of prize draws in general and the positively Wagnerian scale of this mailing in particular.

First, we have an outer envelope, duly marked with a digest of its contents and the statutory mating call, 'Open Now'. Then, two reply envelopes, with the first of which I can say yes, or as the proprietors would have it YES; and with the other I can say NO. Not that the CA will quite take no for an answer, for there is a tuck-in slip in the envelope for naughty negatives which starts, 'Don't say No now' and repeats it immediately with all the plaintive pleading of a hero hanging from a cliff top while the bad guy treads on his fingers.

But to continue. The letter is indeed an epistle of four pages and there is a broadsheet summarising the wonders of *Which?*, promising *inter alia* to keep my household *au fait* with adhesives and men's raincoats. Then a four-colour flier summarises the prizes for the third time to date and a Prize Draw Selection and acceptance Certificate which lasers my name, address and postal code to great effect and introduces me to my six draw numbers. It also repeats the nature of the prizes just in case I'd forgotten them while I was reading the first part of the mailing the week before.

And that's it, with the exception of the additional three fliers which advise me respectively of a free mystery gift, an earlybird which apparently offers four and not three issues if I move smartly enough, and lastly, five testimonials from grateful *Which?* readers in places like Frinton.

> If genius is an inexhaustible capacity for taking pains, then the CA just got itself a Nobel Prize.

Phew! Or dare I say phooey? For here in one envelope is the summation of an entire industry. Here is the technology, the creative skill, the promotional investment, the excitement, the sheer determination to make sure that nothing is left out. If genius is an inexhaustible capacity for taking pains, then the CA just got itself a Nobel Prize. I should be left reeling with the scale of it all, shaking just a little as I thrust whichever piece of paper is the reply device into my YES envelope. In fact, I'm bemused, irritated and the sort of hard-core-non-respondent who isn't even going to use the NO envelope, Freepost or no Freepost.

I'll tell you for why. I know it's a fast-moving world we live in, but am I the only one who finds a Prize Draw promotion on this scale from a Consumers' Association just a teensy-weensy bit uncomfortable? Am I the only one who sees the whole thing as a conflict between media and message, an uncomfortable marriage of distinct promotional traditions which surprises me as much as it would to learn the Folio Society were doing a tie-up with the *Sun's* bingo competition?

But maybe the ethical side just makes me a sentimental old fluff. What I can suggest professionally is that more, in direct marketing as elsewhere, does not mean better. Is the obvious investment scale of this promotion, with its super-colossal unit costs in origination, printing and enclosing, really going to be consistent with the likely return? Could the same result not have been achieved with six pieces of paper rather than eleven? And has the sheer irritation potential of this package been quantified? Sorry, Consumers' Association, but I have to accuse you of having swallowed the textbook.

Actually this saddens me for I know the folk at Buckingham Street to be level-headed individuals of some probity and no little sagacity. And I had also better point out that the last time I waxed negative about a Consumers Union promotion from the States, an earnest young lady in the audience told me that it was the most profitable ad that they had ever run. No, I'm always willing to eat humble pie especially if the CA tells me that the Sainsbury's version is edibly superior to the St Michael's one.

This time, though, I doubt that I'll have to. I don't believe that this promotion will prove to be cost-effective. I haven't responded to it anyway. There's a distinct dent in my doormat where the recruitment package arrived and, with the cost of coconut matting as it is, I just daren't risk getting on their active list.

Why intermediate status housing is a cinch for personalised lawn mowers

May 1982

On the subject of systems for classifying consumers George was never likely to be other than an agnostic, at best.

You remember the days when you used to scan the exam results when they were pinned on the board at school? Well, I hope you do, though it dawns on me that the idea of exam results, let alone pinning them on boards, marks me off as relic of a bygone age.

It all comes back to me when I hear of a new survey that aims to classify the population into almighty all-seeing computer segments. I go rushing to look up where I stand this year. Where am I on the Chancellor's new tax tables? How does my salary compare with those amazing managerial figures peddled every year by the Institute of Marketing? And, now that we have ACORN classifying our every neighbourhood, where do I live this year? These days you have to be interested. It was all right for my dad to remain obliviously C2 all his life before he declined unknowingly into DE status on retirement, but I can't afford to be oblivious. I need to know, I tell you.

So it was with trembling hand that I opened the new ACORN Users Guide. Sure enough, woe awaited me. Despite the sort of upward mobility that has the burglars queuing up at my Chubb lock, I still find myself apparently grubbing it out in Group C or even Group H. My housing is distinctly older, unarguably of intermediate status and, yea, it is a multi-racial area. So, according to the ACORN co-ordinates, my neighbours are typically elderly, typically suffering from a lack of family accommodation, typically lacking large gardens and typically engaged in service trades, often in a self-employed capacity.

The fact that they spend their time mowing their enormous lawns, spawning lots of little Barnabys and Emmas, dressing them in Laura Ashley and forever buying poncey new fireplaces, is a perception denied ACORN. So, too, is the fact most of my black neighbours are either running flourishing import/export businesses or are lecturing on Renaissance drama at the local polytechnic. That's when they're not serving as pillars of the local church or buying poncey new fireplaces, of course.

> These global decisions are as pernicious in thought as they are hapless in execution.

The truth is that most of urban Britain and a good deal of what's left of rural Britain is thankfully pluralist. Walk down any of these mean streets described by ACORN and you may find heiresses, world-famous dramatists and MPs. Investigate affluent suburban housing and you will find many an old spinster on supplementary benefit. And the high-status non-family areas (these words are ACORN's, not mine) will be found to harbour a good number of low-status large family households. We are not quite Airstrip One just yet, thank God.

Be fair, I hear someone cry, ACORN is just a tool, a discipline – shrewd marketing persons use it merely as a starting point. Do they? Am I the only person to have heard a client's mailing list described as 'typically university towns with a smattering of retirement areas?' Has no one else been party to a conversation where whole swathes of the population were ruled out of order because their immediate neighbourhood of a few hundred thousand was reeking with bad debts? These global decisions are as pernicious in thought as they are hapless in execution. Credit checking and even credit scoring are nasty necessities of direct marketing life; the sweeping social audit that is beginning to be used as marketing shorthand is something again.

I won't labour the point for I've laboured it before. And I don't want to be seen as a curmudgeonly old spoilsport. But maybe some points get made if I offer an exclusive preview of my demographic classification of office types, based on ten minutes intensive research into the characteristics of places of work. Patents are pending.

Office type A: nineteenth-century warehouse-type accommodation.

Often found in Northern industrial towns. Staff are comparatively underpaid and typically come to work by public transport for car-parking facilities are minimal. Expense accounts are relatively unknown and most eating is done in grimly decorated canteens. Members of the public are often seen in reception areas.

Office type B: pre-twentieth century administrative block.

Often found in the centre of London, such offices are frequently shabby despite occasionally impressive exteriors. Individual accommodation is typically substandard and improvised. Kettles are often boiled in lavatories for lack of communal catering facilities and many offices are underused.

Office type C: affluent new trading estates.

Car parks are typically full of new registrations. Often purpose-built, offices such as these are light, warm and usually bustling. There is usually much evidence of mechanisation and investment in new technology; a computer installation is often found. Personnel typically refresh themselves at nearby Italian restaurants and wine bars.

The first is a reasonable depiction of the British Mail Order

Corporation, the second of the Home Office and the third resembles what I can remember of Aeonics. So whom would you sooner do business with? Fact is, you can't read a book by looking at the cover let alone scanning it with a laser.

Imitate the action of the gerbil or something

September 1982

This was at a time when there was lots of gossip surrounding Scotcade and Kaleidoscope. So what's new, did I hear you say?

First messenger:	The news from Shropshire is grave, sire.
Second messenger:	Aye, and from other parts of the realm.
Third messenger:	Tis said that many a once-proud merchandiser Is drinking the sour lees of downside risk. That accountants throughout the land are recasting Their oft-revised projections. That bankers Swooning with fright, foreclose their promises.
Second messenger:	The centre cannot hold nor yet the holding companies.
Third messenger:	Baleful times indeed! Whence the swagger of years past? Whence the brio of countless seminars, When men of vision would come forth armed With rhetoric and zeal and mighty regression analysis The future to command? O sorry business!

And sorry, too, to burst into mock-iambics like that, but it does seem that the epic scale of current developments in our business demands positively Shakespearean treatment.

For tabarded messengers, read telephones. I don't know about you but the instrument on my desk has been buzzing for weeks past with messages from far and wide about the demise of this enterprise and that; usually supplemented with some uncalled for observation about how said collapse could in turn lead to the collapse of this service company, this agency, this mailing house, this printer.

Not to put too fine a point on it, there's a whole lot of gloating going on...

Prurience is often a very good thing in short measure, but there is an unhealthy degree of pleasure being conveyed by some of this reportage. There is a distinct whiff of 'lo, how are the mighty fallen', and 'I could see it coming' and 'it couldn't last'. Not to put too fine a point on it, there's a whole lot of gloating going on, which is as dumb as it is unhealthy.

Even in a highly competitive and parochial business, I fail to see how anyone can derive pleasure from the current difficulties of some of our leading flagship operators. (I write this at a time when it is difficult to be precise. By the time you get to read it, you'll know more than I know in writing it.)

If some of these operations go under or even submerge untidily for a while, it is bad for everyone in this business, nothing less. It will mean that direct response trading and the relationship that it has assiduously built with a new buying class will go back quite a few steps. It will make life that little more difficult for the survivors, no matter how many hot lists come into the market in the next few months as a result. It is bad news, not to be distilled with any small pleasure that you or your company was not in the firing line this time round.

Having said that, the lessons should be applied with vigour.

We now have formally to acknowledge that the country is deep in recession, that spending power has been reduced, that people's extraordinary willingness to part with significant sums of money for marginal purchases via plastic currency has at least seized up for a little while. The party is over.

At least this sort of party is over, the kind where guests were transfixed by an equation that started in Taipei and led to the Cayman Islands via Gray's Inn Road. Perhaps now it will be acknowledged that most people actually don't read colour supplements. Perhaps now it will be acknowledged that what Stan Remington said two years ago about running a business on fifteen percent and borrowing money at twenty is indeed a central truth. Perhaps now it will be acknowledged that it is daft to pile on operational costs for reasons of corporate aggrandisement. Perhaps we are all a little wiser.

The joy is, or course, that the debacles and the discomfitures which are persuading marketing journalists to froth at the mouth and telephone gossips to pile on the third-party agony, concerns only a tiny sliver of the direct marketing business. All sorts of other enterprises go on ploughing profitable furrows, often oblivious to what a journalist told me recently was 'the sexy end of the market'. The scale of these enterprises, whether it be measured in fiscal terms, in technological terms, in terms of talent, expertise and experience, enables one to get recent happenings into perspective, a necessary task for journalists and direct marketing folk alike. Listen too hard to the current Babel and you could be forgiven for confusing a little local difficulty with the apocalypse. Bad it is, apocalypse it ain't.

We are all going to have to think a bit harder: about products and margins and costs and lists and opportunities. That doesn't faze me and I don't see why it should faze you. So let's end with a little more bardish braggadocia.

First messenger
(for it is still he):   The nation groaneth under the weight
Of pocket calculators, briefcase and
luggage sets.

> The merest stripling can boast with hearty zeal
> Of cassette recorders that make the tea and tell the time.
> Our Sunday journals saunter oblivious to the wound
> They have effected. The time is ripe for change.

Second messenger. Verily, you speak with the wisdom of ages.
Where to now, sirrah?

Third messenger. Heaven forfend we shall cease this hard-lived tale.
Let's go to brainstorm via a glass of ale.

EXEUNT OMNES

Let us now praise semi-famous men

October 1982

Guy Stringer and Harold Sumption are both sadly now deceased but they were giants of the UK fundraising scene and very fine individuals too. Both were around and active when George penned this piece and would have modestly shrugged off the praise therein, but he speaks for all of us when he records with due deference the debt we owe them.

Because direct marketing is still a very junior business and because it is also a jealous and spiteful business on occasion, it is rare indeed for anyone of us to find the opportunity to stand up and sing the praises of anyone else. I am not talking about the annual awards hooley and neither am I talking about the habit of our American cousins of conferring an annual award on one of their number. I am talking about the occasional ability to commemorate the achievements of individuals as opposed to organisations. Not in any context of spotlights and dinner jackets, nor yet in the private conversation of individuals who may seek to agree over a pint that so-and-so is indeed a hell of a guy.

But there comes a time when such things need to be said at least semi-publicly. And, in the absence of any more palatable arena, this column will have to do. For I really do think it about time that we created an interval in this fevered and vigorous business wherein we can salute some of our elder statesmen. Not because they are elder and only accidentally because they are statesmen, but because all of us genuinely owe a lot to the generation that went before.

Many people seem to imagine that direct marketing was invented round about 1976 and that its invention was preceded by an uncertain piece of pre-history where a few untutored souls wandered around like cave men fashioning the tools which later civilisations learned to use and develop. Which, of course, is bunk. While it may be difficult to imagine a world without a trade magazine, a trade association and a seminar circuit, the fact remains that an awful lot was happening as quickly, as dynamically and as profitably as anything that has happened since. Those of us who knocked around in the sixties may not have known that we were in something called direct marketing but we were, and the experience we gained in those relatively unrewarding years has certainly coloured anything we may have achieved since.

So I ask you, metaphorically at least, to put your hands together for two gentlemen who have quietly been presiding over the development of direct marketing for a great many years without, I sense, quite appreciating it. Both of them are shortly going to fade into semi-retirement and it would be wrong if they went unsaluted. They are astonishingly similar gentlemen (and I use the latter word quite deliberately), they are both well into their sixties, I think, and they will both be astonished and maybe slightly rattled to find me writing about them here. Their names are Harold Sumption and Guy Stringer.

Harold, you will probably know more of. He is currently chairman of an advertising agency whose name escapes me, is involved with the Franklin Mint and with the International Direct Marketing Symposium, is quite clearly involved with such charity accounts as Help the Aged and ActionAid and keeps his hand in with Oxfam. For all I know, he also runs the World Bank on Thursday afternoons for it is certainly difficult to find a certain kind of pie which has risen triumphant without the Sumption digit.

There can in fact be very few charities over the last twenty years or so who have not profited by Harold's advice, often freely given in every sense. But to typecast the guy as a charity and fundraising specialist is to miss the point that this is actually one of the old-style polymaths. When I went to work for him twenty years ago, he had already worked with GUS, had already done a stint with a printer, was writing highly effective copy and was handing over scribbles to art men which only required a sheet of tracing paper and a broader range of pencils to turn into highly presentable client layouts. He stopped doing this Da Vinci act as he came to be surrounded by zesty young acolytes such as myself, but that solid grounding in practicality never left him and probably still drives this year's acolytes quite barmy.

> Both of these men are wise in a sense that few of us can ever expect to be and certainly both are loved and admired in a way that fools may think sentimental.

Guy Stringer of Oxfam is a bloke with whom I have never directly worked but it is obvious what he has done with Oxfam in the twelve or so years that he has been there. Because Oxfam is by now such an institution, it is probably difficult to get an objective measure of its phenomenal achievements.

It is not my brief here to describe those achievements, merely to record that Guy Stringer has presided over and provided the temperamental fuel for the last few chapters. The fantastic retail explosion of Oxfam shops in the seventies, the honing of their direct mail into a fine art, the continued insistence on a campaigning edge to Oxfam's work – Guy Stringer was and is an unlikely figure to have presided over such events but few would want to deny him much of the credit. It helps to have such an old-fashioned feeling for a better world and to be able to back it with the physical resilience that had him more or less single-handedly running aid supplies into a very hairy Cambodia a few years ago. But to Guy, the ability to shake sense out of international bureaucracies and the ability to shake shekels out of the great British public are the same thing; both are born of passion and a joy in what one is doing.

Both of these men are wise in a sense that few of us can ever expect to be and certainly both are loved and admired in a way that fools may think sentimental. And it seems to me that they both have gifts that the rest of us would do well to re-explore. If I could list them, I would nominate decency in their daily doings, the ability to motivate other people along positive lines and, above all, sheer, unstructured common sense. It is an unassailable combination when it is backed by such a degree of personal integrity.

I'd better point out that I'm not writing an obituary. Guy, I gather, retires from Banbury Road next year and Harold's version of events will inevitably be a gradual re-gearing of hyperactivity called semi-retirement. But they will each of them fade just slightly now from centre stage and it seems entirely proper that we should raise our glasses before they do. They have never been the flashiest operators around and they will not emerge as the best heeled. But their quiet and level-headed contribution to direct marketing will be obvious to anyone who has ever known either of them. The best of heroes often go unsung; this is just a little trill to help rectify the balance.

An initial reaction to CLS and OM (other matters)

December 1982

This seeming rail against the growth of the acronym in British public life was actually a timely though affectionate pop at our transatlantic cousins. At least, George thought so...

Picking your way between the acronyms on 9th November was not easy. It was the high-powered launch of the New Consumer Location System (CLS) by the Post Office (PO) at the Royal Lancaster Hotel (RLH).

We have representations from CCN, IMS and, of course, CACI. Then a gentleman told us about BMRB and TGI, which were at least familiar initials to the media hacks in the audience. All, of course, in the interests of ACORN from whom we all trust giant oaks will grow. The RW (red wine) was admirable and TOS (things on sticks) world class. A GT was had by all.

It seems to me we can all save a lot of time and typewriter ribbons by communicating in acronym. The agencies are rightly ahead of the field here with HLY, O&M, MSW and THBW already in common parlance, though Wunderman International would seem to have another identity crisis with their initials. Client lists are studded with the likes of BCA, BMOC and S and T for whom we mull over the CPTs (cost per thousand) and the CPRs (cost per reply). All this under the tutelage of BDMA, DMPA, MUA, MOPA and the rest. Add in the NPA, PPA, NRS and the CA and we seem to be living in some kind of video game. Maybe we are.

Even the slang end of the business is getting truncated. My

very own colleagues (of whom the merest paste-up man is an MBA or PhD) invented the term OTB (on the bung) to describe a particular kind of shifty client or print rep. Then again, they are crude enough to have invented the deplorably sexist WWO, WWS and NWAW to categorise the attractions of the female gender. I don't know where to put my ears sometimes.

All this is by the way, though. What I wanted to write about was the Americans. It was brought on by my partner coming back on TWA from the DMMA in LA and opining that our American cousins were getting a bit above themselves. I precis of course, for her reportage is studded always with *bonhomie*, never with blandishments. Her gist was the extent to which the Americans light on the merest achievement and trumpet it to the heavens. In short, that there is something peculiarly American about presuming that anything that moves in direct marketing is a world-shattering event, to be lauded beyond its rightful place.

> You see it in their trade press with the most mundane of operations being interviewed as if the pope were being asked to talk us through transubstantiation.

You see it in their trade press with the most mundane of operations being interviewed as if the pope were being asked to talk us through transubstantiation. You see it in a lot of American platform presentations where you are led to believe that direct marketing is at the forefront of a social revolution. The language and style of American commentary on their own business is characteristically overwrought; hype lies at the heart of it. And the interesting thing is that hype becomes self-belief, which actually makes Americans better salesmen than us.

But ask yourselves: when was the last time you saw a piece of creative work from the States that really impressed you?

When did you ever read an American textbook as valuable and as entertaining as Drayton Bird's recent second book? When was the last time you were able to pluck an idea from the States and use it for your own business?

I guess there are some honest answers to these rhetorical questions. Certainly the Americans, being longer in this business, and bigger in this business, have a lot to bestow. But I have a sneaking feeling that right now there is more intelligent reworking of direct marketing themes in the UK and in Europe than there is on the other side of the pond. I certainly see decreasing need to stare in awe across it.

Don't get me wrong – I am not preaching a jingoistic anti-Americanism. I worked for Americans for two years and they taught me how to communicate and, therefore, how to do business. But we are in danger of presuming idly that Stateside experience and Stateside rhetoric is the fount of all wisdom. And anyone who still clings to that belief is the same sort of star-struck punter who thinks that Norman Mailer is better than Graham Greene because he writes bigger books and does more television.

So, in this year of the Falklands, all I'm suggesting is a little more GSTQ and a little less GBA. After all, if you do an anagram of BDMA and DMMA you can get Bad Mad Mm... Need I say more?

TTFN.

An everyday story of direct marketing folk

January 1983

Drayton Bird's now classic *Commonsense Direct Marketing* makes a favourable first impression on George.

I mentioned Drayton Bird's book *Commonsense Direct Marketing* almost in parenthesis in the last issue and the great man actually rang up to say thanks, an event as unexpected as it was pleasurable. What follows is an unabashed puff, born not of the courtesy of the author's phone call, more of a re-reading of the volume concerned and a gradual awareness of just how damned good it is.

You ought to know for a start that I hate textbooks. I have them all. They sit behind my desk and occasionally they are taken down, dusted and handed over to new staff. They also afford the occasional crib for seminars and conferences when you get stuck but that's another story.

The main negative about textbooks is that they are too big and too pompous. They consist very largely of lists and bromides derived from lists. You know the sort of thing – 'thirty-seven ways to catch your prospect's attention', an inventory which usually sounds like an expanded Seven Deadly Sins, ending up with a homily to the effect that you should remember that your customers deep down are really human beings just like you or I.

Stratified common sense in other words but usually stretched over too many pages and offered up in a prolix style that suggests the *Book of Revelations* rewritten by the Office of Fair Trading.

Drayton's book makes no such stylistic mistakes. It's chirpy, unceremonious and anecdotal. It's not afraid of the first person singular, unabashed about relating stories both positive and negative from his twenty-five year career. It has lists all right, for they do help shape material, but the lists are both pertinent and suitably terse – I particularly recommend the three simple facts about mailing lists; pithy to a fault, but if people just observe them as the truisms they are it would save such a lot of expensive jabber. Above all, the book is entertaining, a good read, scoring thousands of good points in the Della Femina tradition, a technique that might just convince its readers that direct marketing practitioners are hard-working hacks and not spiritual gurus. For this relief, much thanks. Its other bull point is that it is based on recent marketing history in the UK and not on what happened in Wisconsin during the Roosevelt years.

> ...but if people just observe them as the truisms they are it would save such a lot of expensive jabber.

All in all, Drayton has written the authoritative textbook for our business for a decade or so. If you haven't heard of it yet it's called *Commonsense Direct Marketing*. If Drayton hadn't given it to me in the first place, I'd have bought it myself – and I can't say fairer than that.

With that, it's hello 1983 and ta ta 1982. It wasn't such a bad year, was it? Give or take a few receiverships, everyone seems to be making a few bob. Faces that were strained and gloomy in spring turned out to be beaming just slightly in the autumn. The great British public's proclivity to join clubs, send for catalogues and test our systems with their infernal orders seems to go on. The crowds in Oxford Street are beating down the doors of the department stores and a sociologist turns up on the BBC's Radio Four to offer the profound truth that fifteen per cent unemployed means eighty-five per cent in work and spending. It is a grubby truth but one that still leaves us with a living to make. As a *Guardian* space rep once said to me: 'Every morning I wake up, it's a bonus'. These days, we'll all settle for that.

NB this piece is actually about textbooks and Drayton Bird's in particular, rather than whatever its title suggests.

Drayton Bird has been a legendary UK direct marketing figure for the last four decades or so. His first book, as George rightly says, made a huge impression when it came out and is no less good today. Jerry Della Femina wrote a couple of great books on advertising and marketing from Madison Avenue, including *From Those Wonderful Folks Who Gave You Pearl Harbor*. Professor Peter Tomkins is a direct marketing academic. In Debrett's he lists his recreations as squash, skiing, jogging and charity work.

Has direct marketing fallen into an information vacuum?

March 1983

On lies, damned lies and the absence of reliable statistics.

A very considerable business journalist was recently assigned by a very considerable marketing magazine (no names, no pack drill, but they do put on a very good lunch) to produce the authentic overview of direct marketing in the eighties. You know the sort of thing: 'Whither the coupon kings?' Or 'Direct selling boom punctures as retail soars.' The journalist was briefed to try and get together a once-and-for-all survey of direct marketing, produced and annotated with the precision and maturity that a fledgling industry was beginning to demand.

Some of us, you see, had savaged the ignorance shown in conventional coverage of our unconventional business. We had made the point over the aforesaid lunch that we wanted out of the special supplement ghetto into which we seemed to be thrust. We were big business, we said. We dealt in millions where some of the front-page acronyms in the same journals dealt in tens of thousands. We were seasoned marketing professionals operating at the furthest limits of data processing, technology, para-psychology, interactive doodads and all-round aplomb. We needed, nay we deserved, to be taken more seriously.

Hence the commission of the very considerable business journalist to report back on our doings. Those of us who found ourselves being interviewed or telephoned for some input on the subject will have been left with two distinct impressions: first, that we were being asked the wrong questions and second: that we were having to give some pretty naff answers.

The questions were mostly global in breadth or profound in depth. How much has mail order grown this year? Is direct mail using up all the money that used to be used for off-the-page? Why do you think people are buying pots and pans or joining book clubs or indulging in commemoratives? Well, what would you have said?

If the figures are not readily available, they can be convened by hearsay, validated by sample analysis and generally trumpeted by interested parties.

You would probably have done what I did – extemporise some highly subjective opinions and offer some third party telephone numbers which might offer some greater wisdom. And in a fortnight's time you would have received another call from the journalist, bewailing the lack of availability of some of your nominees, protesting the lack of hard information from anyone and castigating the trade association for not making like the Economist Intelligence Unit. You could only have been sympathetic.

There are two problems here. The biggest is undoubtedly the insistence on expertise-by-numbers. By which I mean the myth of expertise, by no means confined to direct marketing or marketing at large, that insists that the only usable analysis is the analysis that has numbers attached to it. It is a myth convened by politicians (inflation down, unemployment up), fostered by pressure groups (one in six children is from a broken home) and inculcated by journalists anxious for a headline summary of a complex story (*Direct Response* falters in last quarter). If the figures are not readily available, they can be convened by hearsay, validated by sample analysis and generally trumpeted by interested parties. Think about some of the grander examples you see quoted and you make take my point: how, in reality, can the government know precisely how many people are unemployed? How can anyone actually figure the number of broken homes or the number of endangered species? And how, to bring it all home, can someone solemnly add up the couponed ads in the colour magazines and in *Barclaycard Magazine* and extrapolate the current state of direct marketing from it? We are all too easily subdued by unquestioned statistics.

But I mentioned two problems, and the second is the one we can do something about. Diffidence is a fine thing and a proper diffidence is unusually relevant in a close-knit, look-over-your-shoulder business like ours. But *total* diffidence? Can we offer no greater information than that things are looking up, or stabilising, or coming out of a downturn or, indeed, are as tough as hell? Can we never offer precise sales figures? Can we never have the confidence to go public on our successes and failures within the same year as such events?

For, without such candour, we have an information vacuum. And an information vacuum gets filled by false information of which there is plenty. Thus a media owner can sell space on the claim that the such-and-such company has done 'astonishingly well' out of that new test facility. A producer company makes hay with the claim that the product has 'pulled its head off' in another catalogue. A list broker can assert that this list or that is 'always successful for charities'. We deserve such useless bromides and the cost of them – until such time as we are prepared to release a little of our experience to others.

Having said all that, I note that a thundering new EIU survey on our business is now on its way. Given its source and its cost, it can only be definitive. But am I the only one chuckling over the fact that its survey covers the likes of Aeonics and Foster Callear? Pity the poor statistical analyst faced with crazies like us!

The customers always write

April 1983

A delight this, particularly if you have ever submitted draft copy and timidly awaited reaction from a client or a higher-up. The first of the two articles featured here appeared shortly after the film *Chariots of Fire* had come out, and was written as a direct result of one dreadful client meeting. In 2010 it was chosen for SOFII, the Showcase of Fundraising Innovation and Inspiration.

In the interests of balance, SOFII's editor asked George to pen the article that follows to show that agency types are just as likely to indulge in this kind of gibberish as are members of the client species.

Scene:
the client's office.

Dramatis personae:
Lemuel Sweat, a client.
Nigel Luncheon-Voucher MBS, an assistant brand manager.
William Blake, a wild-eyed copy man.

First draft:
'And did those feet in ancient time
Walk upon England's mountains green?

And was the holy lamb of God
On England's pleasant pastures seen?
And did the Countenance Divine
Shine forth upon our clouded hills?
And was Jerusalem builded here
Among those dark satanic mills?'

LS: Like the first draft, Bill, but I'm a bit restless about this first line. 'And did those feet...' It's too negative. Sounds as if we don't know. I don't think – and this is a purely personal opinion – that the audience should be left in any doubt. Besides, the question marks are bloody irritating.

NL-V: I agree. And I think we've got a problem with the mountains. Scafell's the biggest and it's distinctly sub-alpine. Could cause correspondence...

LS: Yes, Bill, mountains are over the top and I don't want those advertising standards chappies on our backs. Can we make it hills? And I'm not sure about this holy lamb bit. You've really got a thing about lambs, Bill, and they're a bit controversial, post-Falklands. Can we cover ourselves with another word? Cattle?

NL-V: Domestic animals?

LS: Furry jobs?

NL-V: No, too colloquial. I prefer furry quadrupeds.

LS: They're not really furry, are they?

NL-V: True. How about woolly quadrupeds?

LS: Woolly quadrupeds, then. Fine. I think the same applies to the next line. Too negative again. Let's say what we mean. The woolly quadrupeds were either seen or they weren't. There's no mileage in self-doubt.

NL-V: That came up in the seminar I went to. Roger Millington was very good on self-doubt.

LS: Well, he should know. Anyway, let's get on with it.

Anything on the next line?

NL-V: Yes. Countenance Divine. I don't understand what you're getting at, Bill.

LS: Agreed. I can't see them talking about the Countenance Divine in the Rovers Return, can you, Nigel?

NL-V: No. And that's where our customer profile is. C2 DE. *Sun* readers, bingo players, Arthur Scargill freaks. They'd probably think the Countenance Divine was a pop group (peals of laughter).

LS: What are we trying to do here anyway? We're trying to say, and this is purely a personal opinion, that Jesus came to this country. Right?

NL-V: Right.

LS: So why the hell aren't we saying it? We don't even mention Jesus. Just this Countenance Divine bit. Let's spell it out for them. Let's talk about a face if we're talking about a face. And faces don't shine. Any alternatives?

NL-V: Rubber-necking?

LS: Eh?

NL-V: Rubber-necking. Jesus must have come here on a boat. 'Quinquereme of Nineveh' and all that. So he was a tourist. Stonehenge, Verulamium, Glastonbury. All that. Tourists rubber-neck.

LS: Don't like it. Too down market. How about 'had a good look at our clouded hills?'

NL-V: Glanced at?

LS: Not emotive enough. How about beamed?

NL-V: That's nice. There's another prob on this line. We've already used hills.

LS: True. Why don't we call these ones hillocks, just to

differentiate them from the green ones earlier.

NL-V: That's good. Green hills, clouded hillocks. Makes sense. Last bit? I suppose we're stuck with Jerusalem?

LS: Looks like it. But I'm not sure about these satanic mills. In fact, I've got reservations about this whole sentence. We're asking again and we should be telling. Can't we just spell it out – Jerusalem was builded here.

NL-V: Not really. It wasn't, was it?

LS: No, I suppose the bloody lawyers would jump on it – stupid buggers. But let's try and be more emphatic about it. Probably. Almost certainly. Something like that. And can we lose the satanic mills? Sounds more Christopher Lee than Charlton Heston. Okay, Bill, I think it's almost there. But beef it up. More emphatic, more Rovers Return, less Magnus Magnusson...

Second draft:
'Perhaps Jesus walked about
Up and down green English hills
Also, we reckon that divine woolly quadrupeds
Were glimpsed in the fields together with other animals.
Then again, His face beamed quite a lot
At the clouded hillocks.
And almost certainly Jerusalem was constructed
Somewhere round these environmentally awful factories.'

LS: Much better, Bill, much better. Love the environmental bit – should catch the kids' vote. Let's get on to the second para. I've got the same problems really with these chariots of fire. I can't see people queuing up for chariots of fire, can you, Nigel?

NL-V: No way, no way. (Peals of laughter.)

CURTAIN

Just try to keep up, will you?

This follow-up was written by George as recently as 2009, in an attempt to provide a balance to the previous article by indicating that advertising agencies can be just as barmy as clients.

'All the Bollo-vocabulary', George pointed out [his phrase, not ours: Ed], 'comes from the current issue of a leading marketing journal – just in case you thought any of this challengeable on the grounds of believability'.

Scene:
the presentation theatre of Silly Wardrobe, an ambient digital marketing agency.

Dramatis personae:
Dave Bollo, agency, head of brand dissertation and enhancement.
Kevin Raincoat, client, head of fundraising at Ursine Watch, UK (formerly Save the Wolves).

Dave: So let me summarise. We're recommending a revised website content management system, WYSIWYG (what you see is what you get, you'll remember), editing with drag and drop, enhanced corporate branding and a nine-cell grid for the loyalty ladder.

Kevin: Very interesting, Dave, and I'm sure very up to date, but I think I need persuading that it's going to help us raise money cost-effectively.

Dave (sulkily): Well, of course, if you want traditional thinking, we can probably find other suppliers in the *Yellow Pages*...

Kevin: No, we're interested in data management, believe me, but my trustees insist that we raise money at a ratio of three-to-one.

Dave: And how do you define three-to-one?

Kevin: Raising three times what you're spending on the process.

Dave: A little simplistic, that seems to me. I really think you should think longer-term. The brand needs a higher profile – another name change maybe – you've been Ursine Watch for three years now.

Kevin: But our supporters are still getting used to it. Half of them still think of us as Save the Wolves.

Dave: Get rid of them!

Kevin: Eh?

Dave: Get rid of them. They can't be proper brand guardians if they can't cope with a name change every few years.

Kevin: But they're the people who send us money!

Dave: That's just one index for support. But they should be capable of campaigning on ursine issues, texting the BBC, decrying the new *Wolfman* film for offering species stereotyping – that sort of thing. And you'll probably find that they are promiscuous and give money to other charities.

Kevin: Well, of course they do. They're nice people.

Dave: (explosively) Nice! What's nice when it's out? Does it enhance deliverability, promote information architecture, migrate content? Does it have a hub? Anyway, how old are these people?

Kevin: Forties, fifties, sixties....

Dave: Oh my God! How can you promote a brand with people who grew up with the Beatles, in the Second World War?

Kevin: But they love wolves. And they've given generously in the past....

Dave: Do you share your KPIs with them?

Kevin: What?

Dave: Are your CIOs and CMOs working together to develop a marketing technology architecture?

Kevin: What?

Dave: Kevin, I have to tell you that we at Silly Wardrobe don't seem to share a language with you.

Kevin: Too bleedin' right, mate. Where's that *Yellow Pages*?

CURTAIN

'O Challock! We who are about to use long words salute thee...'

May 1983

One of the best, this, we think, with an opening line to die for. It goes downhill from there, which is what makes it so great. You will be truly amazed.

It was always my secret wish that Kaleidoscope or someone would run an ice pick in their catalogue so that I could get away with the line 'guaranteed to break the ice at parties'. Then again, I always wanted someone to run a promotion for a seed company that ended 'rush now while phlox lasts'. All of which proves two things. First, that I still have a terrible personal problem when it comes to keeping a straight face. And second, that I was brought up on postal bargain ads.

Indeed I have remained a keen student of the five-point stuff in the weekend papers to the point where I would like a sabbatical year in which to produce a world-class monograph on the subject. You know the sort of thing: *The fusion of the superlative with the prosaic: British postal bargain advertising 1950-1980.* Are you listening, University of Lancaster? It could be yours for the asking. Rustle some folding money out of Gulbenkian and the limits of human knowledge would be moved on outwards.

All art forms have a golden age, of course, and the golden age of postal bargains, like all others, seems to have coincided uncannily with my childhood and adolescence. They were the days when the papers were stuffed full of ex-army surplus underwear, endless devices to deal with incontinence and ho-ho merchandise aimed at raising guffaws at social gatherings of all kinds. They were the days when whoopee cushions were sold off the page, depicted by fat cartoon characters being sorely embarrassed as fellow guests chortled. They were the days when the all-purpose phrase 'You will be truly amazed' would suffice as a lead-in to any product claim, when lots and lots of stuff called rubberwear was sold before the innocent eyes of a population to whom Diana Dors was the dirtiest thing you could think of. The days when CAP was a thing you wore on your head on your way to school. Ah, dear, dead days!

For the wide-eyed innocence of postal bargain advertising shines out like a good deed in a naughty, over-complex world.

Mind you, if there is still an extant area of selling activity untouched by seminars and learned magazine articles it is this one. For the wide-eyed innocence of postal bargain advertising shines out like a good deed in a naughty, over-complex world. Who else but a postal bargain advertiser would position an acrylic sweater as 'British-made combat sweaters' and go on to claim '...manufactured to a high standard by HM Government contractors that have made these jumpers so famous right across the world...'? The combination of uneasy syntax with belief in the power of an endorsement by HM Government contractors is deeply touching to all us sophisticates. But to run this ad with a handsome line illustration that suggests that our lads in the Falklands are even now thrashing Johnny Gaucho while sporting their fetching acrylic sweaters is opportunism of the cleverest kind.

I like, too, the necessary compactness of the language. This is an area where every little single column centimetre is counted and it shows in the wonderful telescoping of verbs, nouns, epithets and articles, definite or indefinite. Where else would you meet a phrase like 'Now with lift up base gate for easy compost removal'; or 'Now put an end to toil and blisters'; or the wonderful unpunctuated claim 'combined with stethoscope compact and convenient to use'?

And it's nice to know that the tradition of apparently barmy products still goes on resilient as ever. Mind you, one man's barmy product is almost certainly another man's *sine qua non*. I never did work out who in their right mind would want all those Newton's cradles and personalised gear knobs, but they did and do which, in a fraught world, has to be a very good thing. For all I know toe-nail scissors, book rests ('remains firmly upright with even large directories!') and five-bar skirt hangers are tearing up trees out there. Long may it remain so! I'm not so sure about the black rubber balaclava hood offered by the S B Rainwear Company of Iver, Bucks, but it's a free country and it could be that you don it while reading directories in bed or removing in-growing toenails. Research will doubtless tell.

The likes of the Able Label Company of Earls Barton, Mister Lewis of London E17, Foam for Comfort of Leeds and Top to Toe of Dewsbury may never make the BDMA awards but I found them all on the same half page of the *Guardian* and I say we should salute them. I have the distinct feeling that they are making more money than the more august practitioners of mail order business without ever having graced a conference.

But I do have one special hero in all this and he resides in somewhere called Challock, near Ashford, Kent. For someone on the direct or indirect payroll of Kent Country Nurseries can put together direct selling ads with an aplomb that passeth all understanding. Anyone who can get the word 'furthermore' into a mail order ad is a friend of mine, but here it is, in a reversed out flash at the bottom of an ad which 'guarantees that grass and hedge cutting can be eliminated' and, which, moreover, substantiates the claim of a 'no quibble money back guarantee'. If that, and the accompanying two hundred words were not evocative enough, if you remained immune to the drawing of a family sipping drinks on a lawn that suggests Sissinghurst rather than Surbiton, then you will doubtless be caught by this last clincher: 'Furthermore', it says, 'there's £1,000 to be won in our Stop Gro G8 competition'. At which point you won't need telling that the product is available at 'inflation beating 1980 prices'.

No, what I like about the Challock school is the combination of throw-the-book-at-them selling and distinctly odd verbals. Other rose walls may reach 7ft high; Challock's 'rapidly attains' the said level. The aforesaid Stop Gro G8 is simply mixed with tap water and applied 'as a drench'. And nowhere have I seen the native cadences of a market trader better reflected than in the immortal line: 'Not £8 each. Only £5.85 each'. It's the sheer vigour of all this that I like, and if a cherry tree can be sold via the information that the relevant berries were once part of the staple diet of Red Indians then that's all right by me.

I think I'll pay a little pilgrimage to Challock. There are caves and a narrow gauge railway there as well you know – the ad finds room to tell me. But I'll probably come back with a cornucopia of goodies, backed each one with no-quibble guarantees. Chances are, I'll be truly amazed at something. I think I'll buy a combat sweater for the journey and a black rubber balaclava hood for the coming back.

Confessions of a closet inner-directed

June 1983

George may not have heard of Maslow's hierarchy of need, but who cares? Bogus sociology apart, clearly we should be proud of our nation's high concentration of ABC1 buyers of cat food.

I confess. Last month I was slightly waspish about the new ACORN classifications just because I was upset at still being an intermediate status sort of chap. But then Montreux intervened and I went to a presentation that gave me insight into my unruly reaction. I was uptight, I think, because I am at heart one of the societally conscious of the inner-directed group. There aren't too many of us according to the research, so we can be forgiven the occasional outburst. Especially the Capricorns among us.

All right, I'll explain. The presentation was about a new form of lifestyle research called VALS. The presenter was an American gentleman of academic gravamen who has assisted in the building of a sociological model that reassembles the American population, not in terms of their income, their location, or their age group but in terms of their lifestyle characteristics.

The opening gambit is a sound one. When you go to a party, he said, you don't necessarily start chatting to your fellow professionals, people on a similar income level, or people who live in the same street. You start talking to people with whom you share an interest. It may be cricket (or should be), it may be hang-gliding, it may be cookery and, in intermediate status country at least, it is likely to be children. What binds people together, in other words, is as much to do with what they do and want to do as it is with more objective characteristics. The lifestyle, in fact, is a cross current over the basic seas of standard demographic data that is often well worth exploring.

So far so good. The evidence of one's eyes does indeed confirm that there is little class or geographic significance in many interest areas, particularly the more recent ones. Video ownership is already a notorious example of a marketing trend unlikely in pure income-level terms. So, too, is photography where there is little correlation between level of income and purchasing habits.
A lot of new marketing opportunities have to do with aspiration on behalf of statistically unlikely people to enjoy the better things in life – food, drink, travel, etc.

Taste and aspiration may be difficult to quantify but they do indicate proclivity to buy with quite as much accuracy as do standard demographics.

But the VALS presentation went quickly over the top as these things tend to. A lot of bogus sociology was being thrown around, stuff that segmented the population into need-drivens, outer-directeds and inner-directeds, all with sub groups. You know the sort of thing, I'm sure, and it always strikes me as a pity that these new research techniques should be so over sold and over literalised. I don't think I was the only audience member in mild contortions at the news that the societally conscious sub-group of the inner-directeds had a distinct purchasing proclivity for cat food. But that's what the man said. Then again we ended with a little preview of a VALS-defined Europe, country by country, giving us national percentages by sub-group. Your breast will swell with pride when I tell you that the UK has got more (three per cent) of the top group than anyone else in sight. 'Integrateds' they were called, by the way, suggesting a sort of new breed of H-G-Wells-type stock cleansed of needs and anxieties, smiling at each other with suntanned visages living to about a hundred and forty and, of course, very heavily into cat food and affluent new housing somewhere near Esher.

The serious side of all this is that I know of no significant UK research in the area of lifestyle. And, if there is none, there should be. Our society is changing very fast indeed, as some politicians will have discovered before this article reaches print. Taste and aspiration may be difficult to quantify but they do indicate proclivity to buy with quite as much accuracy as do standard demographics. We started with our basic socio-economic of ABC1s etc, we now have ACORN to give us the geography of a database and we now need something that tells us more about lifestyle. Maybe the Post Office should be funding some early work into the subject. I certainly sense that, within three to five years, many direct marketers will be looking for some new research tools in this area. Anyway, I must be off, I intend to shed some avoirdupois and go for integrated status by Michaelmas. It'll be a hard slog, so I'm stocking up on cat food just in case.

Stap me vitals, the colonies are preening themselves again

July 1983

Once more George offends the Americans, even in jest. Why not? Someone has to.

A few months back I ventured to suggest that maybe, just maybe, the Americans did not know it all. What I meant was that they knew quite a lot, could fairly be credited with having originated much direct marketing practice, but should not forever be granted godlike status in these matters. An innocuous aside, I would have thought.

An American correspondent immediately took issue with me, more or less accusing me of being anti-American. The same correspondent then asked me to write a piece for an American journal with the firm instruction not to be rude about them. I obliged with some ease, for I cannot for the life of me see why the occasional aside in these pages should be elevated to the status of a diplomatic incident.

Now, I see that Lester Wunderman, no less, has been having a go at us Europeans. I read in last month's *Direct Response* that the great man is quoted in a German trade paper as saying that, 'Most of the direct marketing activities in Europe remind him of the time he started in business some forty years ago when direct marketing was regarded as a clumsy, ineffective way to sell all sorts of junk'. But there is hope for us yet, for Wunderman ends his philippic with the belief that, 'Europe will catch up with the USA by 1990'. Thanks, Lester. The idea of us plodding around in trilby hats and stiff collars and with gas masks swinging from our briefcases is quite pleasing but bear in mind that Mr Wunderman is a much-travelled man, exposed only to the best-developed end of our industry. Maybe the view of us from the less sophisticated level of American direct marketing is even more pronounced. So let's offer a little pastiche of ourselves as seen from East Jesus, Nebraska.

Scene: a British direct marketing agency. From the windows one can hear street vendors, organ grinders and the like.

Dramatis personae:
Praise-God Epithet, a copywriter.
Samuel Poltroon, an account director.
Nehemiah Fruitslice, a client.

SP: Prithee, light yon candle, Praise-God, lest Master Fruitslice fail to see the craftsmanship of his new announcement.

P-GE: Aye, Samuel, 'tis craftsmanship indeed, and you do well to dwell on't. Methinks Master Fruitslice will become a rich man as a result.

NF: A fig for your banter, scribbler. Many a sovereign have I tied up in the rights to *Foxes Book of Martyrs* and a decent return is all I crave. So, show me your wares.

SP (producing ad): All the new verities from the colonies have been observed, Master Fruitslice. 'Tis a powerful announcement indeed. (He reads) VERILY, A VOLUME TO ENDURE. *FOXES BOOK OF MARTYRS*, LITERARY ENDEAVOUR AND SPIRITUAL REGENERATION FOR BUT THREE SOVEREIGNS.

NF: A judicious assembly of benefits, I warrant. *And* the tariff in the headline. 'Tis the product of many a symposium, I trust, Epithet?

P-GE: I have imbibed at the feet of masters in the trade. There is barely a sage in the realm whose wisdom I have not sought.

NF: And whence goes this announcement?

SP: Progress again, Master Fruitslice. No more handbills or broadsheets. 'Tis no matter for the town crier. We will place this announcement in one of the new coffee shop newspapers. There is one called the *Observer* that offers a most genteel arrangement of advantage to such as yourself.

NF: And the tariff for these wonders?

SP: A pittance, my friend. The quills were squeaking in the counting house last night computing the said trifle, but trifle it be.

NF: And my announcement will reach the gaze of the gentry?

SP: A vast sweep of gentlefolk scan the said journal. Costing four pennies as it does, you are guaranteed of many a bulging purse.

NF: 'Tis done. What now?

SP: We shall call a chair this instant so that your offer will hasten to Master Caxton's for an overnight woodcut.

NF: Such marvels! And prithee tell me, how fares young Master Rowney?

P-GE: Still scribbling endlessly about the Shoppe Front bubble. Methinks the lad is crazed with creditors' meetings.

EXEUNT OMNES

Please don't write, cousins. It's only a joke.

Brush up your database

August 1983

In this piece George was imitating the breathless interviewing style of American trade journals. It wasn't always apparent to sections of his readership that at times their favourite columnist wasn't being entirely serious.

This is Roland Scoop reporting for *Direct Response* magazine. I'm sitting here in the downtown Harlesden office of Dr Ernst Invoice, creator of the new HCF database and segmentation system, the first attempt to set up a computer file based entirely on haircut.

Q: Ernst, what exactly does HOF stand for?

A: Hair Cut First, Roland. As you know, you can't really get into this field without a good acronym. We turned the assignment over to our acronym boys and they eventually came through with HCF – research seemed to confirm that it had the right mathematical feel.

Q: But you dismissed other acronyms on the way?

A: Dozens. We ran a number of group interviews with user groups and HCF emerged after quite a number of sessions. The working title for a long time was, in fact, Tonsorial Input Tertiary System, but a lot of the respondents found this a bit skittish.

Q: Tell me, Ernst, what first led you to hair as an all-important determinant of purchasing patterns.

A: It just struck us as pretty well universal. Things like trousers and glasses were less than ubiquitous and other physical indices like noses and ears were just too subject to change. Hair emerged clearly as the KD – key determinant.

Q: And you now have the entire population segmented according to hair type?

A: Indeed we have. The original survey work that was done at Lancaster indicated some thirty-seven stable hair types that we managed to cut down to thirty-two after we'd finished our sample analysis around the country. They range from toupees to zero options, which is what the research boys call baldies.

Q: And I gather from your press release that the survey produced some fairly surprising data?

A: I'm glad you mentioned that, Roland. Some of the findings were indeed illuminating. We were surprised for instance to learn that a disproportionate number of the longer hair types were in fact women. Then again, the short-back-and-side segment had an undue concentration in places like Aldershot and Catterick. Zero option types were largely found among males above 40 – ZO representation among females of any age was fairly limited.

Q: With data like that coming through, you must have got pretty excited?

A: I don't mind telling you, Roland, there was a lot of excitement at the time. It's not often you see DP men crying into their printouts. The point was that we had a base from which we could extrapolate across-the-board marketing data for a variety of user groups. If long hair types included a good proportion of women, then long hair types would be a perfect module for things like sanitary protection and knitting offers. Long hair types would tend to be mothers rather than fathers, priorities leg shaving rather than any other kind.

Q: Cynics would say that not all long hair types were in fact women.

A: We took that one on board pretty early. A certain number *are* men, which is why we created category twenty-three, the obdurate hippy male or OHM. Category twenty-three is heavily into beards, flowers and exotic cigarettes. And, increasingly, into anti-wrinkle cream and things like Phyllosan and Ovaltine.

Q: You seem to have thought of everything, Ernst. Were the short hair types equally complicated?

A: More so, if anything. They ranged from ABZOs – all but zero options – to new romantics, upwardly mobile young executives, Radcliffe Hall types and old reactionaries. They each have their own psychographics and demographics and so on.

Q: Let me just take you up on that, Ernst. What characterises the old reactionaries, for example?

A: They're heavy television watchers, heavy *Telegraph* readers, light on wine drinking and groups like Status Quo. Conversely they drink a lot of brown ale, are surprisingly keen on Spandau Ballet and tend to tear the wings off flies in summertime.

Q: The direct marketing aspect of all this is obvious to my mind. Where do you go from here, Ernst?

A: We'll be presenting HCF at Montreux next year. And we've got a GLC grant application in so that we can put the system on to satellite, cable and interactive doodahs of all kinds.

Q: And again according to the press release, you're producing a catalogue based on HCF?

A: That's right, Roland. We're doing a joint venture thing with a bright young outfit called Briefcase. We'll be featuring personalised hairbrushes, crimping tools, Macassar oil and hair grips, possibly going as far as earrings. Everything segmented by hair type and underpinned by ink jet. The catalogue's called *Follicles*.

Q: Sounds another winner to me. Dr Invoice, thank you for letting us hear your choice of acronyms.

A: Thank you, Roland. It's been a privilege gibbering at you.

Down there on a visit

September 1983

George is a socialist at heart of course and full of solutions to social injustice that are both moral and elegant. Entertaining too. Here he rallies to the defence of that perceived poor relation of the direct marketing business, the mailing house. Those I knew then usually drove a car, and their children had shoes, as far as I recall.

Not so long ago I was walking around a mailing house, something I hadn't done for a year or two. It was very good for me.

Mailing houses tend to be the same the world over. You start with a reception area that is the merest gesture to gracious business living – a pot plant or two, some imitation pine, some month-old copies of the trade press and signs in Woolworth lettering. At this end of the business, the cloth is clearly cut according to reduced means.

Executives who labour under enormous titles do their labouring in tiny partitioned offices surrounded by copies of *Kelly's Directories* and the *Glasgow Yellow Pages*. There are brown paper parcels, the funny ha-ha signs that you see in lousy pubs and postcards from Majorca. Radio One seeps through the factory floor.

And it is on the factory floor that the experience becomes distinctly olfactory, if you'll forgive the phrase. The smells, I mean! The wood of pallets, the twine of parcels, the post office sacks, the printing ink, the dust covering the surplus brochures, the filled ashtrays, the cowboy plumbing – here everything smells of one great nasal experience that could only be a mailing house.

It is a long way from the cleansed temples in which we have our conferences, seminars and working lunches. It is even further from the air-conditioned and Perrier-laden rooms in which we have business meetings. For this is an engine room, peopled by working mums called Ada and Doreen, who tell you that they'll be glad when they see the back of that charity job that came in last week, and by youths in T-shirts who look balefully at you as you pass. It is a world where twenty-year old executives are called guvnors and where lunch hours are for getting the family shopping in. It is an area of our business that we all take totally for granted.

> It is a long way from the cleansed temples in which we have our conferences, seminars and working lunches.

In saying as much, I am not making a dewy-eyed plea to remember the Adas and Doreens of this world, nor reporting Mayhew-like on the working conditions of mailing house personnel. I am not suggesting that the tone of our great industry is lowered by imitation pine or by Radio One. But I am coming to believe that mailing houses do not make enough money.

This was brought on by receiving a sudden wave of mailings from mailing houses, peddling their wares with a variety of presentations that ran from mighty folders to photocopied sheets (some of them would have qualified for any Silly Mailing of the Month Award, though there is a clear winner this month in Lord Redesdale's earnest advice on BDMA letterhead that my career would be well served by a spell at the diploma course at Kingston). But what caught my eye about most of these mailings was an unusual candour about prices and the nature of the prices themselves: £18 per thousand? £15 per thousand? £8 per thousand? It is obviously as competitive as hell out there. What sort of margin can there be on doing a thousand of anything for half the hourly cost of a freelance copywriter? What sort of volume business do you need to add up sums of money like this and pay staff, electricity bills and petrol costs? If upfront postage costs help ease cash flow, how do you swing the problem of weekly-paid staff and outworkers on piece rates?

Rhetorical questions all, for I do not know the answers. With a few big-name exceptions, mailing houses are a sort of alternative economy of which the rest of us know little. We need them when we need them, we complain about their lack of professionalism, we query that the mailing actually went out when we are not flooded with replies, we remain deeply suspicious of what goes on down there. And we pay them at rates of £15 per thousand. Look at the component costs of a test mailing campaign – the creative costs, the origination, the postage, the print – that figure at the bottom of the list, the one in the low hundreds, is the lettershop component. Doesn't it look a bit bleak as a fraction of the whole?

Right now must seem a fairly hysterical time to be suggesting that marketing should pay more for its lettershop services. Nevertheless it seems to me that there is a clear relationship between the age-old complaint as to the lack professionalism in British mailing houses and the money that we allow them to earn. It also strikes me as no coincidence that the best people in the mailing business seem to have drifted more profitably into its more sectarian areas – telephone selling, list management, database work, fulfilment and the like. I seem to sense, but I could be wrong, that the old basic mainstream and honourable role of the lettershop is now thought a little passé, merely a residual function on which to graft some soi-disant technology or over-hyped add-on service before it can be sold. If that is so, it is a great pity. If that is so and the reason is lousy margins and no way out, it is an even greater pity.

We need reliable and resilient lettershops. We do not want

them to swap their imitation pine for the real thing, nor to send Ada to Kingston. But they might have become the peasantry of an industry whose squires and barons have become fleshy. A little redistribution of the available wealth might not be a bad thing right now. And I think it's a commercial, not a moral, point that I'm making.

Some people can write and others cannot

October 1983

It's evident that our scribe is a little jaundiced in this piece. Nevertheless he's simply saying what every editor feels at some time, if not on most days. Note the pop at the new phenomenon then termed word processing, and the implication that this insidious arrival was adding to our propensity towards increasing carelessness with words.

I do like a good aphorism to end the day with. When you reach that world-weary part of the day when you wonder what you are doing here, when the combination of nonsense and frenzy overcomes the barrier of good humour that you erect to stay sane, when the mid-life crisis appears like Scrooge's ghost the other side of your desk, then is the time for a nicely-turned aphorism, a semi-literate half-truth that at least turns experience into a pleasing form of words.

The other day had been harrowing and it was in just this mood that I came up with the following. I will not elevate it to Smith's First Law but I suspect a few dozen hacks around town will know what 1 mean.

It goes thus: the time spent on producing direct response copy is in inverse proportion to the client's ability to write it in the first place.

Phew! Pretty offensive, what? A distinct hint of sour grapes, did I hear you say, born of a rough time during the holiday period? Well, maybe. But I insist that there is some version of a universal truth knocking around in that aphorism. And, actually it's a more benign statement than it must appear at first blush.

> ...debating the warp and the woof of the verbiage with a zeal that would do credit to a don undertaking textual analysis on Gerard Manley Hopkins.

What I am trying to report is this: that clients who know their direct marketing business literally know their direct marketing business. They know that part of their business is to hire someone to write the words, to scan the said words and to approve those words. This way, they get their words cheap.

Conversely, other clients feel they participate in the creation of those words, debating the warp and the woof of the verbiage with a zeal that would do credit to a don undertaking textual analysis on Gerard Manley Hopkins. In my experience, this category cannot write. Also in my experience the first category can write.

Afficionados of this column will know that I do not overrate the practice of writing. I see it as technique not art, common sense not science. I think some people can write and others cannot write, just as some people cannot swim, cannot spell, cannot fashion a dovetail joint and cannot tango. There need be no shame in these fascinating varieties of human skill.

But I insist: some people cannot write. Not just direct response copy mind you, for to a demonstrable extent the same folk have difficulty in composing a business letter that says what is meant without undue repetition, obscurantism or lazy cliché. And I repeat: I do not hold the lack of this godgiven skill against them. It is a honourable lack.

But what I must worry about is the uncanny regularity with which those selfsame people cause you the most trouble when it comes to producing the stuff. I am not demeaning the role of a client who tells you that the facts are wrong, that the copy is boring, that you have ignored the brief. These are pragmatic observations to which any piece of writing should constantly be subjected. What does cause me grief is the debate often invoked by discussion on copy that has the client sucking a pencil, staring at the ceiling and wondering out loud whether 'unique' isn't really an altogether stronger adjective than 'unusual'. The writer is forced back on pedantry to explain the difference, the client chortles at the scale of the brainpower he has hired and continues to make the case for 'unique'.

There is an answer to this client, often applied from much of what I see around me. It is to write in cliché, to write copy that uses the basic direct marketing vocabulary with cynical precision. For the kind of client I am describing, this makes the copy a comforting experience. Drugged as he probably is with seminars and textbooks, the appearance of copy that looks and feels so much like the real thing first time around, inoculates him from the debate, assures him that he has bought what he came in to buy.

This explains why so much direct marketing copy might well have been composed on a word processor. It also explains why so much direct marketing goes unread. Like political speeches, it is assumed that some things must be said in a certain order, that this rhetorical statement should be made just here, that an indentation or a pause for breath should occur at this point. The result is predictability, the shortcut to boredom.

I had an example the other week of a short letter written for a promotional piece that had actually been penned by the chief executive of the organisation concerned. And that is how it read – it was pithy, clear and contained a few flashes of verbal colour, sufficient to suggest that it was a real guy writing. It came to me to rewrite, to 'sharpen it up'. I protested the daftness of this process but was persuaded to do a dim version of the sharpening-up process, trying to retain the vitality of the original. I obviously failed, for the next version of the letter I saw contained every comfortable cliché you can cram into three paragraphs. An okay piece of writing has been turned into a dead piece of self-justifying prose,

An equation that has often appealed to me is how much time a writer spends writing and how much re-writing. If you are writing, chances are you are doing it for someone who can write himself. If you are re-writing, chances are you are doing it for someone who cannot write their way out of a paper bag. Am I right, fellow hacks, or am I just a little jaundiced this month?

'Your name has been suggested to us . . .'

November 1983

More harping on the essentially unfair activity of clients appointing agencies rather than the other way round. George must have had a particularly depressing experience or two of this sordid phenomenon around the time that he wrote this. For which we can be grateful.

In the last week, my advice has been sought by a lot of people. I have been asked *inter alia* to offer a promotional strategy for a cuddly toy that boasts a sound suggestive of the mother's womb, guaranteed to send infants asleep within minutes. I have been asked to appraise a mailing piece for, let us say, egg futures. I have been asked by a six-strong panel of a major voluntary organisation what I think of their logo. None of these good folk did I know before, none of them do I work for and, naturally, none of them would think of paying for my reaction and those of my colleagues to the extraordinary questions that they pose.

Anyone who runs a direct response agency will be used to this situation, one where apparent expertise in a particular sector is seen to embrace godlike knowledge in all others. It is no use cutting up rough and shattering illusions with full-blooded reactions like 'How the hell would I know?' Some people can probably get away this. I cannot, being a supine lover of the human race and a wide-eyed Candide-like believer that this week's nutter might just turn out to be next year's Bob Scott.

But brain-picking is becoming a whole alternative industry.

My many consultant friends tell me that they are often called into situations where, within twenty minutes, they know that there is nothing on business-wise but where two hours of free information and opinion are called for as a trade-off for a cup of coffee. There is rarely anything sinister about this, more a total misunderstanding on behalf of salaried chappies that people in service companies and freelancers are a conversational resource to be dipped into occasionally as part of the old learning curve.

With agencies, it is distinctly worse, for agencies are saddled with this extraordinary ritual called a new business presentation. The subject of presentations regularly exercises greater minds than mine in the advertising trade press. And, indeed, the stakes are higher in consumer agencies where unbelievable sums of money are spent in an attempt to convince a prospective client of the agency's claims. I gather that the more sophisticated clients now offer up fees for the real all-singing, all-dancing presentations, but it can only be a contribution to the process, nothing more.

The trouble with presentations is, of course, that both agency and client love them. For the agency it is the equivalent of courtship and the act of love, starting with the first flirtatious encounter, building up through the excitement of the seduction and finally the whoosh of actually doing it. If you think the analogy far-fetched, take a look at an agency man slumped over a drink after a presentation. Post-coital tristesse, physical exhaustion and the need to ask the unspoken question, 'Was it good for you too?'

Clients presumably approach these things on a lower emotional key. But it still has to be fun, doesn't it, watching these agency oiks coming in wearing their best suits, looking for a point for the slide projector, trying to set up their display boards, waiting for their cues? It must be difficult for clients not to exploit the situation, to posture, to role play.

So often it reminds me of the nights I used to spend as a school governor when we were interviewing, say, a new head of geography and there was always a lay governor even dumber than myself who would ask the sweating aspirant whether he really liked maps…

For the content of these events is too often pantomime. A brief is often, but not always, received. The agency labours to do it justice. It presents and is traditionally plied with questions bearing no relationship to that brief, indeed sometimes contradictory to it, posed by people you have never met before and who turn out be the head of stationery buying, invited along because it's a big occasion.

> The silly ritual and the redundant secrecy both militate against honest communication and they can linger after the presentation itself.

Again, there is too often an ersatz air of secrecy about the event. I cannot think of any reason why a short-listed agency should not be told of the other names on the short list. If they did know in direct marketing, where the agencies know so much about their respective strengths and weaknesses, it might well lead to some of us vacating the field on the perfectly sound basis that the other agencies will likely be a better choice for the client concerned. The silly ritual and the redundant secrecy both militate against honest communication and they can linger after the presentation itself. A little while ago we were unsuccessful in a new business pitch. When told so, I rang up and asked who won. My instincts were simple. First, the post-coital curiosity I mentioned earlier and, second, the fact that I wanted to congratulate the successful agency. The client refused the information, which was both offensive to the effort we had put in and suggestive of some shifty behind-the-scenes manoeuvres. Silly, isn't it?

Potential clients of direct response agencies need to do very little to choose their agencies. They can look at what the agency has done, talk to the people they would be working with, and check them out with their existing clients. Speculative creative work is rarely relevant, wholesale marketing recommendations usually completely academic. But, as long as both sides enjoy the process, it will probably continue. Hard headed we may think ourselves, soft cuddly toys we turn out to be.

So you seriously want to be a client?

December 1983

An interesting historical point on the origins of the lead character in this piece, Max Headroom. George says, 'The name came out of a boozy dinner I once had with Miles Kington, *The Times* humorist, in which we tried to think of silly names for a silly novel – you know, Richard Shops, Urban Sprawl – that sort of nonsense. A year later I turn round to find Max has his own trendy TV show...' He did indeed, though it was short-lived. Max was a computer generated fictional artificial intelligence. The idea of clients lining up to pitch to an agency in the desperate hope that they'll take the account is just too delicious, though...

Last month's piece obviously rang bells, touched chords, echoed deeply felt emotions, all that sort of thing. People rang up to say as much, chorusing how the point needed making, how it was about time someone said it, etc, etc.

The point of the piece struck me, in fact, as a slender one as well as a hoary one. It was the age-old nonsense of agency presentations and I was remarking on the peculiar dumbness of selecting a direct response agency via the grisly ritual that bedevils our cousins in mainstream agencies. It was usually irrelevant, inevitably a waste of most people's time and, almost always, an excuse for role-playing all round. This was the banal point I was making and you'd be astonished at the number of good folk on the client side who couldn't wait to agree.

In fact one of them suggested that it would be altogether more honourable if the agencies were to ask for presentations from potential clients on the basis that agency oiks are probably better grounded in the things that matter than client oiks. Whilst reeling aghast from the heresy inherent in this judgement and steeling myself never to be associated with such subversive canards, I have to admit to a quiet fantasy coming on...

Scene: the offices of Headroom and Associates, a specialist direct response agency somewhere in London. Motorcycle messengers lurk among the rubber plants. Writers lie supine on *chaises longues*, brushing madeleine crumbs from their velvet jackets, art directors compare cushion fabrics, account executives ring their brokers, the atmosphere is one of civilised torpor, a bit like the staff room at All Souls when they've filled in their football pools.

Enter: three people, sweating. They carry briefcases, a projector and an easel. They wait in reception for thirty-five minutes, are refreshed with coffee in plastic cups and are then ushered into the agency's boardroom.

Headroom:	Come in, come in. I'm sorry you've been kept waiting but we really are very busy here at the agency right now. You'll be the first to know how difficult it is to choose a new client. Let me just make the introductions. I'm Max Headroom, the MD. This is Richard Shops, our creative director, Beulah Hill, head of gerunds, Miss Swollocks from invoicing and chicanery, Mr Janus from dispatch and research and, lastly but not leastly, Wilf the cleaner. Anything to add, Dick?
Shops:	No, I think you said it all, Max. But I just

would like to repeat how difficult it is to choose a new client. It's been hell.

Headroom: I think that's a fair point, Dick. And I think it's right that the client knows how difficult it's been for us. (Turns to client party.) Okay, over to you. As you know we have short-listed six prospective clients from our original universe of thirty-eight. We've heard a lot about you and look forward to hearing how and why you will be the right client for us to work with in the next few years. So, fire away. (Headroom folds arms, narrows eyes. His colleagues follow suit, picking up pens and clipboards and blowing smoke rings).

The client party presents. They show the ads they have produced to date, graphs demonstrating seven-figure appropriations for the next decade, offer biographies of their key staff, show slides of their factories, extracts from their bank statements, snaps of their sales conferences in Acapulco, ending with a testimonial from Les Shepherd and a commitment to be extremely liberal on production bills. Finally and rather glumly, they remove their coats and are seen to be wearing T-shirts bearing the legend: 'You'll make a few bob out of us all right, Maxie baby'.

Headroom: Very good, very good. I do like to see a little panache in a prospective client. Any questions? Wilf?

Wilf the cleaner: About coffee cups. We have had a lot of problems at the agency with coffee cups, lipstick, cigarette stubs in the saucers, that sort of thing. How do you deal with this, as clients?

Client one: We bring our own cups.

Client two: And wash them up. Bring our own coffee if necessary.

Client three: Or not have coffee at all. Whatever the agency feels is right.

Wilf: I see (makes conspicuously large note on clipboard).

Shops: As a creative bod, I'm naturally keen on super great ads involving location photography in somewhere like Tunisia. Does your account promise lots of that?

Client one: We pride ourselves, Mr Shops, on our ambitious location photography. Not just photography either – we recently had a special PMT run up in Bali that the agency were able to organise for us.

Ms Hill: Through you, Mr Chair, I'd like to ask the client about their attitude on seal clubbing. Do they have a company policy on the clubbing of seal pups, I wonder?

Client two (after a moment's thought): We abhor it. Ghastly business. Certainly never employ anyone who clubs seals. Never.

Ms Hill (shouting): So you would take away the livelihood of Newfoundland fisherfolk, would you? Good, honest, hard-working people who are being victimised by every bleeding heart in the world. I suppose you'd like seals to take over the world, would you, living next door to you, stinking the place out with their smelly wet coats and their stupid moustaches…

Headroom: I really must stop you there, Beulah, I really think the client's attitudes to seals is a trifle ultra vires.

Ms Hill (through gritted teeth): It might be for some (makes very large note on clipboard).

Ms Swollocks:	I was interested in what you had to say about your bank balance. But you confined your remarks to your current account whereas, of course, we have to be interested in other sources of revenue from you. I take it you have deposits, equities, offshore funds, that sort of thing?
Client three:	Certainly we have. Lots and lots of them. Not to put too fine a point on it, we are very well endowed pecuniary-wise.
Ms Swollocks:	So you have no objection to bonding large sums with the agency, for work in advance, that sort of thing?
Client three:	Gosh, no. What's ours is yours if you were to take us on.
Headroom:	Well, I think that's a sensible note to end on. I've certainly enjoyed our little chat and I know I speak for all my colleagues when I say how impressed we've been with your company. But we are seeing lots of clients over the next few days and I can safely tell you that it's going to be a very difficult choice. Our options range from selecting one of you as client, drawing up a further short list or not choosing a client at all. It's as simple as that. But you should hear from us within a month one way or another.
Client party:	Thank you for giving us the chance to present our company and finding the time…
Headroom:	Oh, piss off. Next!

CURTAIN

Unpredictable, this prophesy business

February 1984

It's 1984. Smith is a firm fan of that other George, Orwell, who was of course a fierce pedant on the use of words and had a lot to say about this particular year. GS said of this piece, 'The business is still staring at its own navel, still relatively immune to consumer needs.' It's lovely to see predictions around the coming of things we now take for granted, such as cable television, or that have come and gone, as in, 'the startling success of video'. And even then the prophets predicted the demise of the printed book. Prophesy is indeed difficult, particularly about the future.

George Orwell actually went to great lengths to deny that *1984* was a work of prediction. It was speculation, he said, a description of a society that might happen rather than one he'd personally put his money on. He could have saved his hard-pressed breath. It is currently difficult to pick up a journal of opinion without finding the great man's grizzled features illustrating a piece wherein the saga of Winston Smith is held up to the great crystal mirror of hindsight and found lacking and gauche.

It all goes to show that prediction is still a compulsive subject, even when the presumed prophet is merely a guy trying to screw a few political insights into a narrative and make a few bob the while. But when hacks do actually try their hands at prophecy, it always strikes me as with one eye on the Old Moore market – I'm sure Nostradamus was a potential pioneer of the part-work medium with all those wonderfully open-ended quatrains.

Thankfully no one is suggesting that Orwell foresaw the sweepstake promotion or the laser letter. But direct marketing has had and will continue to have plenty of seers, and not just the Roebuck variety. We have to be interested in the future lest someone nicks a bit of it from us. We are narcissistic too, proud of how far we have come, too prone to believe that our basic cleverness and overall adorability will be enhanced by adroit attention to what someone tells us is the future. This makes trend-spotters of us all.

We should be wary. Prophets are as often false as they are true. Up to the late sixties, it was believed that progress, usually defined in terms of economic growth, was just going to carry on indefinitely. Then came the warning of eco crisis, apparently borne out by the oil price shambles of 1973. Prophecy changed overnight. For progress read doom. For rising standards of living read retrenchment. For a technological future read growing your own lentils.

Or look at particular social prophecies. The Buchanan-inspired projections of growth in car ownership were wildly wrong, leading to the hesitant road-building programme we have suffered ever since. A baby boom for a year or two evokes rabid discussion about population growth, to be followed by a sharp decline in progeny and earnest discussions about the decline in childbearing and the problems of an ageing population. It must be fifteen years since someone informed me that the printed book would soon be a precious relic, usurped by the television screen and the tape cassette. The revealed truth is that book sales rise steadily throughout the world.

But prophesy is a sexy subject and the sceptic is often seen as spoiling the fun. Brian Halsey and I permitted ourselves a few waspish asides about the technological revolution at Direct Marketing Day and umbrage was definitely taken in some quarters. All sorts of people want to believe in the database as the dawn of the direct marketing millennium and I have to say that I don't quite know enough to check their zeal.

But all the talk of the new technology does seem to me to contain an important fallacy. We see it only as increasing our power to sell, not increasing the power of the consumer to choose. Because home computers are becoming ubiquitous, we readily presume that their owners will automatically use them to buy our goods or services. Because cable television is in prospect, we automatically assume that we have been offered market segmentation on a plate, with audiences grouping themselves for our benefit.

Why do we spend so much time on discussing *our* method and not *their* need?

The early evidence of all these things is distinctly mixed. Cable television in the States is a long way from being the sure fire popular success which is sometimes depicted. The startling success of video seems to have achieved a worldwide decrease in television watching. The first generation of domestic computers seem to be sternly applied to educational and games-playing modes. Prestel remains a failure. People aren't quite behaving as they were supposed to.

It could be that the new technological advance will increase the individual's ability to choose, not quench his or her individual freedom of action as the neo-Orwellians would have it. For all the evidence is that social habits, which both cloak and convene buying habits, are formed by the consumer, then amplified and resold by the marketer. No one can argue that the growth in, say, squash, snooker and video itself were marketing-led, no matter how much any of us knew about the growth in leisure pursuits a decade ago.

A continued growth in individual freedom may seem

distinctly un-Orwellian and I'm not particularly pursuing it as a counter claim. But it is at least a thoughtful alternative to what else we hear and it goes practically undiscussed in direct marketing circles. For, if people have greater ability to decide on their own priorities, what are we offering them? Why do we spend so much time on discussing *our* method and not *their* need? The audience is not captive – indeed, it may be more footloose than ever before – and it is unlikely to sit around in its ACORN subsets waiting for our call.

The catchphrase a few years back was the product is hero. Pretty soon now direct marketing is going to have to find a few more heroes. It seems a long time since the last lot stalked the land.

What's in an acronym?

March 1984

George again in his role as champion of the ordinary marketing chap. It seems slightly nit-picky in hindsight but has some historical interest, in that it reflects the perpetual restlessness that surrounds industry bodies. George said of it, 'This upset Michael Schlagman and Michael Manton (the DMSB's top dogs) to the point of buying me lunch. Since then, the DMSB seems to have drifted further and further from the direct marketing mainstream. They have undoubtedly done sterling work but I cling to my original belief that they've told the lads too little about it.' We like the idea of upsetting someone to the point of them buying lunch...

All sorts of direct mail people are getting to be restless about the Direct Mail Sales Bureau. I hope that that simple statement doesn't throw all parties into the sort of industry frenzy where letters flood into the post boxes of the trade press defending the honour of this valiant attempt to reposition our chosen way of life. The DMSB has deployed a certain well-heeled vigour on all our behalves and we should be duly grateful. But restlessness there is and restlessness now needs to be reported. It is all meant in the most positive spirit.

Any criticisms can be grouped under three main heads. First: presentation; secondly: over-promising; thirdly: detail.

The first is probably the easiest to dismiss. Given the genealogy of the Bureau, it was probably inevitable that the publicity was going to emerge in the glossy double-page-spread form that we have all now seen. It could be that the celebrated cucumber motif is just the thing to shake them senseless at Saatchi's or Masius or wherever such material is targeted. I happen to doubt it, but I have to express myself envious of the billing, creative and production values that have clearly gone into the campaign, a fact that probably disenfranchises me and my agency cousins from further comment. I do happen to think that the ads are crass in the extreme but then I think most ads in the trade press are crass in the extreme, so what the hell? Conversely, whoever wrote the copy for the follow-up pack can write. For this relief much thanks.

> But any such philosophical or statistical asides fade by comparison with the great sullen issue of cost.

Then, over-promising. The chosen means of persuasion by the DMSB has been to confront standard agency prejudices about direct mail and to knock them down. Fair enough. But take just one of the DMSB's chosen negatives: 'There isn't a list of my client's target market'. To which the DMSB brochure retorts: 'Wrong. With the new computerised Consumer Location System, we can link TGI data with ACORN to build up a profile of potential customers. Then, through the postcodes and electoral rolls, we can list the addresses of households "most likely to buy" so that you can reach a precise target audience with minimum overlap or wastage'.

To which I reply that the rhetorical question that set off the self-given answer remains unanswered. It is fair enough to talk of CLS as a probe; it is intellectually dishonest to suggest that it can offer a list of a credible target audience per client. TGl, which is one input to the process, deals with 24,000 adult responses on a vast range of purchasing habits covering 4,500 brands or services from over 500 product fields. As such it is a broad brush indeed. Similarly with ACORN on whose fundamental deficiencies I have written before and which I do not propose to elaborate again. Electoral registers are twelve per cent out of true at any given time and the existing classifications are crude in at least urban situations. I repeat: the combination of these acronyms that gives us CLS has value but it should not be oversold. If I were handling Kellogg's or Fiat or Ferguson, I should be just slightly waspish about the claims in this area for they do not coincide with the realities of selling most products.

But any such philosophical or statistical asides fade by comparison with the great sullen issue of cost. Anyone involved in direct mail knows that it is an expensive medium that can be made to work by virtue of the techniques that we all assiduously apply. You cannot idly ask a media planner or buyer to consider an option that is to be measured in hundreds of pounds per thousand when his normal index for cost per thousand is in pence. The basic fact is that direct mail is applicable only to a small proportion of product or service situations where the initial promotional cost is defended by the cost of the product or service being sold. It makes sense if you are selling a case of wine and building a house list the while. It does not make sense if you are an off-licence chain or are dependent on single bottle sales. Direct mail has nothing to offer manufacturers of antifreeze or packets of tea, and I only use these examples to record the point that they are illustrated in the CLS brochure. If the practice of pinpointing likely buyers via TGI and ACORN were valid, then the horrid truth is that we would all be well advised to reach the consumer via door-to-door distribution and not direct mail on cost per thousand terms.

Lastly, detail. There is plenty that has caused concern. I will just light on one detail claim that has surfaced in all the DMSB publicity that has been aimed at mainstream agencies. It says quite simply that direct mail is now as profitable to handle as any other conventional medium. Which can only mean to the aforesaid mainstream agency that it yields fifteen per cent commission.

Well, it doesn't and there is a new generation of wide-eyed direct mail users who believe that it does. I will not dwell on this point for it is a hairy one in that the combination of discounts available from Post Office sources at first or second remove is a fraught area. But it would be nice if the Bureau would tell some of the rest of us what they mean by this oft-repeated statement. I think we should be told.

But then I think the Bureau offers us a report back anyway. It is now eighteen months in operation. It will have forged many contacts, made many presentations, joined up many dots. How much success has it had? How many advertisers has it swung into use of the medium? And with what success? Where are the first CLS case histories? These seem reasonable questions to ask at this stage.

The troops, as I say, are restless. It was always inevitable that the direct mail business would be sceptical for it is a sceptical business (it was a very high-powered direct mail name who reminded me that CLS was exactly the same as something called CQI launched by the old BIA in the sixties). My own personal view is to say that the DMSB deserves all the help we can give it for we all stand to gain by its success.

At the moment, the Bureau is in the position of a crack Guards battalion that has gone off on a shooting competition with the German High Command while the rank and file are slugging it out with the opposing infantry. It may make sense for our war effort, but the rank and file can be forgiven for doubting it just now.

What say you, Michael?

Bridge rolls over troubled water

April 1984

George has enjoyed a minor obsession about award ceremonies for some decades now. A night out at the BDMA awards with George and company was guaranteed to add a grey hair or two and a few laughter lines to boot. Particularly when we took home a raft of gongs. Here he outlines the potential of the DM trade body's annual shindig.

The BDMA awards committee is already hard at it, planning and convening this year's awards night. The Dorchester is being sussed, celebrities are being vetted, menus planned. Your comments on last year's musical interlude are being appraised and the word has gone out that direct marketing needs a dance floor larger than the new *Sunday Times Magazine* format on which to frug its cares away.

There is no point in striking attitudes about the awards ceremony. It is an event that teeters on the edge of the ludicrous but which still manages to convey pleasure, excitement and a very proper *bonhomie* to many people in the business. There is as much point in being waspish about it as there is worrying about the fibre content of the blancmange at a children's party. You can get overwrought about anything if you really want to, but it is not to be recommended if you wish to retain a sense of proportion. Awards are fun, irresistible fun, and five hundred people will be clumping their way to the Dorchester in early December, whatever little bromides they may have offered on the subject in the meantime.

My only submission is to suggest to my colleagues on the awards committee that they would do well to add even more bezazz to the event. The shades of the Academy awards ceremony were quite apparent at several points last December. Denis Norden's truly professional handling of the entire event, the unconfided and universal joy when John Fraser-Robinson walked off with the big one, the regular whoops and squeaks from the WWAV table – all these things had a distinct show-biz flavour. Acknowledge it, say I, let it all hang out, on with the motley. If some pokey little theatre awards can make it on prime time television, then I can't see any problem with the

Stretch this out long enough and the bread rolls should be raining around the room.

BDMA ceremony finding a space on Channel Four, maybe between 'goat rearing in the inner city' and that super new Haitian film that you all missed at the NFT.

It will have to be sponsored of course and *Direct Response* magazine is the obvious candidate – one call to Young Beaverbrook should suffice, in my judgment. Then, we will need a couple of third-rate personalities to interview the great and the good as they come up the stairs. At this stage many of them will still be standing which all helps.

Sample dialogue, third-rate personality: 'It's been quite a year for you, Roger. Are you looking forward to tonight?'

Roger: 'Happen you're right there, loov. I've got short-listing in't best handwriting category. Win this, and ah'll be bankable raht across Kingston.'

Someone of course will have to burst into tears as they receive an award. Others will be expected to behave with an equally predictable gravamen, making the statutory point that the award is really a team achievement and taking time out to thank the typesetters, the artwork boys, the list broker and, of course, the BDMA, that august institution without which none of this would be possible. Stretch this out long enough and the bread rolls should be raining around the room. Then again, someone should refuse to accept an award on some dim ethical grounds, supplying a Chilean refugee to make a twenty-minute speech on the inequalities of the regime. More bread rolls.

And I like the idea of an award winner not being able to make it on the night, being dedicated to a fearsome set of photography dates somewhere in the Mojave Desert. He could appear on video, telling us how he misses us all and wishes he could be with us in good old London, England. By which time the bread rolls would have run out.

All this means envelope opening by some hussy in a low-cut dress. The short-listed candidates are read out, the envelope opened and with a gasp, she says, 'And the winner of the best mailing produced by a motoring organisation based in Basingstoke goes to... the Automobile Association.' Whereupon, Nick Hutton, clad in the appropriate patrolman's livery for the occasion, is seen bathed in the spotlight and is urged with many a kiss and fond hug to venture to the stage to embrace the said hussy and to look suitably diffident and odd. He can then tell us all how they really enjoyed working on that windshield mailing, how this was the biggest thing since the last windshield mailing, etc, etc. By which time Len Ford, now appointed chief usher, is moving around the room with an electric prod to retain a degree of seemliness to the proceedings.

There would have to be entertainment to break up what I'm now seeing as a seven-hour event. The Post Office could bring on the dancing girls, Peter Jupp could wriggle out of a polylope, Nigel Swabey could juggle briefcases, Keith Norman could tell short stories, Stuart Heather could limbo dance. In this business, we could really make our own entertainment, just like people used to.

See you at the Dorchester, anyway. I'm the one in the corner trying to look like Scott Fitzgerald and failing badly.

Say goodbye to verbal clutter

July 1984

George returns to his favourite and most familiar subject. He commented on this piece at the time, 'This is a man living in a glass house throwing stones. I write enough copy of this kind to feel pretty badly about posturing otherwise. But I think the English language is worth fighting for...' Sounds like trouble's brewing...

Presenter: The recession continues, unemployment is still rife but there is one area of British business where growth still seems assured for the next decade. I refer of course to the direct marketing cliché industry. Years of studious plagiarism have now made British copywriters world leaders in this sunrise industry and this week sees the publication of the Annual Survey of Mail Order Clichés and Acceptable Half-Truths published by the Cliché Research Unit at Essex University. At the other end of the line we have Doctor Chicanery who has helped compile the report. Doctor Chicanery, what do you see as the major trends of the last year?

Dr C: Undoubtedly, Brian, the emergence of the adverb. The whole tradition of direct marketing copy has concentrated on the adjective with words like free, distinctive, luxurious and elegant being deployed with a quite breathtaking liberty.

Our research shows quite clearly that the adverb is now thought equally vital.

Presenter: I see. So, elegant is no longer the *mot juste*?

Dr C: No, it would now be classically elegant or indeed elegantly classical. Timelessly classical also has its adherents but you can of course move these words around at will. Truly classical has been spotted and timelessly elegant is not unknown.

Presenter: Where did this use of the adverb start?

Dr C: We spotted a trend a few years ago, Brian, to move away from the traditional verb to a more rarefied version of the idea. The classic case was 'made' as in 'made in polystyrene'.

Presenter: And what would it be now?

Dr C: Crafted, without a doubt. Everything is crafted. Occasionally in upmarket publications, it might be wrought.

Presenter: So the product would be crafted in polystyrene. That sounds silly.

Dr C: Indeed. Hence the emergence of what we in the Unit call the Parasitical Adverb. Products are not crafted in isolation. They are either meticulously crafted or faithfully crafted, and so on.

Presenter: By craftsmen presumably.

Dr C: That is clearly the inference. Taipei is full of craftsmen. On the odd occasion when the craftsmen are British they are of course using the time-honoured skills of bygone days. That sort of thing.

Presenter: And what other examples of the Parasitical Adverb are there? What would you use to qualify 'feminine' for instance?

Dr C: Utterly is very popular. Or you can use any of the

words we described earlier. Simply is coming into favour, obviously when all the others are exhausted.

Presenter: Designed?

Dr C: Beautifully or carefully.

Presenter: Fits?

Dr C: Snugly.

Presenter: But presumably not all the new clichés are adverbs. I'm personally a great fan of coupon copy – rush me the full kit and that sort of thing.

Dr C: Yes, that would be thought a trifle démodé these days. The problem here of course is that the advertisers have to put things into people's mouths without incurring the wrath of the CAP. This leads to what we call the Transferred First Person – Yes, I accept and so on.

Presenter: With of course the random use of upper case?

Dr C: Still very popular. The colour brochure should be FREE or, in extremes, ABSOLUTELY FREE. You should send for it TODAY and open the envelope NOW.

Presenter: And is 'without obligation' still as popular?

Dr C: Indeed, Brian, it now only exists in direct marketing.

Presenter: And what exactly does it mean?

Dr C: Usually seven follow-ups if you don't buy. It comes from the same stable as 'completely satisfied' preceded by the phrase 'if you are not for some reason'. It means you have to write lots of letters and threaten Esther Rantzen. Similarly with 'a screwdriver and a few minutes is all you need' for KD furniture. It means you need a full tool kit and most of Saturday.

Presenter: We only have a few seconds left, Doctor Chicanery. So what's your favourite cliché of the year?

Dr C: Without a doubt, 'makes an ideal gift.' It's an oldie but it's still as popular as ever when the writer obviously hasn't got a clue what the product looks like. We call it the Line of Least Resistance.

Presenter: Doctor Chicanery, thank you very much.

Infra-draws on

October 1984

Ah happy days! Who doesn't recall the Horace Batchelor ads on Radio Luxembourg? But when it first appeared George was worried that this article might offend his old pal and long-time client Nigel Swabey, CEO of Kaleidoscope and other enterprises. So, he actually reassured him that it was meant affectionately. I'm not sure Nigel was convinced...

There is a suburb of Bristol that shall forever remain part of my adolescence. It is Keynsham. That is to say, it is K-E-Y-N-S-H-A-M, spelled out with great sonority by a regular voice on Radio Luxembourg, 'station of the stars', throughout the 1950s.

Fellow candidates for the male menopause will know that I am talking about a man called Horace Batchelor whose regular radio ads for his 'famous Infra-Draw Method' punctuated the crackling reception that the old Bakelite wireless used to afford transmissions from the Duchy.

Horace Bachelor used to do his own commercials, much like those dapper car salesmen who became such an intrinsic part of early Channel Four. Horace had an infallible method for the treble chance, one that had won tens of thousands for his delighted customers, and he was forever telling us about it, eschewing the obvious point as to why he, Horace Batchelor, hadn't already decamped to Tahiti with a blonde if the Infra Draw method was all it was cracked up to be.

Not that Horace sounded a man to decamp with a floozy. The voice suggested a rubicund man of middle years, earnestly philanthropic. Florid check sports jackets he may have flaunted, but one suspected leather pads on the elbows. The Infra Draw Method sounded as much a welfare benefit as it did punters' dream. Horace was integrity packed.

Well, *plus ça change*, as I never tire of reporting. I have before me a clutch of direct mail material produced by his spiritual successors. It offers systems, advice, formulae – short cuts, all, to greater wealth via forecasting with unerring precision the relative performance of canines and equines. The mailings come from places like Swindon, Halifax, Hammersmith and Wetherby. The advertisers include Northern Sports Services, Castle Sporting Services, Wetherby Bloodstock and an outfit who would dearly be as happy to be hanged for a sheep as a lamb called Harry Field and Company, Commission Agents.

The mailings I am describing amount to a month's post for a reformed sinner in this field, a friend of a friend, you understand. As such, he must be a cold prospect to the point of utter frigidity, for he certainly has not placed a bet from the address on the labels for some years past.

Labels, in fact, are obviously the state of the art in this submerged area of direct marketing, for hand addressing is more the norm. The enclosures, too, are untouched by personalisation, second colour malarkey or other gewgaws. Here, the message is simple, stern and transcribed via a yeoman-like Rotaprint. And the message is eternal, vivid, universal, unalloyed by thoughts of CAP or any other white liberal acronyms. The USP from Wetherby and Hammersmith is briefly stated: bung us a few sovs and you will be a very rich punter indeed.

I paraphrase as ever, for the language is rarely as crude as that. Take this opening paragraph, 'As a member of the sporting public interested in the systematic side of racing investments, you must have come across some systems you couldn't possibly put into operation yourself. This reason (sic) can be various.'

Now, this sounds to me just like John Watson rewritten by Arthur Daly, and I love it, especially that 'systematic side of racing investments' replacing the old demotic 'betting'.

Alternatively, an intro that leads in, 'We understand that you are a keen supporter of Horse Racing.' Even better and more shameless, 'I first brought your attention to this system in my Autumn 1983 bulletin but unfortunately some of the dates on the two sheets of paper became transposed, causing many of you confusion.' Our man in Halifax then goes on to apologise for any inconvenience, breezily ignoring the fact that some of his customers may have faced financial ruin as a result of said transposition. Or perhaps not.

The enclosures, too, are untouched by personalisation, second colour malarkey or other gewgaws.

And there is a loveable dignity about much of the phraseology in this missive, suggesting a trade that thinks itself ill served by public reputation. Again the spectre of Arthur Daly surfaces in a sentence like this, 'At a time when old values seem often to fall by the wayside, Racing Club Select is becoming increasingly recognised as a champion of all who strive for excellence in the practice of scrupulosity in dealing with members of the racing public.'

The products themselves are dazzling for those of us who never get farther than the ITV Seven. You can have the Senior Ratings Saturday Yankee, Denmans Saturday Double, The Torpedo Formula, the Dawson System, or ultimately presumably, the Income for Life Racing Revolution.

It goes without saying that all these systems are variable only in terms of the speed with which they confer wealth on you. The claims made for them are unabashed – '50 per cent winners to date', 'average yearly profit £2,477', etc. Nothing mealy-mouthed about this market. And, in case you want a model for your newfound lifestyle, try Alec Bird, '…whom the bookies describe as the most successful punter in the history of racing and they should know, they paid for all the luxuries he enjoys: the moated manor complete with servants, the Rolls and his own personal plane.' Mr Bird's rules for successful betting are contained in a slim volume offered as a premium on an earlybird offer from Castle Sporting Services… You didn't know Drayton had a brother, did you?

But sometimes the facade of professional dignity is seen to break down and the newsletter writers say what they feel about their many competitors. I quote from Northern Sports Services, 'If you get a circular from this liar simply tear it in four, hold the pieces together, drill a hole in the top corner, thread some string through it and hang it in a convenient room in the house.'

Now, that's what I call vigorous positioning. The next time I'm writing an intro for one of Nigel Swabey's catalogues, expect some equally pointed remarks about the products in all those other catalogues. I mean, it stands to reason that our clobber's better than that other tripe-hound's clobber. Let's tell the punters what a lot of porkies the other lot spin. Let's sort them out and make our catalogue a genuine runner.

Okay, Nigel? Not for nothing are you known as the thinking man's Arthur Daly.

The moon and thirteen pence

November 1984

The import and substance of the Great Envelope Debate seems now to be lost in time but George's observations on its triviality have survived.

It is rare for *Direct Response* to find room for a correspondence column. By the time you've put in all those riveting news stories about binding machines and the month's agency formations, you find yourself short of the column inches whereby direct marketing practitioners can score points off each other by way of published letter.

A pity, this. A trade press correspondence column always brings out the best in special pleading and organisational selling done over as objective facts and reporting. The true state of the art you will find in that wonderful parish magazine *Campaign* whose letter column abounds with savage retorts from newspaper publishers whose historic claim on 90 per cent coverage of whatever has been breached by some saucy media owner insisting that the said 90 per cent are to be found more cost-effectively via skywriting, ACORN-related legwarmers, or whatever the first miscreant is not selling. Then, you have the standard agency blather: whether Jerome Fandor actually left OTE before he formed Fandor Direct, who first thought of the creative approach involving a picture of a slow loris and the headline in Latin, who actually paid for that lunch in Langan's. You know the sort of stuff, I'm sure.

The September issue of *Direct Response* (I think it was September for it arrived in mid-October) contained such a correspondence column. There was a letter praising this column with faint damn by exposing the differential between our agency's creative philosophy and the press releases that it occasionally visits on a yawning world. Good sport, I thought that was.

But what I really liked were the other four letters. One was from a telemarketing bod saying that Pauline Marks didn't invent the telephone. The other three were devoted to the Great Printed Envelope Controversy.

New readers start here. Conventional wisdom has it that the way to riches for a mailing shot starts with a printed message on the envelope. I can do no better than quote from the letter on the subject from Mr Littlechild of DRG Envelopes, '...if no headline is printed on the envelope communicating the offer, he can become quickly disillusioned and negatively orientated to the sender company.'

Well, there you have it, with as vivid an illustration as ever underpinned a spiel. Those unheadlined envelopes are creating havoc in Britain's hallways. Grown men are reeling around on their doormats, the day's post clutched in their hands, disillusion seeping through their frames, winding themselves up with negative orientations to the sender of the anonymous envelope. 'This mailing shot has failed in its first duty to put six helpful words on the outside', they are saying, 'my hostility is such that I will not even open the offensive and lamentable piece that I find in my hands. What sort of ACORN code do they take me for?'

Such is the case for the conventional wisdom. But what has now happened is that the venerable Laurence Connelly has said pooh pooh to all that.

He has questioned the orthodoxy in a *Direct Response* article and has evidently unleashed a wave of previously suppressed radicalism in this matter. That master of reticence John Fraser-Robinson sends a short letter that manages to say hurrah and to offer side swipes about laser personalisations and, more obscurely, Drayton Bird. John is obviously a keen member of the terse lobby. Then, another venerable figure in the shape of Norman Hart gets the boot in at greater length. Norman just puts the word 'personal' on the envelope and gets his letters read. All this leaves Mr Littlechild to make the case for envelope messages. And before we all say that he would, wouldn't he, it is fair to report that DRG are currently researching the matter. I'd like a copy of that report, too, please.

Me, I refuse to take sides. One man's wisdom is another man's predilection and I have to say that there are better things to worry about.

Those whom the gods destroy, they first beguile with trivia.

Which is what intrigues me about this rare sighting of a correspondence column in our trade magazine and the nature of the outpourings within it. Direct marketing people are increasingly worried about their professional dignity and esteem. They think themselves badly done by, cast as the Third Division North of the marketing business, perceived as pedlars when they should be seen as scientists. And they are talking about whether you should have words on the envelope.

If we are serious about direct mail in this country, we would do well to stop this family banter about trivia and raise the debate to a higher level, literally and metaphorically. There are two enormous constraints on the growth of profitable direct mail. The first is the appalling state of lists available on the UK market. The second is the remorseless rise in postal costs from our friends at the Post Office.

To the first, I have no answer except prayer. To the second, I have to record a personal belief that direct marketing has never properly bared its fangs at the Post Office and told it what we all know: that we need a reduction in postage costs within which to develop the next stage of postal selling. I have yet to see an informed debate on this issue, let alone sensed an industry will to lobby for such a thing. Until we do, we will remain a very junior branch of commerce indeed.

But perhaps we are simply more concerned with copy on envelopes than £130 per thousand underlying every direct mail equation. Those whom the gods destroy, they first beguile with trivia.

The public ministration of acknowledgement to a direct marketing agency

December 1984

At times readers of George's columns must have seriously wondered what he was on. Doesn't detract from the entertainment though. 'Runcie', by the way, was an archbishop of the time.

I forget why I was reading the *Book of Common Prayer*. Probably looking for a few epithets, I expect. But it did occur to me that here was a book with a service for just about every known human function that can be solemnised. And nothing about direct marketing.

This is an obvious oversight. I can forgive King James' lot for not rising to the challenge, but the new groovey, state-of-the-art Church of England cannot be so lightly forgiven. Put this omission together with the announcement of a new direct marketing agency every ten days and you obviously have the service that fits the bill. We need a little more formality surrounding these new agency entrants and a formal service would seem to offer it. And don't you worry, Runcie, I've even written it for you.

Priest: Hath this agency been already acknowledged, or no?

BDMA spokesman: Not according to the manual records of the Association thereof.

Priest: Who giveth this agency for acknowledgement?

Witness: I, Professor Peter Tomkins (whom God preserve) of

the London Borough of Richmond do hereby
pledge myself to the role of Ubiquitous Official.

Priest (turning to congregation): Dearly beloved, forasmuch
as direct marketing is where it is at and is expanding
all over the firmament in accordance with the
precepts of the prophet, Wunderman; and that the
coupons raineth down like manna in Heaven, I
beseech you to bear witness to this solemn occasion.
We are asked to admit into our fold a new lamb
(here insert name of new agency), so that the
bounteous bottom line which the Lord bestoweth at
this moment in time is spread around a bit fairer.

The state of holy direct marketing is a honourable
one, instituted by God and implemented by a
glittering array of trade associations. It signifieth the
mystical union between we, the experts, and the
punters munificence. First, it was ordained for the
procreation of folding money. Second, it was
ordained as a bulwark for capitalism. Third, it was
ordained for the mutual society, comfort and help
that one party ought to have of the other. Therefore,
if any little spoilsport can show any just cause why
this new lot should not be admitted into the fold, let
him now speak, or else hereafter staunch the
verbals.

All right, lads, any impediments, then?

The congregation shall stay sullenly silent.

Priest (continuing): Okay, (turns to the agency proprieter)
then wilt thou wed thyself to holy direct marketing
to the end of your natural life or 1987 whichever be
sooner? Wilt thou cultivate it, go to all the
conferences, drink Perrier water and generally
trumpet the future of direct marketing as Joshua did
up Jericho with diverse horns? Wilt thou agree to set
up a creative department within the meaning of this

solemn ceremony and not farm it round to every freelance in London?

Agency proprietor: I solemnly plight my troth and my new brochure (hands over new brochure to priest). I agree to cherish direct marketing in all its manifold aspects. Yea, from the laser letter to the MPS, from the window envelope to the Webcraft origami kit, in sickness and in health, for richer or poorer, I solemnly swear that I shall be an all round good egg.

Priest: And wilt thou attend BDMA roundtable luncheons?

Agency proprietor: Though the victuals be plain and the wine straight in from Cana, I shall undertake to be there lest Keith Norman strike me down and turneth me into a pillar of Saxa.

Priest: And wilt thou agree to subscribe to *Direct Response* magazine and the catechisms therein inscribed? To rear your staff in the available textbooks, to ensure that they take the Gospel according to Bird wheresoever they find themselves?

Agency proprietor: The seven copies of *Direct Response* which arriveth on my desk will be liberally circulated to all who pass our portals. We shall multiply Drayton's gospel as your guvnor did the loaves and fishes.

Priest: The congregation shall now rise and repeat the Direct Marketing prayer.

> *Our trade association, which art all over the place.*
> *Hallowed be thy seminars.*
> *Thy invoices come, Thy code of practice be done,*
> *In Montreux as it is in New Oxford Street.*
> *Give us this day our daily fees,*
> *And forgive us our weasels with the CAP.*
> *Lead us not into client conflicts,*

And deliver us from overweening agency proprietors.
For my soul and my expense account doth magnify the
retainer.
And my spirit hath rejoiced in the thought of all that
folding.
For ever and ever.
Amen.

Priest (removes cassock): Well, that's you in, sunshine, Now, have you got a VAT number or do you want it as a cash job?

In these mean conference rooms, a man must pose

February 1985

Reflections on direct marketing stereotypes of the age, such as 'young Ned Wardrobe, the gig-lamped wizard of the sprocket holes'. Ah, would that the sprocket hole might make a comeback... Enjoy.

We were leafing through the latest response figures, segmented as they now are, not just in terms of average order, recency of purchase and method of purchase, but with the height and weight of customers. 'There's something going on here,' said young Ned Wardrobe, the gig-lamped wizard of the sprocket holes. 'Some of these correlations are quite fascinating. It could be that we have the means of beating the control package after twelve years.'

'Pshaw,' retorted crusty old writer Erasmus Mantelpiece. 'It'll take more than your fancy arithmetic to beat that control, young shaver. I remember that morning when Broom-Cupboard and I presented it to young Mr Putz. We were in Kentish Town then, of course. A long time ago, before Broom-Cupboard sold his soul in Basingstoke and we used to come to work in Hush Puppies.' Scornfully, he puffed smoke from his meerschaum.

'Hear him out, Erasmus,' pleaded anxiety-laden, not-so-upwardly-mobile-anymore head of customer segmentation, Ken Lampshade, 'Let's give the lad his head. That work he recently did on pink envelope gum gave us a whole new direction on adhesive colouration...'

'Pink gum, my eye,' retorted the ever-irascible Erasmus. 'Six letters of praise from customers called Julian and you're shipping the stuff in by the vat-load from New Jersey.'

'It wasn't just six letters from Julian,' said the watchful but ever-patient young Wardrobe, 'the pink gum added .007 per cent response to that particular test. Extrapolate that and the extra sales speak for themselves.'

It was as tough as ever at the weekly meeting. I made a mental note that Lampshade wasn't making it again. We needed someone who could close Erasmus down, could bring Wardrobe out, could synergise the synergy that much faster. Lampshade had peaked in early '84 with that idea of his of putting the reply card in a plastic outer with a fragrance of attar roses to bring up the female response. But you can't live on old triumphs, not in direct marketing you can't.

Wardrobe was trying again, cutting through the meerschaum smoke with clipped and terse sentences. More and more, I liked the cut of the young man's jib. Could he be the stats man we'd been searching for since Trivet went to Langley Street to head up long division? I narrowed my eyes and listened.

'I make no apologies to Mr Mantlepiece for saying this, but there are obvious inferences here for tall customers –let's say five ten and over – going for the earlybird in Anglia. Conversely, the thinner customers are passing up the earlybird in favour of the publisher's letter and bangtail package. Especially, if I might say, where they have recently bought on twenty months credit and have Y in the postcode. Test A 26 is absolutely definite on this. The rollout possibilities shriek off the printout.'

Wardrobe sat back, a trifle smugly, I thought for a man of his tender years. I made a mental note to watch out for his smugness.

'Let me try and get a fix on this,' said the hapless Lampshade whose professional banter was as ever six to twelve months out of date. 'What you're telling us to do is to concentrate on the earlybird and target it to the fairly tall. And to sling A 26 to slender credit customers with Y in their postcode?'

'Not quite as simple as that, Mr Lampshade,' said Wardrobe. 'Remember the heavy TV viewership figures in Anglia. We may just have mailed the tall when there was poor programming in the East. Maybe there was little else to do that week in Saxmundham.'

'...the pink gum added .007 per cent response to that particular test. Extrapolate that and the extra sales speak for themselves.'

Mantelpiece was growling now, I knew he would. He always did.

'What a load of bollocks! You come here, fresh from some smart-arsed course at Sussex, with your designer plimsolls and your pink envelope gum and you tell me, *me*, that we'll beat control by segmenting the list according to avoirdupois and hat size and God knows what. We were selling products when you were still playing Pacman on your kindergarten PC, you pointy-headed poseur...'

I had to cut in here. If I ever learned anything about management, it's when to cut in. Lampshade was staring at his pad, Mantlepiece was eyeballing Wardrobe, Wardrobe was polishing his glasses. It was time for the boss to wrap it all up. A time for statesmanship. I cleared my throat,

'Okay, fellers, I think we've given this one all it's going to get this morning. I think Wardrobe's got something but don't expect me to believe in it just yet. I suggest we go with A 26 in Granada when the next snooker competition comes around. Then, I think we fasten on to the thin man syndrome and do some telephone follow up. Let's bring it all back in two months' time and see how it looks then.'

'Remember,' and I narrowed my eyes at this point, 'you never finish testing in this business. So, cut the crap and start punching.'

They gathered up their pads and left the room. I sat and stared at the meerschaum smoke. The phone rang. Osaka on the line. Could I do an hour on 'Whither the window envelope' out there next fall?

Never let anyone tell you it's easy in direct marketing.

All booted up and in a foul mode

March 1985

In case you were wondering why we'd put the old Olivetti on the cover. George, you may now realise, is something of a late adopter of technology. The Sage of Kingston herein referred to is the redoubtable Roger Millington, a well-loved figure in British direct marketing at the time. Reginald Dixon was a theatre organist who died in 1985. He was known as 'Mr Blackpool', and used to remove the bottom board of his organ during a performance so that he could kick the strings and create a thunder effect. We feel that even in the mid 1980s not a lot of George's readers would have known that.

I am sitting here staring glumly into an Apricot screen. My desk is covered with manuals, users guides, microfloppies and the crisp ten-page document produced by the colleague of mine who was designated to take us into the new technology. My battered Olivetti has been taken away and I am now a currently ailing component of a word processing function. I am very unhappy.

First, I feel awkward. I have long clattered away on the Lettera, seeing myself as some latter day eye-shaded Mencken, growling at the occasional errors committed by the damn thing despite my softness of touch and general manual dexterity. Now, I feel like Reginald Dixon sitting at a Mighty Wurlitzer.

Second, I feel daft and namby-pamby. Growl at an error and you feel better for banging out a whole row of simple obliques. Chase the miscreant syllable with a cursor and you lack the good old macho pounding noise that makes you feel better. I can now shift whole blocks around, change a word wherever it occurs, muck about with indents. All very efficient, but I'm a man who likes to pull out a sheet of paper from a typewriter, scrunch it into a ball and miss the waste-paper basket with it.

No, I am not quite at one with this new mechanical world, I am sure I'll survive, I am sure I shall develop a style to cope with future inadequacies in the typing department. But my steely-eyed colleagues practically assured me that I would be able to play Space Invaders on the thing and it is already clear that they have fed me this charming untruth in a cynical attempt to counter my known reactions to anything invented since 1910.

In the three hours since the beast has inhabited my desk, nobody has come into my office. This is unusual if not unprecedented and can only mean that the news that I have been saddled with the thing today has percolated around corporate headquarters. I suspect them of sniggering in corridors. I think I hear them warning each other not to go into his office just yet because he's just got his new beastie and you know what he's like with machinery. Certainly the risk of being decapitated with a microfloppy ripped in anguish from the left-hand drive is well understood. It would be a reasonable assumption in these parts that the Apricot is by now a very battered fruit indeed.

Actually I had one meeting this morning, with a direct mail man of the old school whose technocratic comment on proceedings was the germane: 'Jesus, what the bloody hell's that?' followed by a spirited anecdote about how you could go blind peering into such things. We stood for a religious moment or two staring at the beastie, for all the world like two pensioners on a park bench looking at the punks and wondering what the world was coming to, Then with a final tut tut, we got down to business.

Not irrelevant either. The direct mail man of the old school bears one of the most distinguished names in the business. At a reasonably advanced age he makes quite a decent living by concentrating on one modestly eclectic part of direct mail and treating it like technology had never progressed beyond the pencil sharpener. He's a man who likes maps and directories and can work you out the most geographically precise mailing distribution within a variety of trade sectors. His clients adore him, for he never postures beyond his intellectual or organisational means. He just organises little direct mail campaigns for you. That is to say, he collects names and addresses, puts your letters and leaflets into envelopes and carries them down to the Post Office for you. I am sure his charges are modest and his efficiency unquestionable.

> # Then with a final tut tut we got down to business.

I wonder how much direct mail business is actually conducted at this level. At the back of last year, I was a component of a travelling concert party who did some seminars up North. The audience was pluralist as it always is, ranging in this case from some of the largest in the land to a whole tranche of genuine kitchen table operators. (When will conference organisers, by the way, learn that customer satisfaction at these events is a matter of acknowledging this total difference between conference attendees?)

The Sage of Kingston and I had done our bit on letter-writing and the vital importance of the letter in a package when a bloke came up and said, 'That's all very well, but it'll cost me another £15 to print a letter *and* my wife's then to put it into the envelope.'

The tendency for us louche metropolitans is to snigger over

such reactions. I don't, for it is clear to me that a very great deal of businesses do use direct mail at just this level and always will. But, because it falls below the level where the service side of our business can profitably operate, it never gets reported. A pity for all concerned, it seems to me.

I tell you what we need. A Campaign for Real Direct Mail (CARDY for short). We can campaign not just against word processors and lasers but against franking machines and window envelopes, Sod the volume discounts and bring back big sheets of postage stamps, we shall cry. Who knows, we might even get handwriting reinvented.

Sorry, I'll have to stop there. The Apricot just questioned the word 'sod' and is bleeping querulously at me. The fruit machine just got the upper hand again. But I'll fight back, I tell you. I think I'll go to the opposite corner of the room and design a letterhead for CARDY while it's not looking.

Five years before the mast

May 1985

**A restless yearning for better days seems
to stalk this and other columns, even
though at this stage in his career George
was a young curmudgeon, not yet the
seasoned old one he grew into. Strange
though now to see our direct marketing
Cassandra exhorting readers of his
column to, 'leave people alone'. Then, I
expect too few young aspirant direct
marketers will also get the references here
to ITV's *Minder* series, one of television's
most glittering achievements but sadly no
longer on our screens, another sign of
finer times now fled.**

The young Lord Gnome of Hoddesdon is beside himself this
month. He positively warbles down the phone at me. It is
apparently the fifth anniversary of *Direct Response* magazine,
he says. Try and touch on it in your column. Wax nostalgic.
Wander down the primrose paths of memory and summarise
the history of British direct marketing in the last half decade.
You know the sort of thing. And with a fey promise to pay
for the piece before the next anniversary he was away,
doubtless to organise the next weekend's seminar.

The assignment really needs a more po-faced commentator
than this one. Someone like Pete Hoke, for instance, whose
latest editorial in the stateside *Direct Marketing* reaches new
heights of rhetoric: 'As we most certainly move toward a day
when all, or nearly all, marketing will be direct marketing.
This will be a day when all marketers, no matter what
business they are in, will have and nourish a formal

customer/prospect database as the central management utility.'

As always when Americans inflate interesting observations with apocalyptic language, the English lip begins to curl. We simper and do a wry knowing smile. Which is very naughty of us, for there is a small and valuable truth at the heart of Pete's rhetoric. Database management may be a rather silly expression for much orthodox marketing practice, but the very use of words like it have convinced a whole new generation of client companies that they are in fact working in direct marketing. The bank that sells insurance products to its current account customers, the software company that has counted the cost of having guys on the road, the grocery company which has discovered that you can sell soap on the telephone – these endless examples of simple opportunity costing have driven many, many people into a world that they have discovered to be that of direct marketing. We can barely complain.

This invasion by big name companies is the biggest single new phenomenon I can see in British direct marketing these last five years. Which is not to say that the invasion has been a total and unalloyed success for all of them; there have been significant successes and some spectacular failures. We would be daft to assume that all those blue chip companies who screwed up their courage to attend a seminar and find out more about this thing called direct marketing subsequently rubbed their hands with glee at the fiscal breakthrough that it gave them. I hear a lot about successful direct mail activity for car dealerships. From which I can only deduce, looking at the static state of the car market, that some people's successes must be achieved via other people's failures. Which does indeed make our own little craft seem like real marketing.

The pool of activity has widened dramatically, a fact that has obviously broadened the service base of the industry. The advertising agencies that serve direct marketing are still largely there, though a few initials may have crept into some of the older letterheads. And there is a very convincing new generation of dm agencies, very largely spawned by mainstream agencies. All these agencies are much more elevated business organisations than they were five years ago, much better equipped in many, many more techniques. It is all, quite frankly, a lot more serious than it used to be.

And the physical producers have kept pace as well. We no longer have to go to New Jersey for an ambitious format. We no longer have too short a list of potential suppliers for a certain kind of list updating. List brokers can no longer be fairly classified as so many cowboys. The use of the telephone has gone beyond the dumb script stage. Everyone has grown up a little.

> But, in the UK, we still operate in an atmosphere where direct mail is customarily referred to as 'junk mail'.

It is when you widen the gaze beyond our own village that you begin to challenge the notion that everything has grown apace, got more sophisticated, made a cultural breakthrough. I look back to some of my earlier articles and I am not merely reporting one man's monthly tilting at windmills when I reflect a certain sense of déja vu. When will Fleet Street take direct response advertisements more seriously? When will our trade associations get together? When will the Post Office shuffle its services into a totally reliable whole? When will broadcast media take off for direct marketing? The rhetorical questions echo down these five years, still awaiting the answers to them. We should not let our satisfaction that we now exist in a fashionable business area mask the imperfect structures in which we work.

Pete Hoke may believe that we stand at the margins of a millennium. I may quietly believe a humble version of the same thing. But, in the UK, we still operate in an atmosphere where direct mail is customarily referred to as 'junk mail'. Where the biggest apparent issue in the business is an endless slanging match between the DMSB and an anonymous columnist. Where newspaper proprietors still show a certain distaste for mail order advertisers whilst running editorial offers which run foul of the ASA. Where even a business-friendly government has put through a loopily drafted Data Protection Act so diffuse as to put many mail users in the regular hands of their lawyers. We are not quite monarchs of all we survey.

The truth is, of course, that the British have a cultural distaste for selling. We took Bonaparte's jibe about being a nation of shopkeepers to heart, supplemented it with the Victorian distaste for 'trade' and overlooked the fact that Victorian comfort was underpinned by successful trade. Even now, petty criminal Arthur Daly has to be personified as a used-car salesman to make the joke fit easily. We even choose to sell our houses through nicely suited estate agents so that the awful process may be surrounded with a little dignity.

Much of this distaste rubs off on direct marketers who, after all, have no other *raison d'etre* than to sell things. Thus, the British loathe the double-glazing salesmen, the insurance rep who calls you at the office, the company that sells you all these colourful things you didn't ask for. Direct marketing wallahs are pushy, intrusive, hard selling and finally an offence against British reason. Why don't we leave people alone?

We know and I know why we don't. But I do not think that the British public has learned to love us any more these last five years and I don't expect them to take us to their hearts in the next five. And I do see some storm clouds ahead unless there is some change in the country's cultural reaction to the honourable practice of selling.

Don't ask me for a headmaster's report on the first five years of *Direct Response*. I'm not a headmaster and I don't feel pedagogic. The business has widened, deepened, become more skilled. But it still has a long way to go before our native Hokes can make statements of confidence at the level of Pete's.

Shlurdy shlurdy, we all fall down

July 1985

This is one of our favourites although we can understand why Paul Rowney, publisher of *Direct Repents*, hated it when it first came out. As George said then, the literals in *Direct Response* were getting out of hand and it seemed time to have a go.

I have been thinking very hard about an old enemy of mine. Yours too, I bet, for I know from industry chit-chat that I am not the only reader of *Direct Response* to be haunted by the presence of the great phantom proof reader who lurks unseen and uncelebrated around the production lines of this great organ.

He is the man (or woman, for one should not jump to hasty conclusions in such a matter) who introduces all the literals into any one piece of setting copy that reaches Hoddesdon. He is the body who leaves out negatives so as to destroy the sense of a sentence (my article last month). He is the one who misspells names (any article, any month). He is the one who misquoted our agency's telephone number so as to defeat the hordes of readers who wanted a copy of our newsletter. He, in short, must be punished.

There, I have already begun to assume a male gender for the miscreant. Indeed, I have begun to assume all sorts of things about him. I think I see him. I think he is of a certain age, a shabby veteran of the age of hot metal. I suspect he started his career inserting literals into *Picture Post*. He has certainly served his time on the *Guardian*. Now, in his sere and yellow years, he applies his art to a trade publication. His vigour in misspelling is untempered by age, his ability to deny a sentence its sense remains undimmed, his restlessness when confronted by a piece of English is unimpaired. This man is a true professional.

Let us catch him at the end of a working day. He has just tottered into the George and Invoice in Hoddesdon High Street, hanging his battered trilby on the hat stand. Let us call him Mr Dyslexia.

Mr D: A point of coking biter, please my good man.

Landlord: Certainly, Mr D. Hard day at the office?

Mr D: Trying hard and very. It was press day for *Direct Repents*, the flagship operation of Marco Enterprises.

Landlord: Sounds interesting, Mr D, religious publication, is it?

Mr D: In its own way. The readers obviously enjoy a good disputation. Very long words they use, or try to, Very scientific too. They are heavily into spilt runs and testes.

Landlord: Are they now? Sounds a bit grubby to me.

Mr D: Not at all. They are men and women of great sagacity. They have a large exhibition in Montrose where they give learned papers on data processions and ink jerk printing. That sort of thing. Then again, they argue among themselves about lassa printing and whether you should start a letter Dear Fiend.

Landlord: I'm sorry but they still sound a dodgy lot. I thought lassa was a nasty disease?

Mr D: Some of them say it is. Others say it's the best thing since micro compressors. They have got a medical man, though. Name of Tompkins.

Landlord: He must have his work cut out with such a caseload. Isn't that the guvnor who just came in?

Mr D: Shlurdu, it's Young Master Rowley, the proprietor... (turns to whey-faced youth in top hat and green eyeshade) can get you I to drink something?

Paul Rowney (for it is he): Certainly, Mr D, and Perrier Campari treat down a would go.

Mr D: Up them line then, host mine, guvnor young just he said what bring the shlurdy shlurdy. Day heavy, sir? (Forelock tugs.)

Paul Rowney: Bad too not. Seminar new fixed for Garden Royal autumn in. Marketing Direct and Forces Armed. Winner should be. Lots of qerty speakers. More follows. Shlurdy shlurdy. Taken chair by Fraser Robinson Johns of Worthing in Amherst. Ticket high, up should clean. Brochure out, totally illegible this one. Heigh ho, Here's stealth!

Mr D: Up bottoms! (They drink silently for a moment.)

Mr D: Loved your piece in 'Whether the ABDM?' sir. Yes, that should between the legs hit them. Right serves them for trying to get it together with a mop. Never could I a future see with that murder. Gosh (staring at beer mat) is time that the? Shlurdy, shlurdy, I must go and check your editorial. I don't want to misspell Mr Fricker's name for it is a vulnerable one. And he'll only write you one of his sic letters. Me let bill pay the.

Paul Rowney: Relax, Mr T. All down to company exposes.
　　　　　　Auf revoir now.

KERTAIN

Never have I awaited the setting of an article with greater
zeal.

Ou est le chat?

August 1985

Getting really silly now. Of course we all know who the two coves mentioned in paragraph one are, don't we? Their description gives them away does it not? '...one tall, the other not.' Ah, what a way with words...

I was in the North yesterday, talking with two agreeable coves, one tall, the other not, both nicely chatty. You may hang me by my toenails but I will reveal neither my location, nor the names of their companies nor the incumbent agencies. It was a nice chat and that's all.

In fact, it was so nice that I came to muse on the Inter City home about the role of chat in direct marketing. As one who has always sworn by the value of personal articulateness and remained ever free to make with the verbals to the point of drowning the available world in deeply-felt gibberish, I have never had any problem in communicating with the spoken word. It probably stems from being an only child and having worse spots than anyone else when it came to developing relationships with the opposite sex. A godlike demeanour I never boasted. So it had to be long words, always deeply felt, even if the objective was merely to get Shirley Delaney into the back row of the Peckham Odeon under the guise of seeing the latest Audie Murphy.

As one passed through adolescence, the spots came and went and came back again, the Tony Curtis failed, and the emphasis remained on the words. By age seventeen I was able to look Janice Palmer straight in the eye, give a slight chuckle and say, 'This is incredible, but I think I'm falling in love with you'. I was what was known at the time as a chatty bleeder.

Direct marketing is full of chatty bleeders (for the sake of overall propriety and at the risk of getting this whole edition impounded by the Old Bill, I will refer to the species from here on in as CBs). Yesterday in the North, we had three simultaneous CBs. Most of the people I work with are CBs. Very few clients are CBs. Roger Millington is a CB superstar. Glenmore is a very superior CB, a sort of Horace Walpole of the art. CB-manship is very much a characteristic of the service side of the business. Which, if you think about it, is merely logical.

Failing that, I reserve the right to look into anyone's eyes and tell them that I love them.

Go round a direct marketing gathering and you will be exposed to chat of every kind. It is believed, quite wrongly, that when the eminent are chatting together – say, the platform speakers at a conference – that they must be comparing notes at a very serious level. In fact, it is likely that they are asking for the latest Test score or enquiring the origin of that pert redheaded lady in the third row or complaining about the quality of the hotel plonk.

Serious chat is more likely from the rank and file delegates. Creep around the huddled groups with your fruit juice in your hand and you will hear things like:

'No way can I see PIN overtaking ACORN. The data claims verge on the spurious.'

Or, 'Tim's really electrifying when it comes to matching profiles.'

Or, 'The proposition simply fell to pieces when we applied unitised costing.'

This is CB-manship at the swotty end of the market. When a swot meets a hearty in this business, the hearty nods vigorously and tells a funny story or offers a piece of gossip. In the case of Millington, he will regale you with stories about the jazz band he played with in 1961. In Glenmore's case he will mention what Rosser Reeves told him in Kuala Lumpur. In my case, I will ask the poor group to nominate five football league teams with an 'x' in their names. Failing that, I reserve the right to look into anyone's eyes and tell them that I love them. We all have our fallback chat and sometimes it goes back a long way.

But chat obviously makes the world go round. Sometimes it is mere gossip (can it really be true that Brian has sold to Jane?) and sometimes not. But it is the cement that binds relationships. In direct marketing it is often the prelude to the shameless foisting of a business card. Always it enables one individual to get a reading on another...

Chatty bleeders run the risk of being brazen, otiose, opinionated, vulgar, indiscreet, pompous and downright boring. In coming forth with their verbal raiment, they run the risk of offending the chattee at so many points that one wonders why they bother making with the verbals. The answer is, as so often, vanity, sheer silly old vanity.

And, as always, the clients and the chattees have the last word. You know what Janice Palmer said, don't you?

'Don't be so bloody silly.'

Exit the scribe: enter Bryan the antipope

December 1985

According to George, Bryan Halsey was at the time the most sensible man in British direct marketing. Indeed. I'm fairly sure that George meant that as a real compliment, for though he may deride sensibleness regularly, he also admires it greatly, in others and, I suspect, secretly yearns after it. Sad, isn't it?

This being a valedictory piece, it's good to have a thumping upbeat theme with which to finish.

It was supplied by Bryan Halsey, whose presentation at the back end of Direct Marketing Day was riveting in its logic, provocative in its content, unexpectedly entertaining in its delivery. Bryan spoke for an hour, said nothing that was really new, yet managed to send out a jaded audience gibbering with superlatives. It will have done him good and it certainly did the rest of us good. You can apply no greater praise to a direct marketing presentation.

For years now I have been thinking of Bryan as a sort of lost hero of direct marketing. Dapper of suit, grey of hair, he seems to have been around forever, running a perennially profitable agency, peddling a lucid brand of common sense, apparently taking no prisoners in terms of industry style or fashion. His own man, writ large, adored by his clients, respected throughout the business as a totally honest practitioner, a man who gives forth a pained anxiety that a simple world should be made too complex and starry eyed. Only occasionally will you meet him at Montreux, for instance, – and when he is there his body language gives off unease. You sense that he is deeply suspicious of that throng, that his heart is really back in Richmond where he has yet to hear of how last weekend's split runs worked out. Similarly, his celebrated attitude to BDMA awards, which he obviously finds an exercise in greater skittishness. HLY don't play those games. They prefer their prizes to be won more puritanically.

I have watched him getting pointedly frustrated at BDMA Council meetings when the debate runs off the rails. I have talked with him about the nonsense that is so often uttered in the name of wisdom. I even worked with him on a joint presentation to Direct Marketing Day two years ago when we tried (and I think failed) to make the same point as he made this year.

But on 11 October Bryan got his rocks off. And he did it in style. The basic text was perfectly simple. Whatever it says in the American magazines, whatever new word we saddle ourselves with, the essence of our business is something called mail order. It was good to hear the words said aloud, so unfashionable have they apparently become. And having uttered the dread words, Bryan got back to basics with what a customer wanted from mail order operations.

He did it most entertainingly, offering an undisclosed product to the audience by means of a successive series of overplayed direct marketing techniques. Would we buy it if the coupon was in the right place, if the headline was as the books say it should be, if the paras were indented, the copy duly long, the picture suitably keylined? Nobody in the audience twitched until he offered the good old money back guarantee for his nameless product.

At one time this technique became quite intellectually dazzling, rather like watching someone play chess well and quickly. And, of course, it enabled him to get all that lovely heretical stuff off his chest. Having laboured his very favourite point about a business that keeps its customers waiting twenty-eight days for the product, he got all rhetorical: 'And we want to tell retailers how to sell *their* products?' he declaimed. It was like a revivalist meeting at that point.

He was honest enough at the end to trail a disaster story that his own agency had presided over, when they themselves had fallen so far in love with the project and the idea that they had forgotten to ask the basic and beautifully simple questions about margin and marketability and answering the great mail order question – who wants this product and why? It was great stuff from start to finish, even managing a timely nudge to tell us that newspaper advertising is inherently more promising than direct mail on the basis that more people get to see the offer.

> At one time this technique became quite intellectually dazzling, rather like watching someone play chess well and quickly.

It could be that we have come to a watershed in British direct marketing and that Bryan has signalled it for us. If we take it that the mid-seventies boom in off-the-page, fuelled by endless seminars and textbooks and courses, has given us a sort of papacy with a great deal of Holy Writ, then Bryan stands as the man who went public on the charlatanry and set out a more fundamentalist stall with older scripture. This makes Halsey a rather pleasing antipope, with Richmond standing as Avignon. You must admit, he does evince a certain saintliness.

I've commended a competitor at such length because I think it's important right now that we do get back to basics. We work, all of us, in a fashion business. We beguile ourselves with our cleverness, insulate ourselves increasingly from market reality by our village banter. The Basic Word from Antipope Bryan is well taken that we had better start looking again at customer service, value for money and the basic unease that the public still has in dealing with products that they cannot see, feel or touch. It is a theme that I have probably done to death in this column since I started it five years ago.

Looking back at the pieces I have penned, I see the Halsey theme jumping around like a recurrent melody, interspersed with the occasional bon mot and a regular chorus of sheer silliness. (I make no apology for the silliness for I am happiest when silly.) But now, I'm jacking it in, at least as a regular contributor. All good things must come to an end and it is reasonable to assume that I shall begin to repeat myself more and more, that I shall therefore turn into a curmudgeonly old bore, and that the mots will become altogether less bon. Hail and farewell, then.

When the backslapping has to stop

November 1986

It turns out that this is George's valedictory article, not the last. And serious stuff it is, the last of the DM pieces (for the time being, as George observed at the time). He did get all sensible for a few moments, as if he wanted to make some important points in his parting shot. What he says still makes sense, though you might think he does go on. Shame that he didn't, though, eh?

The last time I opined in these columns, it was on a text supplied by Bryan Halsey. Bryan had done a presentation at last year's Direct Marketing Day which offered Great Truths and which offered them with great panache. I thought it a good thing to report this event and to remind people that Bryan remains the most sensible person in British direct marketing.

Eyebrows were raised as they always will be when one praises a competitor. Was this praising with faint damn or was this a diplomatic prelude to a merger of interests between his great empire and mine? Neither, I insisted – it's just that Bryan was heard saying out loud things that were being whispered decorously elsewhere. His natural reticence would deny him the opportunity to repeat these things and I felt it right to amplify them on his behalf – *c'est tout*.

This summer Glenmore and I were asked to produce a presentation for the Pan Pacific Symposium on the State of the Art in the UK. Born of the panic that sweeps over

speakers a week before the event, we elected to produce a
short video interviewing a small selection of the great and the
good for the benefit of the Sydney audience. Jane Porter,
Simon Roncoroni, Nigel Swabey and Bryan Halsey kindly
agreed to come before the lights and subject themselves to the
inane questioning of the poor man's John Timpson. It worked
a treat, played a storm and spared us having to gabble for
sixteen minutes.

Jane talked about media, Nigel about the joys of cataloguing,
Simon about the next stage of telemarketing. Bryan played the
role I had given him, terse, magisterial, concerned. To be fair,
he protested about me setting him up as the Jeremiah of the
business and I had to jettison some of the excellent reportage
that Bryan offered to substantiate his view of the business. To
that extent I used him, for I wanted his point of view, his
gravamen, his anxiety to embellish my own message to the
Ockers that British direct marketing was not quite the all-
singing, all-dancing bonanza that they might have been led to
expect. Bryan is doing the Pan Pacific himself next year so he
can do his own thing without an interlocutor. But our little
interview this year ended thus:

Poor Man's Timpson: 'So you think we can be accused of
                         being a trifle smug?'

Bryan (magisterially): 'Yes, I think we can...'

Smug! What a terrible word to throw at a buoyant young
profession! Everything we hear, which means everything we
tell to each other, is to do with buoyancy, growth, greater
profitability, the far horizons of technology and creativity.
Everyone is making it simultaneously, the future is ours, for is
it not written in the scriptures according to Hoke that by the
end of the century all marketing will be direct marketing? Can
we just calm down a moment and forget the last blast of
Montreux rhetoric? Can we find the time to acknowledge that
we are a business and not a religion? Can we hit the pause
button?

Already, I am trampling on language. I say we are a business.

We are not. We are a collection of businesses, small ones. The list broker sells to the client or the agency as does the media owner as does the consultant. Given an even political break, they will sell to anyone including each other. This is a Babel of selling, not a vertical industry. It is a collection of interests, vaguely intertwined, always wary one of the other. It is only our deep-seated desire for respectability that persuades us to salute our trade associations and to serve them.

It worked a treat, played a storm and spared us having to gabble for sixteen minutes.

The fact that we have six or seven such trade associations underlines my point. We all make our living in various ways. An industry we are not.

Yet the current fashionability of what we do has convinced us that we are indeed that industry that we are not. The invasion of mainstream agencies into our pastures has amplified this basic untruth and introduced the soppy language of *Campaign*-land. We are now forced to talk of 'billings' rather than pre-tax profits or p/e ratios. And, as Ian Dewar sagely pointed out a month or two back, the apparent equations do not add up. Taken at face value, direct marketing agencies are inherently less profitable than their mainstream cousins. The fact is that they are not – or should not be – for a direct marketing agency's fee income should mean a more resilient remuneration base if the place is sensibly managed. And most are.

But this is an irritating little example of direct marketing currently getting suckered into people's cultural patterns. There are many others and I have written about them before. It would be boorish to keep banging on about them but they do aggregate to a personal view that direct marketing has become overly narcissistic, incapable of seeing the wood for the trees, increasingly vulnerable to all sorts of slings and arrows that somehow never get mentioned for fear of spoiling the party.

I'm doing the party-pooper bit right now because I am aware
that a lot of young people are coming into direct marketing.
There is a new generation around and I welcome it, for they
should be able to take the game into a whole new sequence.
But my fear is that they will be pitching their tents on the
bullshit of a previous generation and not its achievements.
The tuition and the experience handed down in articles, in
presentations, in seminars have been uncritically received by
practically all who have been exposed to it. And all that
learning, and those precepts, has surrounded claims of
wildfire success, often not provable, seldom repeatable.
Listen to the available wisdom and you cannot but believe
that everything works in direct marketing as long as you do it
like those other herberts did it.

This is of course manifest nonsense and we all know it. The
point about direct marketing is its lack of ambiguity. You
know how successful – or otherwise – your promotion has
been. The obvious fact of life is that as much direct
marketing fails as succeeds. That failure is visible and beyond
rationalisation, so why do people pretend otherwise?

Lack of candour about failure is a characteristic of any
business, not just direct marketing. But it is more critical to
us, for we are not often shielded by the corporate structures
and rationalisations which are allowed to fudge failure
elsewhere. The difference between honesty and doublethink
is often the difference between continued profitable existence
and receivership for a company. In 1983, The Economist
Intelligence Unit surveyed sixty-three direct response
companies as part of its report on the UK mail order market.
No less than seventeen are no longer operational to my
certain knowledge and the list would doubtless grow if I could
call some of the smaller ones to mind. Is this really an index
of a fast-growing business?

Where precisely is this growth anyway? If I read a recent
story correctly, Richard Fassbender is quoted as saying that
volume growth of direct mail is up by thirty-two percent from
1980 to 1985 and that the cost per item is up by thirty per
cent in the same period. These figures confirm direct mail's

status as 'the fastest growing medium' apparently, tucking in nicely behind press and television. They do indeed confirm everyone's perception that direct mail has grown apace, but has anyone measured the equally-evident collapse in off-the-page advertising during the same period? And what would the final sum say about the growth of the business? And does anyone care? Where is the authoritative smack of an industry which cannot even compute its own figures and the changing face of its activity?

In fact Bryan, as an old mail order hand, believes that direct mail has been oversold in the last few years. So do I. For the direct mail package has become the industry's staple product, its potential hyped beyond its reasonable means. Direct mail remains the most difficult of media to make profitable for it starts with the highest cost-per-thousand known to marketing man. The many new users of direct marketing in the last decade have largely been sold direct mail rather than direct marketing. They have tried and, too often, they have failed. Which has soured them unfairly on the whole process. The world of direct mail is now littered with excusers, once bitten, forever shy.

It is the exceptions that prove the rule – the newsletter operations, the financial institutions, the cataloguers. I know of these successes and I find it no coincidence that these are areas of activity where the creative standards are often of the highest. For is it not true that most direct mail is precisely what our critics call it: junk? How many pieces cross your desk or your door mat which stay your attention for more than a moment? Do you not sometimes despair that you inhabit the same business?

The horrid central fact of our business at the moment was uttered by Halsey on our little video: that there is little sign of increased consumer demand for what we are selling. Indeed, there is a palpably growing degree of consumer dissatisfaction, if not with what we are selling, then certainly of the way in which we sell it. The business is notoriously insensitive to individual customer satisfaction. We often sell tat, we rarely package anything with pride, we solemnly try to effect delivery in twenty-eight days (and often fail). Some of this is probably inevitable. All of it is not good enough.

Could it be true that the apparent growth of the business is more or less supply driven? We are all in there selling – agencies, computer bureaux, list brokers, printers, consultants, telemarketing companies and the rest. Is there really enough business to go round this lengthening chain of suppliers? Though it might be the darkest and most unwelcome of prophesies, I fancy not. I know that everyone is busy. What I'm wondering is whether everyone is profitably busy? For, if this Babel

> But my fear is that they will be pitching their tents on the bullshit of a previous generation and not its achievements.

of intra-industry selling is not reflected in a genuine growth of actual customer activity – which is what I suspect but cannot prove – then we have a rather typical British economic situation on our hands.

I am being querulous, not apocalyptic. I sense that the party, as lazily defined over the last decade, is beginning to be over. I worry about lookalike creative work, the lack of new products, the increased customer resistance to much of what we do. Above all, I worry about our continued habit of navel contemplation and lack of intellectual marketing progress as opposed to technical production progress. I certainly worry about the relevance of our previous creative postulates to that hardnosed street-wise generation which is now coming through as big customers, ready with credit cards and whole new cultural habits.

I think we have to be brighter than we currently are to conquer the new world of retail support, of public services, of leisure products, of recruitment advertising even. There are many new fields to be conquered, but they will not be conquered by waddling into them with the jaded vocabulary and shoddy practice of previous campaigns. We have turned quickly into a yuppie village. It could as easily turn into something less buoyant. Overweening and misplaced pride often comes before a fall, they say.

**Such is life: observations
in the corridors of the almost
powerful, from various sources**

What *are* we talking about?

Date unknown/Local Government News

George Smith on tribal patois and verbal machismo enters a plea for English as she is spoken.

It's a good job that Neil Kinnock is known to be that rare creature, a Member of Parliament with a sense of humour. Otherwise, the following sentence that recently dropped from his lips would win the David Coleman Prize for Hysterically Mixed Metaphors.

The Member for Bedwellty is currently shadow education spokesman, a function that gives added edge to this wonderful pronouncement:

'I think,' said Neil, 'we can convince the hawks in the Government that they are actually sitting ducks and, by such means, divert their course. It is not the first time in the history of Tory governments that they have effected a U-turn and if we can speed them up in that U-turn we will be happy.'

Wow! There's enough going on it that sentence to make a Walt Disney feature. Four colourful metaphors in just over fifty words, each one a cliché, colliding with each other in a mini-masterpiece of nonsense, breathlessly devoid of meaning to anyone except fellow politicos and the assembled hacks. Well done, Neil.

The occasion was a press conference to mark the Labour Party's campaign against public expenditure cuts, a campaign that I happen to think both honourable and promising. When I confessed to such partisanship last month, I also indicated a predictive horror at the language that would be used in the coming great debate.

Apart from the shadow education spokesman's surrealism, we

have that sturdiest of politicians, Stan Orme, coming through with 'the greatest challenge to the welfare state since its inception'. Word perfect, Stan, thanks for joining us on the show.

Then we have Roy Hattersley, another politician otherwise credited with a little native wit, transfixing the Scottish masses with the news that £18 million has already been cut from Strathclyde's revenue budget. And, finally, a statement that can only stem from a Transport House press release, to the effect that Labour councils forced to put up rates to save services will receive national backing from the Labour party – which being translated, means that you'll be supplied with a wordy resolution from the National Executive to wave at impoverished ratepayers.

...in contemporary politics, this decay of language has become critical.

Yes, the show's on the road again, and the language is as arid as it is meaningless. And in contemporary politics, this decay of language has become critical.

To my mind the great English language is now broken down into a series of tribal patois, each of them characterised not merely by a verbal machismo based on the overuse of eclectic words, but also by downright sloppiness and insensitivity. It happens because our society, far from becoming pluralist, has become increasingly sectionalised into interest groups, with those groups having less and less interest in purveying their thoughts and ideas to others.

The language of public utterance, in particular, has become brutalised, stripped of its power to convey passion, conviction, persuasion, intelligence. Extract these qualities from the political process and you are left with the politics from which we currently suffer, a ho-hum ritual of clashing power blocs.

It is typical that the left's reaction to the Conservative's election victory was to pour scorn on the conspiratorial workings of Fleet Street and Saatchi and Saatchi. For, when all is said and done about proprietorial imbalance in the Street and the size of Central Office budgets, it is surely true that the Conservative party were seen to cut through years of political claptrap and say simple things rather well.

The fact that the case they argued was pretty unholy needn't blind us to the skill with which they played on the national nerve system. They said what people wanted to hear, that we pay too much tax, that there are too many bureaucrats, that we are against scroungers, that we're a bit fed up with things as they are. Admittedly there's nothing here to stretch the brain cells, but it was all manifestly good stuff and, as I remember, it was mostly conveyed in pretty demotic language.

> And there has to be a lesson here for anyone trying to defend local government services from current government policy.

And there has to be a lesson here for anyone trying to defend local government services from current government policy. For a start, stop talking about 'the cuts' that's our language, not the man in the street's, and in any case 'the cuts' as an issue is at least six years old to my reckoning. Stop talking about budgets and other things which are meaningless to anyone who's never waded through a rate forecast. Stop talking about greatest challenges and savage attacks and the most reactionary government for fifty years (historical precision suggests Callaghan's in any case). Stop using, in other words, all the predictable imagery and go for ideas and words that can fairly and vigorously illuminate the issue.

How about: 'Did you really vote to have your hospital close down?' Or: 'Don't you think it's disgusting that they're taking your schoolchildren's food away?' Or: 'Are you really going

to let them charge you a subscription to your local library?'
Who knows, the use of such language might actually give the
campaign a popular base and give it a chance of succeeding
that it cannot have while it relies on the language of the
committee room.

And, while we're at it, what about convening a Campaign for
Demotic English? The only reason I can think of is that
nobody would know what the hell you were talking about.

Say what you mean

Date unknown/Local Government News: Such is life

George shows how the incorrect use of words can deflect their true meaning.

Now, I'm a great fan of words. They enable me to say what I mean, and they enable me to understand what other people mean. Sometimes, that is. For words can be used as a screen for lack of thinking quite as much as they can be used as an articulation of thinking.

Politics, as always, is quite the worst example. When a prime minister poses the question, 'What sort of society do we want?', it has the correct statesmanlike ring about it. But Jim wasn't posing a genuine rhetorical question there – the poor man is genuinely nonplussed. It sounds convincing and deeply felt. It means that the man's buggered.

Keen students of politics can translate this cant: fifty-five million others stay confused or apathetic. A pity for those who value words, a vast pity for those who don't know the rules of the game of verbal politics.

Words can be used for a variety of reasons, and the primary one of articulating meaning, seems less and less fashionable. In fact it could be argued (which is treacherous writing indeed because I'm damn well going to argue it) that words are increasingly used not to articulate meaning, or amplify meaning or increase understanding. Nor indeed, this side of Dr Goebbels or the US Senate at least, actually to purvey falsehood. No, the big new use of words lies in a whole new commodity area: the deflection of true meaning.

And what, you may cry, has this to do with local government? Plenty, is all. For you lot have got it down to a very fine art. Take the word – and you often do – 'community'. It means ... 'A society of people linked together by common conditions of life'. That makes it an abstract noun, properly to be used as a metaphor.

But look around and see what you have made of it. We now have community workers, often apparently working in community teams. We have a whole new sub-science called community development. We have some academics pottering away somewhere producing community studies and, of course, we have community centres.

Now we've all played a role in this nonsense.

A recent situations vacant ad I saw headlined two posts with this well-honed piece of news-speak: 'It's sheer initiative that turns community centres into centres in the community'. If you're not sent into a dead swoon by this powerful thought, you could go on to read the following piece of verbal baroque: 'At... social services we're concerned, not just with creating a true community environment in our day centres, but with developing each centre's role as part of the community at large. So that each is very much an integral part of the community.'

As always with candidates for Pseuds Corner, you sense that whoever wrote or commissioned this amazing rubbish was thinking deeply about it. And you want to believe that they at least know what they're talking about.

But the deft abolition of the English language that's going on here goes way beyond the use of jargon. For any trade has its jargon, and outsiders must be expected to acquire it. My argument is that no one knows what precisely they mean by community, and that that is very dangerous.

I won't say that some of my best friends are community workers. But I do know some, and they seem totally confused about what people expect them to do. They utter a few bromides along the lines of 'identifying needs', or 'relating to the needs of the local community', 'liaising with other bodies in the area', and so on. What it actually means is that they attend lots of meetings, often with each other.

Now we've all played a role in this nonsense. When I was a councillor, we were very hot on the community concept. I can hear myself saying even now, 'We must put this proposal to the local community.'

We talked incessantly about participating with the community, listening to what the community said. We set up community libraries, community facilities – and one occasion we demanded of the local squash club that they give us community access to one of their courts during lunch hours. Oh, horrors! So this is one politician willing to admit that politicians started it, in exactly the same way that they invent most of the world's cant. But I have to say to my local government officers, even in this mood of self-flagellation, think about it!

Because, what has happened is that a metaphor has become literalised, uselessly so. Community just means people, no more. It isn't a thing, it isn't a fact, it shouldn't be a point on a flow chart.

A community is just people, people who almost without exception think of themselves as friends, family, neighbours, ratepayers, West Ham fans but just people, and not, thank you very much, a Community.

For it's our word not theirs, an administrative concept not a perceptible fact, a piece of imagery – no more. If you don't believe me, try substituting the word people' for 'community' wherever you see it in the next month. People worker, people centre, people facilities… doesn't sound half as impressive, does it?

And, of course, having re-launched a word, we've created a new industry with thousands of intelligent people having to believe in the community concept quite as god-fearingly as medieval theologians believed in the seven circles of hell.

Fascinated by old rope

May, 1979/Local Government News: Such is life

This was written just before the election – that election, the one that still makes some of us shudder.

This month the reader has a distinct advantage over the writer. I refer, of course, to the events of 3rd May. By the time you get to read this, Maggie will have replaced Jim, or Jim will be beaming onward into the eighties, or David Steel will be drinking his own weight in whatever beverage is offered at number ten when chicanery time comes round. The swingometer will have been packed away, the opinion polls will be rationalising their errors and leader writers will be uttering at their most tendentious.

Meanwhile all I've got to go on is what the media tells me. And what the media tells me bears a distinct resemblance to what the media told me last time. And the time before that.

I refer not to their prognostications about the winner – that's easy with a dozen polls offering up reprint material. Neither do I refer to their partiality –the ugly facts of political media imbalance make a sorry tale, but an over-familiar one. No, what fascinates me about media coverage of elections is that standard complaint about the content of the campaign.

You know the sort of thing I mean. Headlines that say, 'Let's concentrate on the Issues', stories that bemoan the 'slanging match', editorials which suggest that 'never before can a British general election have been fought at such a low level as the current one'.

It fascinates me because it is tantamount to a gaggle of whores complaining about the incidence of pre-marital sex; and it fascinates me because it is a load of old rope.

It stems, as do so many things in Britain, from a gloriously imperfect nostalgia, from that wonderful ability for national self-delusion that somehow things were better a little while back. You hear it in ordinary conversation, you see it mirrored in the wickedly distorting lens of the media.

I know people who insist that pop music went into irreversible decline after Frankie Laine/the Beatles/Cream.

My mother will go to her grave believing that we had beautiful weather throughout the last war; any football fan's answer to any current problems of English football will be to hark back to those wonderful days of Matthews/ Finney/Mannion or Charlton/Moore/Stiles.

I know people who insist that pop music went into irreversible decline after Frankie Laine/the Beatles/Cream. That we all develop tastes and enthusiasms in our youth and insist on them thereafter is no more than human nature and innocuous and charming with it.

It is the converse that worries me: the inability to see the virtues of the weather this Easter, Ron Greenwood's England team, or the Tom Robinson Band. Or, even, let it be whispered, Jim Callaghan, Maggie Thatcher, or David Steel.

Because politics are important.

If we let the basic silliness of nostalgia infect one's judgement about politics and politicians, then we all lose.

Hence my resentment at the sight and sound of the national press in their treatment of contemporary politicians and politics. They seem to suggest a golden age of politics when politicians were statesmen, when the whole damned process was conducted on a somehow more elevated, honourable basis. Such cant defies all the evidence of recorded history: politics is what it always was – the game of acquiring power and deploying it for your own class interest. It is the game as

played by Peel, Gladstone, Disraeli, Lloyd George and
Baldwin, and to say as much is not to decry the nature of
British politics – it is to emphasise what it is there for.

The passing of the years inevitably lends enchantment to the
politicians of previous generations. In my political life I have
watched the metamorphosis of
Aneurin Bevan from the man-
you-love-to-hate to an
apparently elder statesman.
(Watch out for the
magnificently meaningless line:
'the Labour Party is no longer
the party of Aneurin Bevan'.)

> Lloyd George and
> Churchill are
> popularly credited
> with having some-
> how won their
> respective world
> wars – both were in
> fact magnificently
> eloquent
> charlatans.

Lloyd George and Churchill are
popularly credited with having
somehow won their respective
world wars – both were in fact
magnificently eloquent
charlatans. Even now I have this
horrible feeling that Harold
Wilson is only a very few years away from some similar
deification as a working-class Macmillan, the cheeky chappy
who saw us through the swinging sixties. And if that prospect
doesn't make you groan, nothing will.

And, in case you want consoling, step back into Victorian
history. The fact that all those politicians finished up as
statues, with revered reputations and examination questions
needn't insulate anyone from the basic historical facts, that
they were politicians jockeying for power, born of whatever
synthesis of class interest, intellectual conviction and innate
pragmatism that kept them going.

The lovably roguish Palmerston transformed himself from
high Tory to fierce radical when he saw the way the cards
were falling. Gladstone decided he was heavily into Irish
home rule after a full fifty years opposition to it. And, best of
all, Disraeli contrived to introduce a highly democratic

reform bill within twelve months of slanging the Liberals much more modest bill out of existence. To call the government front bench 'a range of exhausted volcanoes' is better rhetoric than referring to the opposition as 'yesterday's men', but the idea is quite the same.

In fact fully a century divides the two insults. Which only goes to demonstrate the agreeable continuity of our politics, or anyone's.

I sense no difference in the nature of politics, no deterioration in the quality of public life. I do acknowledge the difference that the mass media have brought to these things. More words are uttered, more statements made. Our politicians cannot disappear as readily as their Victorian counterparts to their country estates or to their clubs. They are on show at all times, quizzed ruthlessly by a new breed of public invigilator on every phrase that they utter, every idea that they dare float.

The net result of the process is that contemporary politics are about claiming the middle ground, whatever that is.

What it means is saying and doing enough to enliven your own natural supporters without positively upsetting too many of the others. And this is a wholly new phenomenon, tempering what you think in favour of what you can't quite say.

It is a new form of political inhibition that runs through all levels of British society. Nobody says quite what they think and if there is scepticism abroad, it is probably because of this one single fact.

If enough people had said early enough and vigorously enough that devolution for Wales was a load of old garbage, then we would have been spared a lot of verbal and physical expense. The people of Wales never seem to have had a single doubt.

The fact is, that politics is about the defence of interest. And the nature of interest changes. The established Church is no longer a force in British politics, the established trade union movement quite certainly is. And within that trade union movement, whatever the rhetoric that blesses the whole process, there is a clash of interest.

For, what the teachers are saying with their pay claim is that they think they are worth more than industrial workers. What skilled industrial workers are saying is that they think they are worth more than unskilled workers. No amount of windy talk about 'parity' or 'justice' can mask the fact that people remain envious of other people and resentful of privilege, real or assumed.

> For it could be said that what is wrong with British politics is not the politics themselves but the hypocrisy that surrounds them.

It was ever thus, and it will never change. What is new is the mealy-mouthed presentation of these eternal human instincts.

For it could be said that what is wrong with British politics is not the politics themselves but the hypocrisy that surrounds them. We will have better politics when we have more honesty. We will have more honesty when more people say what they think, rather than what they think people want to hear.

Politicians share a part of the blame, but not, I would submit, a major part. For they are only representing the collective views of the people who vote for them. Only when those people are prepared to be more honest with each other, will politicians of greater vigour be allowed to emerge and flourish.

Meanwhile, we are stuck with the true heirs of Disraeli and Gladstone. And for what it's worth, I don't think Gladstone would make a better fist at running the country than anybody around at the moment. And neither do I think that Stanley Matthews at his prime would win the next World Cup for us.

Reflections on our euro-indifference

July 1979/Local Government News: Such is life

What appears to be euro-scepticism is really indignation at the antics of experts.

What a naughty nation we are. All the apparatus of democratic Europe was put out for us to play with on 7th June, and we all sulked instead of playing. Tut, tut, my countrymen, don't you know that you'll only grow up strong and healthy if you learn to play nicely like those other European children. Carry on like this, my *méchants*, and it'll be tears before euro-bedtime, that's for sure.

Well, the nursery school analogy seems pretty fair after the European elections. We have been told off rather a lot, haven't we? I mean, everyone went to such trouble for us, spending a million pounds of our money on telling us how important our votes were, shipping Radio Four to Europe for the duration, and even getting that nice Petula Clark to come and sing the Ode to Joy to jolly us along. And still only one in three of us wanted to play. Can you blame the leader writers and the euro-nannies for telling us off? I mean, how ungrateful can we get?

Yes, the British people are being sneered at again for being sensible and I resent it. One of the least-reported phenomena of British electoral politics is the inexplicably sophisticated pattern of turnout. To an extraordinary extent British voters vote when they know it matters, and stay away when they know that it doesn't. Anyone who has ever worked a council election knows the widespread divergence in turnout figures in safe wards and marginal wards. Heaven knows how people know which is which, but their collective instinct is uncanny. Psephologists and politicians have theories about differential turnout and some of them apply – Tories always like voting more than Labour supporters, the Conservative machine is always better endowed than any other, and local issues do make a difference. But all these things are both traditional and marginal when you look at the facts of truly fifty years of electoral history, facts that say that about 35 per cent will vote at a borough council election, 40 per cent at a GLC-type election and 75 per cent or so at a general election. The electorate has an instinct for the important decisions.

Which makes a 30 per cent turnout for Europe just about right. For what the experts and euro-fanatics choose to see as the apathy of the British people might just be their shrewd and measured judgement that it doesn't matter a metric jot who represents them in Europe. After all, they voted emphatically to stay in Europe with Wilson's referendum, and they did it on expert advice, for rarely can an electorate have been subjected to such unanimous pressure for one side of an argument. All the good responsible people advised us to say yes, only the bad guys and the eccentrics advised us to say no. The good guys won the argument and the election because the rest of us chose, on balance, to believe what they said. And here's the salient point – they were wrong. None of the promised benefits from Market membership accrued. New jobs were not created, British business did not make inroads into whole new markets, French wine and German cars did not come through any cheaper. No doubt there are expert reasons for the sad anticlimax of Market membership but the British voter knows only that he was sold a pup.

No doubt there are expert reasons for the sad anti-climax of Market membership but the British voter knows only that he was sold a pup.

And now, of course, we are treated to the unedifying spectacle of the experts bawling out the electorate because of their judgement on the experts. This seems to me to have about the same moral force as a group of Fellows of All Souls berating a crowd of dustmen for not buying enough T S Eliot poetry. The significance of the European election is prized only by the experts, it is lost on the rest of us. And for the experts to complain of our insularity and xenophobia, for them to insist that we've somehow let ourselves down, is to misjudge the strain of common sense that always lies at the heart of the British body politic. For it could be that the electors knew that the European parliament has no real powers, it could be that they resented the idea that one person could sensibly represent half-a-million people, it could be that they were dismayed by the bunch of nondescripts, carpetbaggers, hustlers and no-hopers who offered themselves for election. And it could be that they were right on all counts.

> The significance of the European election is prized only by the experts, it is lost on the rest of us.

Expertise has taken an awful battering in Britain over the last decade or so, and it is a dangerous phenomenon. For there is no value in scepticism, no joy in disbelieving everything you are told. Yet people's opportunity to respond to what they are told has been dulled by years of rotten advice. And the blame is widely dispersed – among architects who built tower blocks, among England football managers who managed not to qualify for the World Cup, among every Treasury hack and front-man politician who ever got a fiscal forecast wrong (which appears to be all of them). Experts should learn to shut up and to admit what is obvious to most of us for most of the time: that we don't know. We may hope, we may suspect, we may feel, but we don't know. Reasonable human doubt needs to be made respectable again in public life. If it were, a little greater credibility might re-enter the process.

There was an interesting example on Budget day. After the inevitable rhetoric of Sir Geoffrey's pronouncements and those curious zoological noises that seem to accompany

Commons broadcasts, a junior Treasury official was asked whether he really thought that Sir Geoffrey's proposal to give us some income tax back so that we could give it back to him in the shape of VAT would fire the nation into a frenzy of building more machine tools (it wasn't quite put like that, you appreciate, but that was the gist of it). The junior Treasury man replied along the lines of how-the-hell-should-he-know? So nonplussed was the interviewer by this sudden outbreak of candour that he put the question again, to receive the same blunt answer. I just do the sums around here, said my hero, how on earth do I know how fifty million people are going to behave in the next twelve months?

Now, that's the sort of expert I like, a man who knows his limits. Would that there be more of him. And would that the EEC boasted a few spokesmen prepared to admit that they had misgivings about the vast and inexplicable bureaucracy that is its only public face. Would that the leader writers would stop telling us how glad we should be that France and Germany haven't gone to war in the last thirty years. Would that experts would stop shouting at us, would stop exhorting us to be enthusiastic about something so inert, would stop insulting our intelligence by wooing us with Petula Clark and the Ode to Joy. The EEC is the greatest historical achievement of the experts to date, and the British people have just passed judgement on it. You can't blame the audience for not applauding a lousy show.

Disgruntled and gruntled of SE5

August 1980/Local Government News: Such is life

Something simple to believe in. There are some things that can't be solved by a few choruses of 'We shall overcome'.

Once, when I was a young man, I was full of views. Show me an issue and I would give you a view. Talk to me of the weather and I would give you an attitude. Try and discuss football with me and I would offer you a perception. Merely mention Godard's latest movie and back I would come with a critique. I was heavily into views. Turn Smith upside down, it was said, and views would fall out.

By the mass, I was intellectually comfortable in those days. Bliss to be alive, heaven to be young, I can tell you, as we stomped along from Aldermaston. The Tories were in office and the world was full of bad things and bad men. By the time we reached Reading, we had cleared up any last nuance of unilateral nuclear disarmament. Slough on the Saturday night, and we'd be fine-tuning the principles of public ownership. At Turnham Green on the Sunday night we were able to close the file on racial prejudice (how's that for a phrase that dates me?), and as we marched down Whitehall on the Easter Monday it was small wonder that we were cheered to the echo – we were after all the new generation on the march, coherent in our belief in the future of reason and decency, enthusiastic in our pursuit of goodness. And, if a few deadheads and Neanderthals called us weirdos, then that merely fortified our joyous valour. We were as articulate as the latest paperback in our rain-sodden duffle coats, secure in the belief that there was nothing, but nothing, that couldn't be solved by a few choruses of We Shall Overcome.

Well, you know the rest. The world was not quite that simple, after all. The oppressed natives in the colonies turned out to be feckless, irresponsible hooligans just as the crusty old blimps had predicted. Those nice Russians we wanted to be friends with kept on killing people and invading places just as that silly old Macmillan insisted they would. And worst of all, the very chaps we canvassed for on doorsteps proved as risibly inadequate as the other lot. What was a zealot to do? Like many of my

> ...I kept my head down, had some banns read, spawned some progeny and became a creditor of the Abbey National.

kind, I kept my head down, had some banns read, spawned some progeny and became a creditor of the Abbey National. All very bourgeois, I know, but an upwardly mobile young executive really would feel a bit gauche in a duffle coat, don't you think?

I'm treating you to this couch job of a political confession because I want you to know that I'm trying to evolve a view of the current furore about the Inner London Education Authority. The Tories, you will have read, want to break it up on the grounds that it tends to be Labour. That is to say, the population of Inner London, being rather short of Tory voters, ILEA tends to emerge from the quadrennial electoral choice as a Labour authority. Having studied this eccentric and unfortunate phenomenon in depth over a period of some hours, Mr Carlisle, Mr Baker and sundry Central Office spear-carriers draw the obvious moral conclusion and prepare to put the chukka boot in.

Now, to declare my interests. The previously reported progeny are being educated by ILEA. The lady whose banns were read with mine is a teacher with ILEA. Every third friend I have seems to work for ILEA. In these parts, the Inner London Education Authority looms as large over the social horizon as General Motors does in Detroit. And yet,

my first, calculatedly heretical, attitude is to view the
impending dissolution of the authority with mischievous glee.

Anyone who says that ILEA is a bureaucratic monolith gets
my nod of agreement. Anyone who says it wastes money on a
prodigious scale finds one ally at Smith Towers. And anyone
who wants to make an education
authority as accountable as the
rest of the local authority structure
gets my vote. As a parent, a
school governor, a councillor and
yes, though the very word sticks
in my craw, as a ratepayer, I have
had experiences which tell me to
bat first wicket down for any team
that wants to shake County Hall
out of its smug, dream-like self-
satisfaction. I try to rest my case.
That is my view. Small is beautiful, say I, and big is nasty.
Disgruntled of SE5 says to hell with ILEA.

> Time was, when I'd have developed a view on ILEA like a cat develops a view on whether to lap the cream.

And yet, and yet ... I can't really bat against my own side, can
I? I do still dislike the Carlisles and the Bakers with an
intensity which passeth all understanding. I don't really want
school children in Kensington and Wandsworth to have to
buy their own slates and be forced to join the OTC at the age
of seven. I don't really want handicapped children to be
thrown on the parish and (maybe this is the clincher) I sure
as hell don't want fourteen different directors of education
littering the great wen. So, Gruntled of SE5 says thumbs-up
to ILEA. I won't wear a badge, mind, but I will offer a view if
the subject comes up.

Oh, to be back at Turnham Green! Oh, the freedom of going
straight for the pros without being confounded by the cons!
Oh, to have something nice and simple to believe in. Time
was, when I'd have developed a view on ILEA like a cat
develops a view on whether to lap the cream. This time
round, I even ask other people for their views and study *New*

Society for information. A man of views can't get much more confused than that!

It is entirely probable that this pre-menopausal anxiety about being so anxious has been brought on by all this sudden talk of the resurgence of the nuclear disarmament issue. The Campaign for Nuclear Disarmament is understood to be swelling in membership, preaching the Auld Religion to packed houses throughout the land. And, indeed, young men with more hair than a chap my age really likes to see have been seen sporting that wondrous badge in neighbouring watering holes. They seem confident enough – they thrust tracts into my hands as I once thrust tracts into others. They are young, of course, naive in the ways of the world, doubtless rather simplistic in their understanding of things. And yet, and yet ... I am on their side, aren't I? Even if they do waste my money by studying sociology and flying around the world on subsidised fares, never knowing what an honest day's work is. Yes, I think l must still be on their side despite everything.

I tell you something. If it wasn't for the kids, the new video recorder and the Abbey National Building Society, I'd be right there with them. Probably with a 'Hands Off ILEA' badge, as well.

Having your cake and eating it

January 1982/Local Government News: Such is life

The Inner London Education Authority seems to be troubling George again. So possibly we should be glad that Margaret Thatcher abolished it.

The word 'meretricious' is a strong one. It stems from the Latin for harlot and it has come to mean showily attractive or alluring by false show. It has yet to generate a noun, at least one that has the approval of the Oxford English Dictionary, and that I find a pity, for meretriciousness is the very word I need to describe the current goings on about local government and local government democracy and local government spending. [George got his way, meretriciousness has made it into the OED, even if my computer's spell check doesn't recognise it: Ed.]

Yet this unthinking allegiance to non-sense still underpins the public debate, a debate that is now entering new levels of passion and therefore danger.

I have written before about the appalling news-speak that sets in when politicians and town hall wallahs begin to transpose the two words 'spending' and 'service'. The elision is pernicious for its suggests that the two words mean the same and calls on one's automatic allegiance to the second to blur one's vision of the first.

I am not suggesting that there is no relationship between the two words. It is obvious that services cost money. It is equally obvious, albeit to a slightly different frame of mind, that not all spending provides services. To believe as much is to have an extraordinary faith in the complex maze of financial practices that underpin our municipal services. Are debt charges services? What about semi-statutory consultants fees? Or arrears write-offs? Or straight financial losses? We are already a long way from the public's understanding of what constitutes services and we have yet to dwell on the sheer administrative burden which makes a service provided by a local authority a regular collision between financial balance sheets and perceived common sense.

Yet this unthinking allegiance to nonsense still underpins the public debate, a debate that is now entering new levels of passion and therefore danger. I have before me a leaflet that was thrust at me at an otherwise delightful Christmas fair at a local primary school. It is headed 'Government attacks London education again' and it is about Heseltine's new bill. It is published by an ad hoc committee called 'Save Landon's Education Service' and it details the horrors to come from Heseltine's latest and silliest ploy – nursery classes cut, no new books, school meals to cost a lot more, larger classes etc, etc.

As a parent and as a still reasonably benign individual I don't want any of these things to happen. The difference is that I don't accept that they automatically have to happen if ILEA is subjected to cash limits.

For non-ILEA readers, a few facts may be in order. ILEA is, in anyone's book, a high service authority. It spends £700 million a year and this year refused to make cuts. Heseltine withdrew £125 million of central government grants, with the net effect that ILEA is now totally financed by its ratepayers. In a more rational world, this simple state of affairs might seem entirely agreeable – it is rare, after all, to have such a neat compact between an authority and its constituency. The rub is, of course, that Heseltine wants ILEA to spend less anyway and is proposing to take legislative powers to make this possible.

And it is at this point that both sides are being meretricious. Having accidentally stumbled into a situation of such a clear-cut relationship between ILEA ratepayers and its services, Heseltine would be advised to shuffle off and mind his own business. If we think that a pupil/teacher ratio of 8:1 is worth paying for, then we can vote for it without intervention from Whitehall.

> This is a perfectly respectable argument, but is conspicuously absent from the leaflet in question.

But this is not the burden of the leaflet from the Save London's Education Services. In their words the issue is 'about whether the Government will give proper financial support to local authority services like education'. In other words, the simple financial democratic relationship which pleases me doesn't please ILEA at all. They want more subvention from the Government and freedom to decide their own spending. Which, in the opinion of one whose cash is being carved up by all these arguments, means having your cake and eating it.

This latter attitude is caused, of course, by ILEA's growing awareness of the political reaction to further rate increases. Unwilling to examine the nature of its own services and politically committed to defending every jot and tittle of the status quo, it wants the Government either to mask the cost of those services or to act as scapegoat for the unpopular actions which will undoubtedly be necessary after years of arid inaction. What in reality the pamphleteers are saying to the public is: give us some of your taxes to add to your rates so that we might defend the status quo. This is a perfectly respectable argument, but is conspicuously absent from the leaflet in question.

In a funny kind of way, they must know the truth of the situation that is far more to do with the dislocation of financial effort and reward than it is to do with the Government attacking London's education. Public expenditure is a maw into which our personal contributions vanish, never to be seen again in any recognisable form. The only way you can begin to get a fix on reality is to carve down the relationship into personal terms. My own rates bill is now near enough £1000 a year – not a particularly unusual sum in inner London. I live in a long road and a road that must be bristling with high rateable values, and I would assess the total rate income from that road at about a quarter of a million pounds a year. Dare I suggest that we could run a modest school for that sort of money? (I appreciate that the rates pay for everything else as well, but education is by far the largest spender and a lot of the rest is still subsidised by central government). I'm sorry, but one does want an explanation of why we are surrounded with talk of cuts in service in a situation where every ten houses down my road are paying by way of rates the salary of a decently paid teacher every year.

Some one will tell me this is over-simplification. So it is. But I only simplify in an effort to make clear the scale of the dislocation between reality and rhetoric. And, in case anyone thinks that I am regurgitating Tory thinking to an unholy extent, I had better make the well-known point that rates are a regressive tax that fall far more harshly on the poor.

It would be an ugly thing to suggest that the real issue is a contest between the nature of our public service and the ability to pay for it by the poorest section of our community, and it would certainly be a paradoxical thing to suggest.

The clumsy foolishness of Heseltine equates with the hysterical half-truths of my pamphleteers. The spending juggernauts roll on. And the poor get poorer.

Dream on

March 1982/Local Government News: Such is life

Race relations is a sensitive subject at any time. Back in 1982...

There are distinct advantages to being my age – just turning into the early forties if you really want to know. Too young to have suffered national service, young enough to have witnessed the birth of rock and roll, old enough to remember Laker taking his nineteen wickets and interested enough to revel in Botham's current feats, my generation can already be seen to have had the best of what can easily be seen to be two different worlds.

In the years of growing up, which I guess chronologically were the late fifties and early sixties, the world was simpler. There was idealism around, there were good guys and bad guys, there was a job at the end of whatever level of the educational process you agreed to subject yourself to. The Tories had been in power since forever and, for people like me at least, political common sense began with the Labour Party and the belief that the decency, the morality, the progress of the world we wanted to live in was enshrined in something approximately called socialism and the values we were willing to believe would flourish under a Labour government.

Well, you know what happened. But it is not my text to write about the inevitable disillusion that inevitably sets in when the wide-eyed vision of youth collides with the hard-faced reality of life with an upper case L. Nor do I intend to draw any large-scale political analysis from the phenomenon, though I suspect that what I am describing underpins much of the current volatility of British politics, for there are at the very least millions like me.

The issue I am going to leap on – foolishly and fearlessly, given its nature – is the question of race. No other issue, to my mind, symbolises so clearly the difference between my young world and my middle-aged world. No other issue better underlines my own despair at the growing nihilism of political thought and debate. No other issue, in short, makes me feel so old.

A brief biographical note is in order before I get shouted at. I grew up in Brixton and I later found myself representing a piece of it on the local council. I went to school with blacks and without descending into verbal breast-beating of the 'some of my best friends are...' variety, I think I can honestly say that I never found the difference in skin colour to be a problem at any part of my lifestyle. By which I mean to record nothing more grandiose than the fact that I had black friends, colleagues and neighbours, that we would drink together, indulge in sports together and look after each other's kids.

But then I never expected race to be a problem.

But then I never expected race to be a problem. We were aware of what used to be called racial discrimination, which was why we uttered loud huzzahs at Labour's legislation in this area. We were aware of the evils of apartheid, which was why we marched, leafleted, campaigned and boycotted Outspan oranges (we still do, incidentally). We were, it seems to me now, old-fashioned liberal integrationists, wanting equality for blacks or, indeed, anyone, cheering at what was going on in Montgomery, Alabama, looking forward to a day when we could forget all this nonsense about race and move on to more sensible issues.

How long ago that all seems. For now the world is one of riots and Scarman commissions and race relations advisers and talk of positive discrimination. Race is a more important issue than it has ever been before (witness how the very word has replaced immigration as the access code to all the available prejudices) and this is the direct contrary of what one had hoped for. For the scale and the nature of the debate now begins to place me on the reactionary side of the arguments, sounding like a refugee from the Peter Simple column, railing against what that brilliant parodist is happy to call the race relations industry. It is not my instinct to find myself in that company and I resent being forced there.

The picture of Brixton as a poverty-stricken Harlem is simply fraudulent.

It's a subject I've been uneasy about for some years now, but it took the reportage of the Brixton riots to alert my jaded faculties to the nonsense that we were in risk of swallowing out of blind deference to apparent liberalism and an unwillingness to say what we were beginning to feel. The riots, you may remember, were ascribed to police behaviour (great truth in this) unemployment (some truth in this) and, to round off what was becoming a ritual incantation, bad housing and amenities – an incantation which has now rolled unchecked from a thousand expert tongues. And exactly the sort of judgement that dismays me. For the facts of Brixton life, from the point of view of one who served the area for a number of years, are that the claim of bad housing is difficult to justify where Lambeth Council has long ago cleared the area of practically all slum properties and where it has actually built some of its more intelligent public housing. There are in fact few slums and no tower blocks in Brixton.

Similarly with amenities. Brixton at the time of the riots, boasted two active cinemas, a full-service public library, innumerable pubs, a first-class recreation centre and a considerable number of youth clubs, most of them, it has to be said, used by young blacks rather than young whites, plus a giant sports centre currently under construction. I am not suggesting that this makes Brixton amenity rich. I am suggesting that I can think of lots of other parts of London much less favourably endowed.

The picture of Brixton as a poverty-stricken Harlem is simply fraudulent. A news report in the local paper demonstrates the speed with which nonsense gains momentum. For, if you truly believe Brixton to be under-endowed with amenities, you owe it to yourself to suggest the amenities that will help bridge the gap. The post-Scarman process is well under way and it is inevitably bringing forth a rich store of daftness. For Lambeth council, *inter alia*, are currently looking for premises in which young blacks can hold late-night parties. One can see how the tortured logic emerges: noisy parties are a source of friction, the friction takes racial form, therefore a facility for noisy parties should be part of the community's services. As so often, I object less to the principle of the thing than the language that surrounds it. A black youth worker is quoted as saying, 'Black youth is angry. We need places to hold our parties but the council doesn't want to accommodate us. I think they want us to forget our culture.' Which strikes me as a quite extraordinarily debilitating remark to make about a section of the community. I do not happen to believe that late-night parties are a particularly central part of anyone's culture. They are about as relevant and as central as, for instance, sex shops appear to be to the indigenous culture. And should sex shops be seen as a social service?

Someone somewhere will actually answer yes to that rhetorical question and, of course, you can argue just about anything into the public sector on exactly the same basis. But we all have our sticking points and this is just one of mine.

For what is happening to race relations in the country is that blacks are being taught to think of themselves purely as blacks, and not as our fellow citizens. The available wisdom says that being black endows you from cradle to grave with special problems, special handicaps, special needs of all kinds. And it is just because I recognise that there is small truth in all these things that I refuse to countenance the view they aggregate to a major and blinding truth that depicts a world I do not recognise though it is visible from my own window.

I can no longer find myself on the side of ILEA's courses for unqualified blacks to enter the teaching profession ahead of their white contemporaries, for I resent the idea that blacks are somehow incapable of acquiring those qualifications. I am against the idea of special old peoples' homes for blacks which has recently surfaced in Lewisham, for I do not accept that black pensioners are so very different from my own parents. And I am against sound-proofed council-run venues for young black parties, for I know that it is as possible to tell young blacks to make less noise as it is to convey the same message to young whites.

By which time, I will already have depicted myself as a hopelessly middle-aged dreamer. But we used to think that a pluralist society was what we were striving for. Is it not possible even now, to step back a few paces and decide what sort of society we want? For ghettoes are a bad thing, no matter how apparently rational the thinking that brings them about.

Ulcers, a pink shirt and the gallows

July 1971/New Society

This penultimate published article, in which George endures the ignominy of being fired, is the earliest of all the pieces in this book, and it's followed immediately by the most recent. They make for an interesting contrast, providing the bookends of a long and successful career. So we think they are a fitting ending to this tribute to George Smith, a great writer and an all-round good bloke.

Advertising men are the people at parties who apologise for their profession. 'I'm an advertising man, I'm afraid.' 'For my sins I work in an agency.' In some ten years of agency life, I'd certainly done my defensive share. And if an ad man's posture is defensive and guilt-ridden, then you'd expect the rationalisations to be pretty glib, too.

My standard conflicts with social worker or teacher friends had come to be well rehearsed. They would tell me I was worthless. I would agree. They would tell me I was vastly overpaid. I would, nod, smugly. They would rue that an intelligent, progressive person like me should earn a living whoring after fat industrialists in expense-account restaurants. And I would sigh, knowingly but helplessly.

I always had just one riposte. Security. All right. I would say, so what if I am earning three times what you're earning and I'm twenty years younger. What if I do swan around international airports and five-star hotels while you're slipping on your bicycle clips. At least you've got security. I could be out on my ear tomorrow. No job, no pension, no anything. Advertising's a young man's profession and I'm nearly thirty. My day will come.

Well, it has. I was fired very suddenly on a Friday afternoon, along with a dozen others. Nothing personal, you understand, just a question of billings and profitability and 'slimming'. At that historical moment I just happened to be in one of the most vulnerable places in the agency.

Advertising men secretly love this sort of thing. A total lack of job security is part of their mystique.

Advertising men secretly love this sort of thing. A total lack of job security is part of their mystique. Agencies depend almost completely on the commission they derive from their client's media expenditure. If that spending is curbed or diverted then the agency is stuck. Because few agency client relationships are binding, a client can promise to spend £100,000 on the agency, persuade it to hire staff to handle the business and then decide to spend the money on other forms of advertising like giveaway plastic daffodils. Whereupon exit the newly hired staff and, traditionally, a few others, also.

This sort of thing happens all the time and it breeds a distinctive gallows humour that is as much part of the agency lifestyle as ulcers, wine bars and pink shirts.

My own position within the agency was equivocal. Labouring under an enormous title, I combined a vague responsibility for some entirely notional international operations with a quasi-administrative job, which involved regular hiring, occasional firing, cogitating less than convincingly over the purchase of typewriters and filing cabinets and generally acting as a sort of familiar to a managing director whom I genuinely liked and respected. All these things represented a visible forty per cent or so of a working day.

My secretary was getting through fifty small print pages of Tolkien a day before I had finally been obliged to recognise my own vulnerability.

I knew the agency was under pressure. The boss and I had many a talk about our billing problems, our cash-flow problems, our accommodation problems. I had batted back his anxieties with what I saw as keen-eyed understanding and what he no doubt saw as servile ignorance. We had discussed staff cutbacks before, noted a few names, suggested a few dates. The solution that was emerging to our problems was an outright merger with another agency and that meant sizeable redundancies right through. At that point our dialogue ceased abruptly. We confided no more. I took the point and began to buy the *Daily Telegraph*.

> We confided no more. I took the point and began to buy the *Daily Telegraph*.

The rumours began both inside and outside the agency. We were going into liquidation. We were buying another agency. We were firing half the clients. Half the clients were firing us.

On the eve of what was now confidently expected to be the day of action, an ex-colleague rang me at home. Fifteen people would be involved the next day, he said, and did I know that my name was at the top of the list. This was good going for a man working on the other side of town, but I chose to thank him with a worldly knowingness.

The agency was in a predictably hysterical mood the next morning. No work was being done, small groups were gathering in assorted offices and the first bottle appeared at 10.15. Internal telephones whispered and confirmed the names of colleagues as they disappeared into the boss's office at regular intervals. But by twelve o'clock I had heard nothing and went off to a pre-arranged game of squash with the media manager and research man.

The media man was sardonic and restrained, a veteran of such occasions. The research man, a provincial graduate whom I'd hired three months previously, was gleeful and excited. Such drama was, after all, the life stuff of the advertising mythology to which he was now a keen subscriber. And besides, he knew who was involved. Someone had told him just after breakfast that morning. We need not worry, he said, our names were not on the list. His smugness was made all the worse for being based on complete ignorance.

> ## His smugness was made all the worse for being based on complete ignorance.

In mid-afternoon we spilled beerily out of the cab. The expected message awaited me. 'Can you go and see the boss?' All the other deeds had obviously been done. The reception area was full of the newly redundant, mostly drunk, some already clutching personal possessions.

The boss had all the briskness that comes with a repetitive job.

'George, I've got to fire you. I think you know that I've got a lot of respect for your ability and I'm genuinely sorry. But you'll know the reasons and I guess you're not really very surprised.'

I tried a wearily understanding gesture. 'This envelope contains your cards, a redundancy claim form and a cheque for a lot of money. The money's tax-free. You make your own arrangements with the Inland Revenue but if you play your cards right it'll stay tax-free. I'm sorry, what'll you do next?'

'Almost certainly get right out of this business.'

'I think you'd be very sensible to do just that. You'll make out, I'm sure.'

We shook hands, me unemployed and flushing, he employed and embarrassed.

How long did that last? Two minutes? Three? After nearly eight years. But the prevailing emotion was bravado, not bitterness, a bravado fortified by the digits on my last pay cheque. People were coming out of nearby offices, wringing my hand and expressing disgust, astonishment, sympathy and a range of emotions they'd forget by Monday morning.

There were more dramatic scenes elsewhere in the building. One girl tried to scream the place down and a unisex young executive succeeded in smashing up his office. But generally it was anti-climactic. After all, only thirteen had gone, instead of the expected twenty-five.

The booze-up afterwards had an air of somewhat contrived celebration, the sort that usually masks a real unease. The unease was not quite that of insecurity demonstrated once again. It was rather the realisation that another set of human relationships had been disjointed. Yesterday's senior executives were now Monday's job hunters. The conversations of close friends had become blocked with stilted expressions of sympathy: 'If I hear of anything, I'll let you know.'

Someone leaned across the bar and said to me, 'Well, I expect you'll be starting your own agency now!'

Tales from the pitch

November 2000/Financial Times Creative Business

PowerPoint may be the new Cow Gum, but some bad habits – sorry, principles – will always apply, according to George.

God, I'm old. So old that I can remember when the spend was called the appropriation, when production was a matter of half-tone blocks, and when the agency's dirtiest jokes came from something called the dispatch department, where you learned to master brown paper and the uncertainties of the Sellotape roll. Hands up who remembers Cow Gum!

And the pitch was known as the presentation, thank you very much. It's thirty-four years since I attended my first such ceremony, dragged from below stairs on the honourable basis that I had provided the lead that had an exciting new client prospect in the agency boardroom.

I was given no role, no lines. Indeed I was probably told to wash carefully, to make sure my parting was straight and to observe the behaviour of my double-barrelled colleagues so that I could glean a little professional savvy; in those days, being from Peckham, you had an evens chance of making progress controller in less than five years, if you really showed willing.

I gleaned well that day. The prospective client was about to introduce heated hair rollers in the UK. Their team was hard-bitten, latterly part of John Bloom's direct-selling sales force, bristling with impatient contempt for advertising agencies staffed by public schoolboys who had probably never sold on the knocker in their lives.

It was bad, very bad. My peers trundled through the

agency's wonders for an hour or so, climaxing with a case history wherein we had applied different daily wrappers to Sunblest bread to justify the line 'Our Daily Bread'. Believe me, this was cutting-edge creativity in 1966.

And it provoked the already-surly prospective client into a memorable utterance. The managing director – and she a lady – threw down her agency pencil and said: 'What the fuck has sliced bread got to do with heated rollers?'

> The memory of the suits trying to salvage the ceremony of presentation for a further hour, is still with me.

Unfair, of course, but still deeply comic. The memory of the suits trying to salvage the ceremony of presentation for a further hour is still with me. Ironically, we actually won the business and I found myself handling it – doubtless on the basis that only Peckham stock would cope with the Cricklewood Tendency.

Moral: never bore the prospective client. Never posture as being smarter or superior to people who know their own business. Always make content relevant and work hard to find the relevance.

They are still there, the agency suits still wondering whether your coffee needs topping up. And these days they labour under the new self-given lash of the PowerPoint presentation, a technique that reduces every message to eight-word bullet-prompted paragraphs. With mantra whizzing tiresomely from left to right in the given rectangle.

These days I sometimes find myself part of a client team confronted by the pitch ceremony. PowerPoint ennui is a recent problem, one that brings out the subversive in me. Recently, somewhere north of Oxford Circus, I was shown a frame that said 'financial relationship?' To which I said: 'Well, currently, the client pays the agency, but we are very flexible in this.'

The 20 seconds of anxiety from the agency team were well worth having. So was the relieved laughter as it dawned on them that flippancy had entered the room. Old habits die hard, especially bad ones.

Expect the unexpected, punctuated by jollity

Though never published, this piece demands inclusion for it describes an experience all travelling public speakers will have a version of, and which others who are not should at least understand before they fill in their evaluation forms at that next conference. The name Darth Vader really was just a mispronunciation of Daft Ada, was it not?

'Ah, good, you are with us. Now you should be in the lobby for the coach at 19.30.'

The point about Sweden is that everyone almost speaks English. That is to say, everyone speaks English perfectly but with an uncanny knack of one wrong word or inflection per sentence. We cannot sneer; but we must always be slightly unnerved.

The phone call to my room at the Gothenburg Sheraton was from the Volvo lady. She had phoned me in London, inviting me to the sales dinner and had left a message at reception that hadn't been given to me.

'I must talk to the Sheraton. This is very typical.'

More verbal instructions followed. 'Please do not dress up. It is very informal. I myself will be wearing slacks.'

Knowing a little about what is informal in Sweden, I elect to go without a tie. The three guys in the lift confirm my thesis – Volvo badges, suits, three different kinds of aftershave. One of them, though – the one with the musky sort of aftershave –

is also tieless. We half smile at each other, the way strangers do in lifts. The collective fragrance is overpowering.

In the lobby backs are being slapped, hands are being shaken. My hostess, indeed wearing designer slacks and a great deal of informal jewellery, introduces me to my fellow guest-speaker – a media man from a large London agency. Within minutes we become soul mates – he too, is wondering what the hell he is doing there. No, he doesn't work for Volvo either. They phoned him, too out of the blue. Could he talk on 'Media in the Year 2000?' He lives in Reigate and shares my unease at the *bonhomie* now going on around us.

We are two grey middle-aged Brits with no badges. When the Volvo lady claps her hands, we go to the back of the coach and make jokes about works outings. It is indeed a high-powered works outing for everyone seems to know each other. Little Chinese chappies lean over seats and joke with Frenchmen. The Brit Volvo contingent belly laughs a lot. The quarter of the coach that is Swedish looks very pleased with itself. The Volvo lady comes to the back of the coach. 'We knew that everyone would be depressed when we adjusted the conference from Paris to Gothenburg. So tonight we are going to be very unexpected.'

The coach starts. There is an intercom. We have a host. His name is Jorgen Crabbe. I'd met him before when he was wearing a short-sleeved shirt in his air-conditioned office. Now he sports an informal Burberry beneath which I can see an informal cravat.

'Welcome, everyone,' says Jorgen. 'Tonight we are going to be very unexpected.' Cheers, clapping, ribaldries. The coach moves on to a holding pattern in a traffic jam. What follows is a twenty-minute coach journey around Gothenburg, punctuated by jollity from Jorgen. To get the flavour, repeat the phrases in authoritative sing-song Swedish English.

'Tonight we are going somewhere really dirty (roars of approval). 'Oh, I am sorry – there are ladies with us. So we should not go somewhere dirty.'

(Groans.)

'In fact, we are taking you to a new restaurant. We do not know that it is at all good, so we are giving you plastic bags just in case.' (Is the laughter getting less spontaneous and more dutiful?)

'On your left you will see a very famous restaurant in Gothenburg. It is very good but you will need a fortune. So we will not go there.' (Yes, the laughter is getting more dutiful.)

The Volvo lady comes to the back of the coach again. 'You see, I said we would be unexpected. If we were in Paris, we would just have gone to a dull restaurant. Here is much more fun.'

We nod vigorously.

The coach is now in the middle of the dock area. It is very dark. Jorgen tells us all about it.

'Gothenburg is a very famous fishing harbour. Only one thing now, there are no boats. Catching fish without boats, this is difficult.'

By now the laughter is confined to the Swedish delegation.

The coach stops.

'Oh, what is the matter now? The coach has stopped. Oh, the driver will not go any further. I think we must go down.'

The coach party lines up alongside a dark shed. You can see silhouetted cranes, hear the lapping of water, smell fish. 'Must be the fucking harbour,' says the fellow guest-speaker.

The party is hustled around the shed and shuffles to a stop at what is undoubtedly a quayside. The crowd, I have to say, is still determinedly jolly. Only the two guest-speakers stand outside the groups of laughing Volvo people. The rest are certainly finding it all very unexpected and keep telling each other as much. They seem immune from the Baltic wind blowing up one's arse and oblivious of the fact that fifty people in casual suits are now standing in complete darkness at a location where you could remake *On the Waterfront.*

Suddenly, a door slides back in the shed, throwing some welcome light on the proceedings. To applause, a small Swede jumps out. Clad in sou'wester and tarpaulins he is obviously Chief Wag for phase two. His name is stencilled on his apron. It is Knut.

'Welcome here to Gothenburg. As you can see, I am a real fisherman. You will hear a lot about niche marketing tomorrow, but now I must tell you about fish marketing' (laughter, applause).

The wind is obliterating many of Knut's one-liners. From what I can see from the back, he is making great play with knives and nets. Judging by the responses, I can only deduce that there are a lot of Volvo house jokes going on. People's names are being mentioned, all greeted with loud laughs.

The fellow guest-speaker is getting gloomier. 'How long is this going to go on?' he says. 'I need to get back to practice my piece for tomorrow.'

Tomorrow, we both perform for this lot. Volvo has asked each of us to produce an exciting presentation, rather unexpected presumably. They asked me to do amazing things with interactive doodads and keyboards and VDUs and things. I said I wasn't that kind of boy. No technological tomfoolery with this punter, I said, a couple of jokes, a few mottos, a bit of mock-irreverence and lots of pictures – all delivered with gravitas. Sod your keyboards. I make like wise and provocative. Take it or leave it. Stuck with me, they took it.

The media man has taken them at their word. Lumbered with a title like 'Media in the Year 2000' he had run together some satellite commercials, nicked some footage from *2001* and agreed to come on dressed as Darth Vader. He is not one of nature's Darth Vaders. He is certainly rueing the day that he agreed to be Darth Vader. Standing on the quayside, leaning forward with a fixed grin for Knut's japes, he looks like a man wondering about the first plane back in the morning.

Knut has now been joined by another fisherman. They are picking up a crate and making great play of levering the lid off.

Cheers and applause. The crate contains glasses.

Second crate. More cheers and applause. It contains bottles.

We all shuffle forward and drink a strange blue drink.

An intense German tells me that it is champagne and blue curacao. He is not sure, though, and seems to want my opinion.

Thankfully, Knut's at it again, He climbs to the top of the crate and claps his hands.

'Now you know we have a party here. We have the drinks. And now we shall have the music.'

To further enthusiasm, an oom-pah band shuffles around the shed, playing their socks off. An accordion, a guitar, euphonium and drums. The band are also dressed as fishermen. They also have their names on their aprons. They are called things like Stig and Bengt and Bonk.

A soft drizzle begins to fall as the first community singing starts. Everyone seems to know the song, so maybe it's a Volvo house song. The guest speakers beam, unknowing. Everyone else is having one hell of a time.

Now, we are ushered down the quayside and into a shed. Gasps of delighted surprise, we are going to have dinner in a canning factory!

And so we do. We proceed to random places where we are greeted with a hymn sheet bearing the words of a great Swedish drinking song. I know it is a great Swedish drinking song because a Danish neighbour tells me so. 'This is a great Swedish drinking song,' he says. 'You will watch them go crazy when they sing it.'

We eat crayfish, eels, prawns, lots of smoked things. We drink beer, wine, acquavit. The band oom-pahs on ten feet away. Knut makes announcements. We sing 'happy birthday to you' to the Singapore dealer who is given a lobster in a box. We shout at each other over the noise and crane forward to the replies, cupping our ears. I discuss football with a Dane, direct marketing with a Swede. An American tells me about the problems they're having on the 7000 series with central locking and the distribution problems they have with GM. I nod.

We sing the great Swedish drinking song sitting down. Then we sing it with linked arms. Then we sing it with linked arms and swaying from side to side. Then we sing it with alternate sitting down and standing up per table. Everyone looks shagged out as well as pissed. I don't think we have to sing it any more.

In fact, I think it is nearly over. Stig, Bonk and the boys are now giving us 'Auld Lang Syne' and Knut and his mates are carrying an enormous tuna to one of the sinks which lines the canning factory where we are having the Volvo sales dinner.

Knut gets major chortles as he manhandles the fish.

'And now we fishermen must go back to work and you must go back to your hotel. I hope you have enjoyed our simple hospitality here on the harbour and that you will all sell lots of cars (great roar). But now we must chop this fish. And we have another three hundred to chop this night. So you must go to your coach.'

Everyone stands and applauds. Knut waves from the sink and does a little dance. I wondered if he would actually chop the fish. I should have known better. Seven swipes of an enormous cleaver separates the tuna's head from its body. Blood and organs everywhere. More applause. Such japes!

Back in the coach, the Volvo lady shimmies up again. 'You see, I said we were unexpected. When we get back to the Sheraton go through the lobby, up through the casino, turn left to the disco. There we have the nightcaps.'

The guest speakers make an excuse and leave the party. They drink coffee and brandy in a bar where a pianist is playing 'South Pacific'. Conversation is minimal. Tomorrow, one of these people is going to be Darth Vader.

To make the presentation theatre, we have to be in the lobby at seven o'clock. The conference is, logically, at a brewery some way out of town.

On arrival, Darth Vader is beside himself with anxiety. I do a quick slide run through, cue up the video and find that the AV man is called Bjorn. He smokes cigarettes, which makes him a very low Swede indeed. Darth is convinced that Bjorn doesn't understand that his commercials are to run in groups of three, that his presentation starts with '*Also Sprach Zarathusa*', that he wants the house lights down when he enters, that he wants a spot to illuminate his sudden appearance as Darth.

Jorgen Crabbe does the intro. A Frenchman tells us about sponsoring horse jumping. A Dutchman says something impenetrable about a joint promotion with Philips. They should each have been twenty minutes. Together, they make fifteen. I am on, early.

I make an early joke. It is greeted with glassy-eyed stares. They are all making notes. I make no further jokes. I finish. The applause seems genuine enough.

Coffee break. Darth is worried about his script. It won't go under his cloak. Can I put it on the lectern as the previous speaker sits down? Sure, I say, and wish him good luck with an air of post-coital smugness.

The first speaker after lunch is the UK man. He has twenty minutes and talks for fifty. He, too, is a wag. For the first half hour, he tells stories about who did what to whom last night at the disco. He brings the house down. Encouraged by the response, he cuts loose. 'I only know two jokes about breweries.' He says. 'The first is about Watneys Beer.' It's the old one about fucking near water. Everyone falls about. On he goes. No, he won't shut up, he says to the Volvo lady making agonised waving motions from the back of the hall. 'They're enjoying this.' Indeed they are, stomping him on with every dirty joke. The man has talent, I can't deny. With a check sports jacket and a piggish upper-class face, he looks creepily like the young Evelyn Waugh. Knows his audience, though.

Trouble is, Darth Vader, is pacing the corridor outside, half an hour late for his appearance. I pop out for a pee and there he is chain smoking in full regalia. You never saw Darth Vader smoking, did you?

Finally the UK man tells us something about his text. He gets down to riotous applause and I slip Darth's speech on the podium. Jorgen does the intro. The lights go down. No one is on the platform. Voice from the back: 'He's not very tall is he?'

Kubrick's rockets and spheres flicker on to the screen. Up comes Richard Strauss on the PA. And, then, yes, in comes the media man, helmeted and be-cloaked, walking slowly to the platform, standing by it with his arms folded.

The spot comes on. Darth speaks.

'May the Force be with you,' he says.

Genuine, professional applause from all round. Darth has passed the Unexpected Test. Bjorn did the business. Thank god for that!

Good, solid presentation too. All that worries me is that Darth Vader is from *Star Wars* not *2001* and that he never talked about the Force anyway – Alec Guinness did. What a dreary mind I have.

At lunchtime we are taken on a trip through the brewery. Apart from the approximate smell of cereals, it could pass for a Volvo plant. But it is very historic. At one point we pass through a room of relics and I say to the Volvo lady, 'What is this piece of wood?'

And she says, 'It is a very historic piece of a tree. As you can see it has been burned. I will ask the people at the brewery and write to you about it if your are interested.'

A week later, I am still waiting for the origin of the charred log. So much for making small talk with Swedes.

But, whatever it was, I'm sure it was unexpected.

Glossary

ACLU
American Civil Liberties Union.

Aldermaston
a village in Berkshire and site of the Atomic Weapons
Establishment. From 1958 until 1963 the Campaign for
Nuclear Disarmament organised a 'ban the bomb' march
each Easter from Aldermaston to London to protest against
the proliferation of nuclear weapons. The marchers were not
only from the UK but from all the over world and all sorts of
backgrounds.

Aldershot
an army base in the UK.

Aeonics
a mail order firm in the 1970s.

Akabussi, Chris
British gold medal winner in the 1992 Olympics in Barcelona.

Anderson shelters
in November 1938, the prime minister appointed Sir John
Anderson to be in charge of air raid precautions; and in
February 1939 the first Anderson shelter was erected in
Britain in a garden in London. Anderson shelters were half
buried in the ground with earth heaped on top to protect
people from bomb blasts during the Second World War.
They had enough room for a family and were safer than
staying in a house.

Atherton, Mike
England cricketer from 1989 to 2001; former captain of the
England team.

BDMA
British Direct Marketing Association, now the Direct
Marketing Association, (DMA).

Birmingham
the Institute of Fundraising in the UK used to hold its
national convention in the UK city of Birmingham, or rather
at the National Convention Centre just outside the city.

Bloom, John
during the 1960s Bloom's innovation was to sell washing
machines directly to the public via coupon advertising at
around half the cost of retailers. They were also sold largely
through affordable hire purchase agreements.

Botham, Ian
England cricketer from the 1977 to 1992, generally
considered to be the England test team's best all rounder;
former captain of the England team.

Catterick
an army base in the UK.

Coleman, David
a sports commentator with the BBC for forty years, he is
remembered for his many on-air gaffes such as, when talking
about the runner Linford Christie, '… has a habit of pulling it
out when it matters the most'. *Private Eye* named its sports
blooper column Colemanballs – a word conceived by
Coleman himself.

Della Femina, Jerry
famous advertising executive and, now, restaurateur. He
wrote a couple of great books on advertising and marketing
from Madison Avenue, including *From Those Wonderful Folks
Who Gave You Pearl Harbor*, which has been cited as a major
source for the television series *Mad Men*.

Daly, Arthur
the dodgy businessman in the BBC comedy adventure
Minder, first aired in 1979.

Dixon, Reginald
organist at the Tower Ballroom in Blackpool from 1930 until his retirement in 1975.

Dors, Diana
British film star and sex symbol during the 1950s. In later life she became a significant character actor until her death in 1984.

Drayton Bird
has been a legendary UK direct marketing figure for the last four decades or so. His second book, *Commonsense Direct Marketing*, as George rightly says, made a huge impression when it came out and it's no less good today.

EIU
Economist Intelligence Unit.

Ford, Len
a former secretary of the BDMA.

Foster Callear
used to sell brass-mounted barometers/clocks through mail order; now collectors' items.

Fraser-Robinson, John
direct marketing luminary of the period when George was writing, head of the agency Amhurst Direct.

Garnett, Alf
a character in the UK's 1960s sit com *Till Death Us Do Part*.

Giro
a payment transfer from one bank account to another instigated by the payer and not the payee. In the UK and in other countries the term Giro may refer to a specific system once operated by the British post office, originally known as National Giro and, confusingly, was adopted by the public and the press as a shorthand term for the Girocheque, which was a cheque and not a credit transfer.

The Great Wen
disparaging nickname for London coined in the 1820s by
William Cobbett, the radical pamphleteer and champion of
rural England.

Gulbenkian
rich financier who allegedly drove around London in a
chauffeur driven taxi, of which he famously said, 'It can turn
on a sixpence, whatever that is'.

GUS
Great Universal Stores.

Hoke Pete
founder and chairman of *Direct Marketing* magazine in the
US and said by some to be the father of direct marketing.
Peter Hoke snr was, we are reasonably sure, father of Pete
Hoke jnr.

ICFM
the Institute of Fundraising Managers, now the UK's
Institute of Fundraising (IoF).

IFRW
International Fund Raising Workshop, now the International
Fundraising Congress (IFC).

IVS
International Voluntary Service.

Goldsmith, Harvey
impresario, in 1985 produced Live Aid with Sir Bob Geldof,
which raised £140 million for famine victims in Africa.

Headingley
Yorkshire cricket ground.

Kingston
Kingston University London.

Laker, Jim
will always be remembered for his bowling in the test match
at Old Trafford in 1956, when he took 19 Australian wickets.

No other bowler has taken more than seventeen wickets in a first-class match, let alone in a test match.

Lord Gnome of Hoddesdon
George was constantly having affectionate swipes at Paul Rowney, owner of *Direct Response* magazine. The original Lord Gnome is supposedly the proprietor of the satirical newspaper *Private Eye*. Direct Response's offices were in Hoddesdon.

MacGregor, John
Secretary of State for Transport from 1992 to 1994.

MCC
Marylebone Cricket Club, founded in 1787, the world's most famous cricket club.

Medley, George
formerly head of fundraising at WWF. First chairman of the ICFM.

Montreux
for many years the great and the good of direct marketing used to gather together at a conference in Montreux, Switzerland.

Mullin, Redmond
one of the founders of the UK's Institute of Fundraising, co-creator of the NSPCC's Centenary Appeal in 1984 and a grandfather of British fundraising.

NCCL
National Council of Civil Liberties now known as Liberty.

NCVO
National Council for Voluntary Organisations.

NSFRE
National Society of Fundraising Executives now the Association of Fundraising Professionals (AFP).

Newton's cradle
desk toy.

Noordwijkerhout
the location of the International Fundraising Congress (IFC) in the Netherlands.

Old Bill
the Metropolitan Police.

Pseuds Corner
a column in the satirical magazine *Private Eye* that features pretentious comments made in the media.

Remington, Stan
former chief executive of Book Club Associates.

Scargill, Arthur
leader of the National Union of Mineworkers during the 1984-85 miners' strike.

Scarman, Leslie, Baron Scarman, OBE, PC
English judge and barrister, who served as a law lord until his retirement in 1986. He was best known for his chairing of the inquiry into the Brixton riots in 1981.

Walter Schmidt
a Swiss direct marketer, organiser of the Montreux conferences.

Scott, Bob
founder of Scotcade.

Shetland oil disaster
in January 1993 a tanker carrying 85,000 tonnes of crude oil ran aground off the Shetland Islands in hurricane force winds.

Simple, Peter
pseudonym used by the British journalist Michael Wharton in his column in the *Daily Telegraph*.

Tomkins, Professor Peter
a direct marketing academic. In Debrett's he lists his recreations as squash, skiing, jogging and charity work.

Taylor, Graham
England football coach 1990 to 1993.

Walmsley, Nigel
former marketing director of the Royal Mail.

Webcraft
stateside printer that invented the inline printing process
capable of forming a leaflet with built-in ready gummed,
folded and perforated reply envelope – the stuff on which
direct marketers get their rocks off.

Whitlam, Mike, CBE
first recipient of the UK's charity lifetime achievement award,
director or CEO of many charities including the Red Cross,
Save the Children and the Royal National Institute for the
Deaf.

Wunderman, Lester
founder of the Wunderman agency, he too is also considered
by some to be the creator of modern day direct marketing.